ECHOES AND REFLECTIONS
TEACHER'S RESOURCE GUIDE

Funded by Dana and Yossie Hollander

Anti-Defamation League
605 Third Avenue
New York, NY 10158

© 2005, 2014 Anti-Defamation League, USC Shoah Foundation, Yad Vashem

All Rights Reserved. Published 2005
Printed in the United States of America

ISBN: 978-1-936542-00-0

Credits
Photos, illustrations, artwork, and video images throughout this resource guide are copyrighted unless otherwise indicated. Additional credit information as follows: Lesson 2 photos 196/220, 196/221, 196/223, 1599/232: Reprinted with permission from Ernst Hiemer, *The Poisoned Mushroom* (Nuremberg: Der Stürmer, 1938); Illustration 6284_34: © Deutsches Historisches Museum, Berlin. Reprinted with permission from Elvira Bauer, *Trust No Fox on Green Heath and No Jew on His Oath* (Berlin, Germany: Deutsches Historisches Museum).

For permission to reprint content from the *Echoes and Reflections Teacher's Resource Guide* contact the Anti-Defamation League at info@echoesandreflections.org. For permission to reprint any video images contact USC Shoah Foundation at sfiaccess@usc.edu or call 213-740-3756.

ADL
Anti-Defamation League®

605 Third Avenue
New York, NY 10158-3560
212-885-7700 / 885-7800
212-867-0779 / 490-0187 (Fax)
adl.org

USC Shoah Foundation
The Institute for Visual History and Education

University of Southern California
Leavey Library
650 W. 35th Street, Suite 114
Los Angeles, CA 90089-2571
213-740-6001
213-740-6044 (Fax)
sfi.usc.edu

YAD VASHEM
The Holocaust Martyrs' and Heroes'
Remembrance Authority

P.O. Box 3477
Jerusalem 91034
Israel
972-2-644-3400
972-2-644-3623 (Fax)
yadvashem.org

About ADL

The Anti-Defamation League (ADL) is one of the nation's premier civil rights and human relations agencies. ADL fights anti-Semitism and all forms of bigotry here and abroad, combats international terrorism and domestic extremism, advocates before Congress, helps victims of anti-Semitism, develops educational programs, and serves as a public resource for government, media, law enforcement, and the public.

When ADL was established in 1913, its charter stated: "The immediate object of the League is to stop, by appeals to reason and conscience, and if necessary, by appeals to law, the defamation of the Jewish people. Its ultimate purpose is to secure justice and fair treatment to all citizens alike and to put an end forever to unjust and unfair discrimination against and ridicule of any sect or body of citizens." With its National Headquarters in New York City, ADL has a network of Regional and Satellite Offices throughout the nation and Jerusalem.

For more information about the Anti-Defamation League, visit adl.org.

About USC Shoah Foundation

USC Shoah Foundation–The Institute for Visual History and Education is dedicated to making audiovisual interviews with survivors and other witnesses of the Holocaust and other genocides, a compelling voice for education and action. The Institute's current collection of nearly 52,000 eyewitness testimonies contained within its Visual History Archive preserves history as told by the people who lived it, and lived through it. Housed at the University of Southern California, within the Dana and David Dornsife College of Letters, Arts and Sciences, the Institute works with partners around the world to advance scholarship and research, to provide resources and online tools for educators, and to disseminate the testimonies for educational purposes.

For more information about USC Shoah Foundation–The Institute for Visual History and Education, visit sfi.usc.edu.

About Yad Vashem

Yad Vashem — The Holocaust Martyrs' and Heroes' Remembrance Authority — was established in 1953 by an act of the Israeli parliament. Yad Vashem acts as the Jewish people's memorial to the six million Jews murdered in the Holocaust and embodies the Jewish people's ongoing confrontation with the rupture engendered by the Holocaust. Containing the world's largest repository of information on the Holocaust, Yad Vashem is the principal global actor in Shoah education, commemoration, research, and documentation. Situated on the Mount of Remembrance in Jerusalem, Yad Vashem serves over one million visitors annually, through the International School for Holocaust Studies, the International Institute for Holocaust Research, the Archives, the Library, the Hall of Names, and its museums and memorials. An additional 12 million visits a year are recorded at the Yad Vashem website.

Yad Vashem is recognized internationally as a beacon of warning against antisemitism, hatred, and genocide and has been granted NGO status by the United Nations. Yad Vashem stands as a unifying symbol for people all over the world and serves as the voice and conscience of the Jewish People, strengthening the commitment to the State of Israel, Jewish continuity, and the protection of the basic human values that were undermined during the *Shoah*.

For more information about Yad Vashem, visit yadvashem.org.

Movies: Denial
Paragraph 175

Path to Nazi genocide
video on ushmm.org
or on youtube

From it's origins
to the Holocaust video @

Boys in the boat → book
Some were neighbors → book

mo → rewatch
Counterfiters
The Reader

all on webpage
added resources there, too

videos on website
mostly for teacher Bk
not students

CONTENTS

Procedures for each unit not on website

Remove from printable from website

LESSON 3 NAZI GERMANY   67

LESSON 4 THE GHETTOS   91

▌ LESSON 10 THE CHILDREN   259

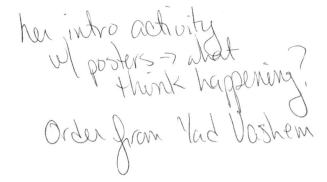
her intro activity w/ posters → what think happening? Order from Yad Vashem

INTRODUCTION

About Echoes and Reflections

Echoes and Reflections provides US secondary educators with professional development and interdisciplinary print and online resources to teach about the Holocaust in today's classrooms. Echoes and Reflections combines the resources and competencies of three world leaders in education—the Anti-Defamation League's experience as a leader in the development and implementation of educational programs and materials; USC Shoah Foundation's Visual History Archive, pedagogical expertise in teaching with testimony, and its digital educational tools, including IWitness; and Yad Vashem's International School for Holocaust Studies' historical, educational, and pedagogical expertise and access to primary source materials—resulting in the most comprehensive Holocaust education program available.

Echoes and Reflections aims to enhance the content knowledge and pedagogical skills of teachers who include Holocaust and genocide studies as part of their curriculum. The program models active learning and practical instructional strategies. The standards-based print and digital resources equip teachers with the tools they need to help today's students study the Holocaust as a significant event in human history, to recognize the complexity of choices made by individuals, and to define the role and responsibility of the individual to uphold the principles of a democracy and moral and ethical behavior.

The goals of Echoes and Reflections are as follows:

- To enhance educators' content knowledge on major topics about the Holocaust, including antisemitism, Nazi ideology, ghettos, the "Final Solution," and resistance.

- To provide secondary educators with access to superior, research-based professional development with a focus on modeling sound pedagogy and instructional strategies for teaching about the Holocaust.

- To develop standards-based, interdisciplinary print and digital resources that foster knowledge and understanding of the Holocaust and its relevance to contemporary society.

- To promote critical thinking through the study of the Holocaust.

- To support students' development of the skills necessary to examine the effects of prejudice and antisemitism.

- To encourage the use of visual history testimony in the classroom, thereby exposing students to the narratives of those who were witnesses to history and providing opportunities for them to examine their own personal narratives.

- To support educators across disciplines as they integrate Holocaust and genocide education into their course of study.

About the Teacher's Resource Guide

The *Echoes and Reflections Teacher's Resource Guide* includes ten multipart lessons and a DVD with over two hours of testimony of survivors and other witnesses to the Holocaust from USC Shoah Foundation's Visual History Archive. Seamlessly integrated into the lessons, visual history testimony provides an opportunity for teachers to address digital and media literacies while teaching about the Holocaust. The modular design of the guide allows teachers the flexibility of using an individual lesson, a specific part of a lesson, or several lessons; the interdisciplinary nature of the lessons make them suitable for a range of disciplines including history, social studies, English/language arts, fine arts, and religion.

Replete with primary and secondary source materials, the *Echoes and Reflections Teacher's Resource Guide* encourages students to analyze a wide array of materials from many perspectives in historical context. Photographs, artwork, diary entries, letters, government documents, maps, poems, visual history testimony, and other source material help students construct an authentic and comprehensive portrait of the past as they frame their own thoughts about what they are seeing or reading, resulting in a deeper level of interest and inquiry.

Overview of Lessons

Each of the ten instructional lessons in the Teacher's Resource Guide is divided into two, three, or four parts that relate to an overall topic. Used sequentially, the lessons provide students with opportunities to investigate major themes associated with the Holocaust in an order that is roughly chronological. All of the lessons provide both historical context for the topic under investigation as well as numerous visual history testimonies and other primary source materials, including additional online multimedia activities in IWitness. Each lesson is designed to help secondary educators teach about the Holocaust while addressing rigorous national, state, and local standards in meaningful ways.

Each lesson begins with **Preparing to Use This Lesson.** In some cases, the notes that have been included in this section elaborate on the suggestions listed in the "Teaching about the Holocaust" section below and are specific to the contents of the lesson. The material in this section is intended to help teachers consider complexities of the Holocaust and to deliver accurate and sensitive instruction.

Each lesson ends with **Making Connections.** This section provides ideas for additional activities and projects that can be integrated into the lesson itself or that can be used to extend a lesson once it has been completed. The topics lend themselves to students' continued study of the Holocaust as well as opportunities for students to make meaningful connections to other people and events, including relevant contemporary issues. The suggested activities—which encourage students to use both print and digital resources and present their work in a variety of forms (written, oral, visual)—may include instructional strategies and/or techniques that address academic standards in addition to those that were identified for the lesson.

Teaching all ten lessons in this resource in the order in which they are presented is ideal. However, the modular nature of the Teacher's Resource Guide allows teachers to choose lessons suitable for their classroom and learning objectives. When teaching any of the lessons, it is important to provide accurate context for the material; therefore, teachers are strongly encouraged to review the additional lessons that have been identified in the descriptions below.

Lesson 1: Studying the Holocaust

This lesson provides an opportunity for students to discuss the value and importance of studying human catastrophes, in general, and the Holocaust, in particular. The lesson also provides an opportunity for students to consider the importance of examining both primary and secondary source materials when studying historical events and to begin to develop a common vocabulary for studying the Holocaust and other genocides. (See Lesson 3: Nazi Germany.)

Lesson 2: Antisemitism

This lesson provides an opportunity for students to learn about the origins of antisemitism. Students will also learn about prewar Jewish life in Germany and antisemitism in Nazi ideology and its similarities and differences from pre-Nazi antisemitism. Students will also examine propaganda methods that were used to exploit antisemitic attitudes among the German people and to create an atmosphere of terror. (See Lesson 3: Nazi Germany.)

Lesson 3: Nazi Germany

The purpose of this lesson is for students to learn about the Weimar Republic's fragile democracy between 1918 and 1933 and to examine historical events that allowed for the complete breakdown of democracy in Germany between 1933 and 1939, which led to the unfolding of anti-Jewish policies. Students will also investigate primary source materials in order to understand how legislation, terror, and propaganda isolated German Jewry from German society. Students also have an opportunity to consider the role and responsibility of the individual in interrupting hate and the escalation of violence. (See Lesson 2: Antisemitism.)

Lesson 4: The Ghettos

This lesson provides students with an opportunity to learn about the ghettos established throughout Nazi Europe and understand that the ghettos were one phase in the continuum of Nazi racial policies that sought to solve the so-called "Jewish problem." Students will also learn about the conditions in most ghettos and how those conditions severely limited Jewish life and led to feelings of humiliation and loss of dignity. Using several primary sources, students will have an opportunity to learn that despite severe overcrowding, starvation, diseases, and grief, Jews still did their utmost to conduct their lives and retain their human dignity. (See Lesson 2: Antisemitism, Lesson 3: Nazi Germany, Lesson 5: The "Final Solution," Lesson 6: Jewish Resistance, Lesson 9: Perpetrators, Collaborators, and Bystanders, and Lesson 10: The Children.)

Lesson 5: The "Final Solution"

The purpose of this lesson is for students to learn about one of humanity's darkest chapters—the systematic mass murder of the Jews that came to be known as the "Final Solution of the Jewish Question." This includes learning about the Einsatzgruppen (mobile killing squads), the Nazi extermination camps, and the perpetrators and collaborators who took part in the murder. This lesson also provides an opportunity for students to learn how Jews attempted to maintain their humanity in the camps despite the inhumane conditions and brutal treatment they faced. (See Lesson 2: Antisemitism, Lesson 3: Nazi Germany, Lesson 8: Survivors and Liberators, and Lesson 9: Perpetrators, Collaborators, and Bystanders.)

Lesson 6: Jewish Resistance

This lesson provides an opportunity for students to explore Jewish resistance efforts during the Holocaust—focusing on the period from the establishment of the ghettos through the implementation of the "Final Solution." An opportunity is provided for students to learn about the risks of resisting Nazi domination and the means, scope, and intensity of resistance efforts. These ranged from cultural and spiritual resistance in the ghettos to armed resistance of partisans and ghetto and camp prisoners. At their core, these forms of resistance are expressions of the capacity to preserve what is best in humanity in the face of the worst humanity has to offer. This lesson also provides an opportunity for students to consider the role of personal and cultural identity in their lives. (See Lesson 2: Antisemitism, Lesson 4: The Ghettos, and Lesson 5: The "Final Solution.")

Lesson 7: Rescuers and Non-Jewish Resistance

This lesson provides students with an opportunity to learn about the types of rescue that occurred in Nazi-occupied Europe and to consider the moral choices that non-Jews made in order to help Jews survive. The lesson also examines the obstacles and dangers that hidden children faced during the Holocaust. (See Lesson 2: Antisemitism, Lesson 5: The "Final Solution," and Lesson 6: Jewish Resistance.)

Lesson 8: Survivors and Liberators

The purpose of this lesson is to provide students with an understanding of the political, legal, social, and emotional status of the Jewish survivors. This lesson also examines the role of the liberators following the defeat of the Nazis at the end of World War II. (See Lesson 2: Antisemitism and Lesson 5: The "Final Solution.")

Lesson 9: Perpetrators, Collaborators, and Bystanders

This lesson provides an opportunity for students to examine the complex issues of responsibility and guilt within the context of the Nazi occupation of Europe. Students will also learn about the war crimes trials following World War II and consider the responsibility of the free world to provide a safe haven for refugees attempting to escape Europe. This lesson also provides students with an introduction to Holocaust denial as a contemporary form of antisemitism. (See Lesson 1: Studying the Holocaust, Lesson 2: Antisemitism, Lesson 3: Nazi Germany, and Lesson 5: The "Final Solution.")

Lesson 10: The Children

The purpose of this lesson is for students to understand the effects of the Holocaust on its most innocent victims—children—since targeting babies and children was an important step in the attempt by the Nazis to erase the Jews and their future. Students will also research post-Holocaust genocides and analyze children's rights violations. In addition, students are provided an opportunity to develop a position on whether an event the magnitude of the Holocaust could happen again and to consider the role and responsibility of the individual in seeing that it does not. (See Lesson 1: Studying the Holocaust, Lesson 2: Antisemitism, Lesson 4: The Ghettos, Lesson 5: The "Final Solution," Lesson 7: Rescuers and Non-Jewish Resistance, and Lesson 9: Perpetrators, Collaborators, and Bystanders.)

Lesson Components

Introduction

Suggested subject areas where material in the lesson may be effectively taught or where cross-discipline teaching is recommended, a list of instructional techniques and specific skills practiced or reinforced in the lesson, and a description of the lesson.

Objectives

The anticipated student learning that will occur as a result of the lesson.

Key Words & Phrases

A list of vocabulary words that students will need to know in order to effectively participate in the lesson. All key words and phrases are defined in the Glossary, located on the Echoes and Reflections website. Some terms include phonetic pronunciations.

Academic Standards

A list of the Common Core State Standards and National Curriculum Standards for Social Studies that the lesson addresses. A complete analysis of how a particular lesson addresses Common Core State Standards by grade level and specific skills is available on the Echoes and Reflections website.

Procedures

Step-by-step teacher instructions to implement the lesson. Also included in this section is additional information for teachers to share with students while teaching the lesson. Procedures include direction to teachers for when to show and discuss the clips of visual history testimony integrated into the lesson. Those survivors and witnesses who appear in the video clips are identified in About the Interviewee/s. An interviewee is only identified the first time he or she appears in a lesson; however, if an interviewee appears in a subsequent lesson, his or her biographical information is repeated. The Biographical Profiles, available on the website, provide additional information about the interviewees.

[NOTE: The amount of time suggested for implementing each lesson is approximate and should only be used as a guide. Teachers will be the best judge as to the amount of material their students will be able to manage over what time period. All lessons are divided into two, three, or four parts based on content. Points for breaking up lessons at the end of class periods have not been provided, as class period times differ widely.]

Lesson Resources

The materials needed to implement each lesson are included at the end of the lesson and also on the Echoes and Reflections website. These resources include informational and literary texts, definitions, maps, photographs, artwork, visual history testimony and other primary source materials referenced in the lesson. These pages were designed to be reproduced; however, their use is strictly limited to the educational purpose outlined in the Teacher's Resource Guide.

Instructional Strategies

Many of the methodologies used to present concepts in Echoes and Reflections promote critical thinking and interaction among students in a civil and socially responsible manner. The lessons include a variety of instructional strategies including directed discussion, small-group work, brainstorming, journaling, and the examination of primary source materials, including written and visual history testimony of survivors and witnesses.

Directed Discussion

Every lesson in Echoes and Reflections includes suggested discussion questions. Teachers should decide how many and which questions are most appropriate for their students. Some of these questions test student comprehension of the concepts presented; others ask students to formulate and share opinions, draw conclusions, make inferences, or connect material to parallel situations. These discussion questions probe students' thinking and provide students with opportunities to support their opinions or positions, and to consider important lessons about moral and ethical decision-making in addition to strictly factual information. Such questions, if used consistently in the classroom, become internalized by students as questions that they need to ask themselves. Review and reinforce the value of carefully listening to others during all directed discussions.

Small-Group Work

Echoes and Reflections provides numerous opportunities for students to work collaboratively. Teachers may want to use a variety of grouping methods including randomly assigned groups, self-selected groups, or teacher-selected groups. The experience of working with many different classmates increases the likelihood that students will be exposed to diverse perspectives and communication styles. This instructional technique also gives students time to explore what helps groups work well together and what can interfere with effective group process. To maximize student participation in the small-group process, make sure that all students clearly understand what is being asked of them and hold students accountable for the decisions and actions taken by the group. Emphasize that the goal of small-group work is not for everyone to agree (even though there are times when consensus is required) but to share information that will enhance the learning experience for all group members. Be sensitive to the academic requirements of each lesson and the abilities of your students. Everyone should contribute successfully to the group process.

Brainstorming

Throughout Echoes and Reflections, brainstorming sessions are used as a springboard to begin discussing new concepts. Because brainstorming separates the process of generating ideas from the process of discrimination and judgment, students have an opportunity to contribute ideas without fear of being "wrong." It is important to remind students throughout brainstorming sessions to work quickly, not to censor their own ideas, not to criticize any of the suggested ideas, and whenever possible, to expand on the ideas of others.

Journaling

Every lesson includes at least one opportunity for students to reflect on what they are learning, record their feelings and reactions to the information, and think about how the material has meaning in their own lives and in society. Journaling also serves as a mechanism by which students create their own primary source material. These assignments, which appear under the heading Reflect and Respond, can be presented to students after completing all or part of a lesson, can be kept in a notebook or on computers. The sensitive and emotional nature of the topics may preclude teacher evaluation. If journaling is to be used as an assessment tool, students should be assured that they will not be evaluated negatively for expressing opinions different from others in the class or from the teacher's.

Examination of Interdisciplinary Primary Source Materials

Echoes and Reflections is replete with photographs, artwork, diary entries, letters, government documents, poems, and written and visual history testimony. These materials invite teachers and students to confront a wide array of topics from many perspectives in historical context. Such testimonies, memoirs, and narratives are genuine ways to increase knowledge of the Holocaust and its historical legacy. With primary source materials, students work with the fragmentary and detailed pieces of evidence that historians themselves use as building blocks in gathering evidence about the past. Additionally, primary sources, approached critically, can help students build an authentic and complete portrait of the past, unlike textbook material that tends to be softened for students through editing.

Because Echoes and Reflections provides many opportunities for students to analyze and synthesize primary source materials, it is an invaluable resource for helping students develop the skills needed to effectively respond to Document-based Questions (DBQs) as well as identifying and defending their own conclusions and opinions. It is strongly recommended that students be given ample time to examine primary source materials like photographs, artifacts, artwork, diary entries, and listen carefully to visual history testimony to help them frame their own thoughts about what they are seeing or reading before giving them all of the factual background information associated with the piece. This will allow for a deeper level of interest and inquiry and will give students the opportunity to practice analyzing primary source materials on their own.

[NOTE: Grammar, usage, and spelling have not been altered on primary source documents. With the exception of primary source documents, accents and diacritics are used sparingly throughout the resource.]

Assessment

Student performance on many of the tasks and assignments in Echoes and Reflections lend themselves to traditional forms of assessment; however, other material is highly subjective and teachers will need to exercise caution in determining whether or not a student has been successful in meeting a lesson's objectives. When a lesson provides students with an opportunity to practice skills with which they may have little prior experience or to critically examine difficult and emotionally sensitive material, they should be made aware that it is their willingness to participate and their efforts that are being assessed, not their "answers." Students must not feel that there are "right answers" that the teacher is trying to get them to articulate; instead students should be encouraged to construct an understanding of the Holocaust as the multifaceted event that it was, with no easy answers and a multitude of complexities. Such an examination practices the skills needed for life-long learning.

About Visual History Testimony

Visual history testimony provides students a rare opportunity to connect with survivors and other witnesses to the Holocaust through a digital medium, which capitalizes on the visual culture of the 21st century. Rich and diverse full life stories, visual history testimony not only supports the study of the Holocaust, but also broaches questions of fairness, justice, labeling, and scapegoating, making it a useful tool for inter- and cross-disciplinary study in history, psychology, literature, character education, and civics. As an integral component of the Echoes and Reflections lessons, visual history testimony presents students with multidimensional perspectives of witnesses to the Holocaust that draw on and promote students' cognitive skills and affective domain, leading to a more informed understanding and interpretation of the Holocaust.

For additional information on using visual history testimony in the classroom, access Guidelines for Using Visual History Testimony on the website.

About the Website (echoesandreflections.org)

The Echoes and Reflections website is an extension of the materials included in the *Echoes and Reflections Teacher's Resource Guide,* allowing digital access to the materials teachers need to implement the lessons. The Lessons section of the website includes a Timeline of key events that took place in Germany and other parts of Europe and the world between 1933 and 1945; a Glossary of terms associated with studying the Holocaust; a list of Visual History Clips by Lesson; and links to USC Shoah Foundation's educational website, IWitness.

The Lesson Components page includes the following information and materials for each of the ten lessons:

- Lesson title and description
- Common Core State Standards
- Downloadable lesson resources
- Clips of visual history testimony, links to the full testimonies in IWitness, and Biographical Profiles
- Multimedia activities from IWitness that complement the lesson
- Additional resources, including supplemental assets from the Yad Vashem archives

In addition, the website also provides educators and students with resources to augment their knowledge and understanding of the Holocaust. These resources include information about the Holocaust, suggested resources and activities for Holocaust remembrance, frequently asked questions about using Echoes and Reflections in the classroom, blogs and examples of how teachers are using the lessons in their classrooms, and scholarly articles to help inform Holocaust instruction.

The Echoes and Reflections website also provides links to USC Shoah Foundation's educational website, IWitness, which seamlessly complements Echoes and Reflections. IWitness features over 1,500 video testimonies from USC Shoah Foundation's Visual History Archive and allows teachers and their students to search, watch, and learn directly from the eyewitnesses to history, including the individuals who are featured in Echoes and Reflections. The interactive online IWitness Activities, including Echoes and Reflections-aligned Activities, expand lessons in the guide and can easily be incorporated into the classroom. Students are able to construct multimedia projects within IWitness that integrate testimony clips together with assets from other sources, including Yad Vashem, such as photographs and maps, voiceover audio, music, and text.

Teaching about the Holocaust

Teaching about the Holocaust (*Shoah*) goes beyond understanding the historical fact that six million Jews were brutally murdered along with other innocent victims of the German regime during World War II. The Holocaust is a lesson in what can happen when hate, extreme prejudice ideology, and discrimination are allowed to flourish and become official policy. It is a lesson in the failure of individuals, institutions, and governments to take a stand against injustice. A comprehensive study of the events leading up to the Holocaust, and of the Holocaust itself, provides students with opportunities to realize the relative ease with which fundamental human and civil rights can be denied and to understand the ramifications of stereotyping, prejudice, antisemitism, discrimination, and scapegoating.

Suggestions for effectively teaching about the Holocaust are presented throughout this resource, as part of the **Preparing to Use This Lesson** section that begins every lesson. The content and instructional strategies that comprise each lesson adhere to effective Holocaust instruction and are consistent with constructivist teaching methods—including inquiry-based learning—already being used in the classroom. In addition, general guidelines to plan and implement an effective Holocaust education unit are listed below.

Planning

- Define terms that will be used consistently (e.g., Holocaust, genocide, antisemitism) so that students will all be working from a common vocabulary.

- Provide students with the necessary background on the history of antisemitism and the role it played in allowing the Holocaust to occur.

- Contextualize the history of the Holocaust by helping students understand what happened before and after specific events.

- Individualize the history of the Holocaust by translating statistics into personal stories; use survivor and witness testimony whenever possible.

- Develop a cross-curricular approach to enrich students' understanding of the Holocaust.

- Provide an abundance of primary source materials representing a variety of perspectives.

- Use age-appropriate written and visual content; avoid use of horrific imagery.

- Make the Holocaust relevant to students' lives by connecting what they are learning to contemporary events.

Implementation

- Create an environment where students feel safe sharing ideas and asking questions of the teacher, other students, and themselves.

- Foster empathy by challenging students to understand people and their attitudes and actions in historical context.

- Help students appreciate historical complexity by encouraging them to recognize that simple answers are rarely adequate to understand an event the magnitude of the Holocaust.

- Approach a subject as sensitive and complex as the Holocaust with caution by not using simulation activities; primary source materials have the unique power to engage students in the study of the Holocaust.

- Be aware of and responsive to the concerns and the range of possible and expected emotions of your students when studying this difficult and complex subject matter; allow sufficient time for students to share their feelings about what they are learning.

- Refrain from comparing the pain of any one group with that of another; it is counterproductive. Oppression in any form is harmful to individuals, groups, and society.

- Stress that the Holocaust was not inevitable; it was the result of choices and decisions made by individuals.

- Distinguish between the history of the Holocaust and the lessons that might be learned from that history.

Adapted from Teaching Guidelines (Berlin, Germany: Education Working Group of the International Holocaust Remembrance Alliance). Additional information on these guidelines is available at holocaustremembrance.com/educate.

About Photo

Smoke Rising from the Burning of Bodies in the Camp, Treblinka, Poland, 1943 (2 BO 8)

Yad Vashem Photo Archive

"Some of the people disapproved, but their disapproval was only silence."

– Kurt Messerschmidt, Jewish Survivor

Preparing to Use This Lesson

Below is information to keep in mind when using this lesson. In some cases, the points elaborate on general suggestions listed in the "Teaching about the Holocaust" section in the Introduction to this resource, and are specific to the content of the lesson. This material is intended to help teachers consider the complexities of teaching the Holocaust and to deliver accurate and sensitive instruction.

- Students will likely have a general understanding of what is meant by "the Holocaust," but that understanding may come primarily from movies and a few assigned readings. Determine what students know about the Holocaust and how they have come to possess that knowledge.

- It is important that students have a clear understanding of the vocabulary used in Echoes and Reflections. Teachers may decide to distribute a copy of the Glossary (available on the website) to each student for future reference or point out where students can access the Glossary online. It is recommended that other words in the lesson that may be unfamiliar to students are also reviewed to ensure understanding of the subject matter.

- Help students understand that the Nazis used words and phrases to influence and manipulate the masses. The term *Kristallnacht* is an example of Nazi "language." Translated, *Kristallnacht* means "Crystal Night" (also often translated as "Night of Broken Glass"), a description that hardly captures the devastation and demoralization that Jews faced across Germany, Austria, and in areas of the Sudetenland in Czechoslovakia on November 9/10, 1938. There are numerous other examples of this same tendency in the language of the Nazi perpetrators: *Sonderbehandlung* ("special treatment") for the murder of primarily Jewish victims, *Euthanasie* for a policy of mass murder of individuals with mental or physical disabilities, *Arbeit Macht Frei* ("Work Makes You Free") over the entrance to Auschwitz. When the Nazis launched their plan to annihilate the remaining Jews in Poland in the fall of 1943, they called it *Erntefest*, or "Harvest Festival." While this may have been a code word, it had the same grim irony that was reflected in *Kristallnacht*.

- Teachers are strongly discouraged from using simulations when teaching about the Holocaust and other genocides. There is a danger that students might be excited by the power of the perpetrators or demonstrate a morbid fascination for the suffering of the victims. It may be useful, however, for students to take on the role of someone from a neutral country, responding to events: a journalist writing an article or editorial; a concerned citizen writing to his or her political representative; or a campaigner trying to mobilize public opinion. Such activities can highlight possible courses of action that students can take about events that concern them in the world today.

- Many students will be unfamiliar with the medium of first-person, visual history testimony. Students will react to the visual history testimony in this and all of the lessons in very different ways. This range of responses should be expected and welcomed. It may be necessary for students to view a particular testimony clip more than once in order to feel comfortable with the medium and to process the information presented by the interviewee. For additional information on using visual history testimony in the classroom, refer to "About Visual History Testimony" in the Introduction to this resource or access Guidelines for Using Visual History Testimony on the website.

STUDYING THE HOLOCAUST

About This Lesson

🕐 120–180 minutes

❖ **INTRODUCTION** This lesson provides an opportunity for students to discuss the value and importance of studying human catastrophes, in general, and the Holocaust, in particular. The lesson also provides an opportunity for students to consider the importance of examining both primary and secondary source materials when studying historical events and to begin to develop a common vocabulary for studying the Holocaust and other genocides.

This two-part lesson has material appropriate for history, social studies, Holocaust and genocide studies, and English/language arts classes. Instructional strategies and techniques used in the lesson include large-group discussion, small-group work, brainstorming, vocabulary building, comparing and contrasting information, analyzing primary and secondary source material, interpreting visual history testimony, and journaling.

❖ **OBJECTIVES** After completing this lesson, students will be able to:

- Differentiate between natural and human catastrophes.
- Develop a rationale for studying human catastrophes.
- Compare and contrast several definitions of the Holocaust.
- Define genocide.
- Differentiate between primary and secondary source materials and explain how each is important when studying historical events.
- Summarize the causes and effects of the *Kristallnacht Pogrom* based on analysis of primary and secondary source materials.
- Discuss both the content and the messages in a clip of visual history testimony.

RESOURCES & TESTIMONIES

All of the resources used in this lesson can be found in this guide at the end of this lesson and at echoesandreflections.org.

Visual history testimonies are available on the website or on the DVD that accompanies this resource guide.

Teachers are urged to review the lesson procedures to identify other materials and technology needed to implement the lesson.

❖ **KEY WORDS & PHRASES**

Brownshirts	Gypsies	Reich
collaborator	Holocaust	Shoah
concentration camp	Jehovah's Witness	Sinti-Roma
discrimination	*Kristallnacht Pogrom*	survivor
European Jewry	Nazi	United Nations
genocide	*pogrom*	visual history testimony
Gestapo	propaganda	

all in glossary on webpage

cd resource about holocaust time line is here too

❖ ACADEMIC STANDARDS The materials in this lesson address the following national education standards:

Common Core State Standards

- Reading Standards for Informational Text 6–12
- Writing Standards 6–12
- Speaking and Listening Standards 6–12
- Language Standards 6–12
- Reading Standards for Literacy in History/Social Studies 6–12
- Writing Standards for Literacy in History/Social Studies 6–12

A complete analysis of how this lesson addresses Common Core State Standards by grade level and specific skills is available on the Echoes and Reflections website.

National Curriculum Standards for Social Studies

❷ Time, Continuity, and Change

❺ Individuals, Groups, and Institutions

❻ Power, Authority, and Governance

❾ Global Connections

❿ Civic Ideals and Practices

Procedures

Part 1: Human Catastrophes

1. Begin this lesson by writing the word "catastrophe" on the board or on chart paper. Ask students to define the term and identify what factors they believe make an event a catastrophe. Have students give examples of both natural and human catastrophes. Chart student responses. For example:

CATASTROPHE

Natural	Human
earthquake	Middle Passage
drought	September 11th
tsunami	Holocaust

2. Discuss the difference between natural and human catastrophes. Emphasize that natural catastrophes are most often out of people's control, whereas human catastrophes are the direct result of actions that people take.

3. Divide the class into pairs or small groups and have each group select a recorder. Instruct students to answer the following questions:

- Who is likely to study human catastrophes (e.g., historians, social scientists, theologians) and why?

- What kinds of questions do you think people studying human catastrophes would want to answer?

- How might the questions be different from questions asked about natural catastrophes?

4. Have each group select a reporter to share its ideas with the whole group. [Optional: Chart responses on the board or on chart paper.]

5. Explain to students that they will be studying about a time in history in which a great human catastrophe occurred. This catastrophe, the Holocaust (in Hebrew, *Shoah*), is the name given for the murder of some six million Jews by the Nazis and their collaborators. The Holocaust occurred during what is known as the Nazi era from 1933 until 1945, during which time Jews were persecuted with increasing severity. After the outbreak of World War II in September 1939, and especially after the Nazis and their collaborators invaded the Soviet Union in June 1941, they began the systematic mass murder of Jews in an attempt to kill all Jews everywhere. Although only Jews were targeted for complete annihilation, many others also fell victim to the Nazis and their allies during World War II which lasted until 1945: scores of thousands of Sinti-Roma; at least 250,000 people with mental or physical disabilities; more than three million Soviet prisoners, about two million Poles; and thousands of homosexuals, Communists, Socialists, trades unionists, and Jehovah's Witnesses. Have students volunteer possible reasons why this period of history is studied. Encourage students to consider that this period of history is studied because it is an important part of world history and because many of the underlying causes and effects of the Holocaust have had a profound influence on later historical events.

6. Display the definitions of the Holocaust used by three different organizations. Review the definitions with students, analyzing the cumulative impact of specific word choices. Have students compare and contrast the definitions and consider possible reasons why the definitions are not all exactly the same. [Optional: Divide the class into three groups and provide each group with one of the definitions to study. Follow with each group sharing its findings and then have students compare and contrast the definitions.]

NOTE 1.6

A differentiation can be made between the general meaning of the word "holocaust" and the use of "the Holocaust" to describe a series of events at a particular historic time. Compare the use of "the Holocaust" to the use of "9/11" in that both refer to a specific historic event during a particular time.

7. Write the word "genocide" on the board or on chart paper. Ask students for their thoughts on what the word means or in what context/s they have heard the word used. Ask students for examples of genocides based on material they may have studied in other classes or know from current events (e.g., Native Americans, Armenians, Tutsi, Darfurians).

8. Inform students that the United Nations has defined genocide as a crime. Before presenting the legal definition of genocide, ask students how they would define genocide to include the instigator (e.g., the state), the targeted group (e.g., an ethnic, racial, tribal, national, or religious group) and the intent (deliberate). Present the United Nations' definition of genocide and have students compare their definition to the United Nations' definition. Have students consider which definition they think best fits the Holocaust and consider why the Holocaust fits the definition of genocide.

NOTE 1.8

Provide each student with a copy of the Glossary downloadable on the website or have them bookmark the web page on their computers. Encourage students to refer to the Glossary throughout their study of the Holocaust.

9. Ask students to share what they already know about the Holocaust and to identify whenever possible their source or sources of

information. List responses on the board or chart paper.

Examples:

- Some Jews went into hiding (source: *Anne Frank: Diary of a Young Girl*)
- Some non-Jews tried to rescue Jews (source: *Schindler's List*)
- Allied troops liberated the concentration camps (source: textbook, a survivor of the Holocaust, a relative who fought in World War II)

10. Review the list of sources that was developed. Help students understand the difference between the primary sources and secondary sources on the list, and have them consider primary and secondary sources not identified on the list that might also be useful in studying the Holocaust. Review how the many types of sources (e.g., diaries, letters, historical fiction, written and visual history testimony, autobiographies, photographs, textbooks) may differ in the type of information included. Initiate a discussion on the accuracy of such sources and reasons why source material must be scrutinized for accuracy.

11. Explain that throughout this study of the Holocaust, students will examine many primary and secondary source materials. Explain that the Holocaust is one of the most documented events in human history and that the perpetrators produced much of the evidence. The Holocaust occurred in modern times, and the Nazi system was a highly bureaucratic one. When the historian wants to know what happened, when, and why, there is a sea of official records, private papers, and first-person accounts ready to be investigated. Naturally, sources must be studied carefully, and all require interpretation. The documents reproduced throughout this resource highlight the historian's tools and tasks, and bring the topics incorporated into these lessons into sharper focus.

Part 2: Primary and Secondary Source Materials

1. Tell students that they will be studying several documents related to the same event in order to compare and contrast source material. To prepare them for this assignment, provide students with some or all of the following background on the *Kristallnacht Pogrom*.

About *Kristallnacht Pogrom* From the time the Nazis came to power in 1933 they began isolating Jews in Germany, and passed many laws to that effect. In the first half of 1938, additional laws were passed in Germany restricting Jewish economic activity and occupational opportunities. In July 1938, a law was passed requiring all Jews to carry identification cards. Later that year, 17,000 Jews of Polish citizenship, many of whom had been living in Germany for decades, were arrested and relocated across the Polish border. The Polish government refused to admit them so they were interned in "relocation camps" on the Polish frontier.

Among the deportees was Zindel Grynszpan, who had been born in western Poland and had moved to Hanover, Germany, where he established a small store, in 1911. On the night of October 27, Grynszpan and his family were forced out of their home by German police. His store and the family's possessions were confiscated and they were forced to move over the Polish border.

Grynszpan's seventeen-year-old son, Herschel, was living with an uncle in Paris. When he received news of his family's expulsion, he went to the German embassy in Paris on November 7, intending to assassinate the German Ambassador to France. Upon discovering that the Ambassador was not in the embassy, he shot a low-ranking diplomat, Third Secretary Ernst vom Rath. Rath was critically wounded and died two days later, on November 9.

Grynszpan's attack was interpreted by Joseph Goebbels, Hitler's Chief of Propaganda, as a direct attack against the Reich and used as an excuse to launch a *pogrom* against Jews. The Nazis euphemistically called this *pogrom Kristallnacht,* "Night of the Broken Glass"; the harmless sound of the name disguised the terror and devastation of the *pogrom* and the demoralization faced by Jews across Germany, Austria, and in areas of the Sudetenland in Czechoslovakia.

On the nights of November 9 and 10, rampaging mobs throughout Germany and the newly acquired territories of Austria and Sudetenland freely attacked Jews in the street, in their homes, and at their places of work and worship. Almost 100 Jews were killed and hundreds more injured; approximately 7,000 Jewish businesses and homes were damaged and looted; 1,400 synagogues were burned; cemeteries and schools were vandalized; and 30,000 Jews were arrested and sent to concentration camps.

2. Divide the class into six groups and have each group select a recorder. Distribute one of the documents listed below to each group, and instruct students to discuss and make notes on what they learn about the *Kristallnacht Pogrom* from studying the material:

   • *Heydrich's Instructions, November 1938*

   • *Letter by Margarete Drexler to the Gestapo*

   • *Description of the Riot in Dinslaken*

   • *Magdeburg, Germany, November 10, 1938*

   • *Siegen, Germany, November 10, 1938*

   • Textbook description of the *Kristallnacht Pogrom* [Note: Locate and have on hand a textbook, or a portion thereof, that includes information about the *Kristallnacht Pogrom.*]

3. After allowing ample time to discuss the documents, instruct students to pass their documents to another group. Group members should again discuss and make notes on what they learn about the topic from studying the material. Continue this process until all groups have had an opportunity to analyze all six documents.

4. Have students share their thinking about the six documents in a whole-group discussion. Following are suggested questions:

   • Which of these materials are primary source documents? Which are secondary source documents?

   • What were some of the things your group noticed while studying the two photographs? What questions, if any, did the photographs raise for your group?

   • How is studying photographs different from studying other types of material?

   • What did you learn about the *Kristallnacht Pogrom* by reading Heydrich's instructions?

   • What argument does Margarete Drexler use in her letter to the Gestapo to try to get her money returned? Why is this information important to know?

   • How does the *Description of the Riot in Dinslaken* make the story of the *Kristallnacht Pogrom* a "human story"?

   • What, if anything, did you learn from the textbook description of the *Kristallnacht Pogrom* that you didn't learn from any of the primary sources?

5. Explain to students that another source of information about the Holocaust is survivor and witness testimony. Survivor and witness testimonies, unlike documents or words from a book, communicate the crucial role of the individual's experiences through his or her stories.

NOTE 2.5

Teachers are encouraged to review the document Guidelines for Using Visual History Testimony available on the website.

TESTIMONY VIEWING

About the Interviewee

Kurt Messerschmidt was born January 2, 1915, in Werneuchen, Germany. He was forced to live in the Theresienstadt ghetto and later imprisoned in the concentration camps of Flossenbürg, Sachsenhausen, Golleschau, and Ganacker. Kurt also was a prisoner in the Auschwitz-Birkenau extermination camp. His interview was conducted in the United States. When the war began, Kurt was twenty-four years old.

For additional information about Kurt Messerschmidt, see his Biographical Profile available on the website.

NOTE 2.7

Additional testimony and materials on the *Kristallnacht Pogrom* can be found in Lesson 3: Nazi Germany and on IWitness.

The interviewees in these testimonies are not "simply" Holocaust survivors and other witnesses. They are students, teachers, brothers, sisters, friends, and family members. They tell stories that recount anger, frustration, humor, surprise, relief, and fear. Viewing first-person, visual history testimony is a personal experience—no two people necessarily react to hearing a particular clip of testimony exactly the same way. Tell students that the visual history testimony that they will hear was collected by USC Shoah Foundation. Information about USC Shoah Foundation can be found at the beginning of this guide and on the Echoes and Reflections website.

6. Show students Visual History Testimony: *Studying the Holocaust* and follow with a discussion using some or all of the questions below.

   • How do you feel after listening to Kurt Messerschmidt talk about his experiences?

   • What is meant by the term "testimony"?

   • What role, if any, does memory play when giving testimony?

   • What, if anything, do you learn about the *Kristallnacht Pogrom* from Kurt's testimony that you didn't learn from any of the other materials studied?

   • How does Kurt's testimony reinforce what you learned from other sources?

   • What are the benefits and challenges of using visual history testimony?

   • What role does the testimony collected by the Shoah Foundation play in the study of the Holocaust? How is this role different from the role and responsibility of historians? How is each important?

7. End this lesson with each student completing a "3-2-1 Assessment".

   • List <u>three</u> things you learned participating in this lesson.

   • Name <u>two</u> things that surprised you. [**Note:** Some teachers prefer to use Name <u>two</u> things that you didn't understand.]

   • Identify <u>one</u> question you still have.

Reflect and Respond

Either in class or as homework, have students reflect and respond to one or more of the topics below or have them develop a topic that has meaning for them based on the material covered in the lesson.

   • What thoughts and feelings come to mind when you hear reference to "the Holocaust"? What do you know about this event and how have you learned your information? Discuss your thoughts on the importance of studying the Holocaust.

   • In his testimony, Kurt Messerschmidt talks about helping the cigar shop owner pick up pieces of glass from the street. He says that he was sure some of the people disapproved of what was happening that night, but their disapproval was only silence. Why do you think that people are often unwilling to speak out when they see something wrong happening? What are the dangers of being silent in the face of injustice?

- Kurt Messerschmidt's testimony about his experience during the *Kristallnacht Pogrom* is filled with rich detail and sensory images, and yet is very compact. Describe a particularly important experience from your life, crafting the memory in a narrative with a clear beginning, middle, and end, vivid details, and a sense of place.

Making Connections

The additional activities and projects listed below can be integrated directly into the lesson or can be used to extend the lesson once it has been completed. The topics lend themselves to students' continued study of the Holocaust as well as opportunities for students to make meaningful connections to other people and events, including relevant contemporary issues. These activities may include instructional strategies and techniques and/or address academic standards in addition to those that were identified for the lesson.

1. Visit IWitness (iwitness.usc.edu) for activities specific to Lesson 1: Studying the Holocaust.

2. Have each student or pairs of students prepare a list of three to five questions that they would like to ask Kurt Messerschmidt after listening to his clip of testimony. After developing the questions, students should go to Kurt's Biographical Profile on the Echoes and Reflections website and see if the answers to their questions are included in the text. If unable to answer all of their questions from the Biographical Profile, have students go to IWitness (iwitness. usc.edu) and identify clips of testimony from Kurt's full testimony that may help answer the questions.

3. If the class has a dedicated classroom wiki, have one of the students volunteer to pose a question to the group based on what was covered in this lesson and have other students respond. Another option would be for students to start a wiki based on Kurt Messerschmidt's testimony and his decision "not to be silent" in the face of injustice. Students could then contribute to the discussion; add stories, videos, etc. As the class continues its study of the Holocaust, different students could take a leadership role in posting new material and questions and inviting others to respond.

4. Instruct students to gather relevant information from multiple print and digital sources about a recent catastrophe (either human or natural), including both primary sources (e.g., an interview) and secondary sources (e.g., a news report) regarding the event. Students should then write an informational essay that introduces the topic, compares and contrasts the information gathered from various sources, and explain how, if at all, the use of both types of sources led to a more complete understanding of the event.

5. Have students research how the *Kristallnacht Pogrom* was covered in media, especially newspapers, in their state, city, or town. After gathering relevant information, instruct students to develop an argument to support or refute the idea that this event was accurately covered and reported to the public. [Note: If unable to locate local or state coverage of the *Kristallnacht Pogrom,* research how this historical event was covered in national or international media.] Have students prepare a written or oral summary of their findings and conclusions.

6. As an alternative to the activity above, have students research how editorial/political cartoonists in major national and international newspapers reacted to the events of the *Kristallnacht Pogrom.* Have students develop a PowerPoint or cloud-based presentation (e.g., Prezi), a written report, or decide on another format to present their work. Their presentations should include

examples of political cartoons published following the *Kristallnacht Pogrom*, information about how people responded to the cartoons if possible, as well as their interpretations of the cartoons and what they learned from studying them.

HOLOCAUST DEFINITIONS

United States Holocaust Memorial Museum, Washington, DC, USA

The Holocaust was the systematic, bureaucratic, state-sponsored persecution and murder of approximately six million Jews by the Nazi regime and its collaborators. "Holocaust" is a word of Greek origin meaning "sacrifice by fire." The Nazis, who came to power in Germany in January 1933, believed that Germans were "racially superior" and that the Jews, deemed "inferior," were an alien threat to the so-called German racial community.

During the era of the Holocaust, German authorities also targeted other groups because of their perceived "racial inferiority": Roma (Gypsies), the disabled, and some of the Slavic peoples (Poles, Russians, and others). Other groups were persecuted on political, ideological, and behavioral grounds, among them Communists, Socialists, Jehovah's Witnesses, and homosexuals.

HOLOCAUST DEFINITIONS

Yad Vashem, Jerusalem, Israel

The Holocaust was unprecedented genocide, total and systematic, perpetrated by Nazi Germany and its collaborators, with the aim of annihilating the Jewish people. The primary motivation was the Nazis' antisemitic racist ideology. Between 1933 and 1941, Nazi Germany pursued a policy that dispossessed the Jews of their rights and their property, followed by the branding and concentration of the Jewish population. This policy gained broad support in Germany and much of occupied Europe. In 1941, following the invasion of the Soviet Union, the Nazis and their collaborators launched the systematic mass murder of the Jews. By 1945, nearly six million Jews had been murdered.

HOLOCAUST DEFINITIONS

Imperial War Museum, London, UK*

'The Holocaust' is the term used to describe the systematic and wholesale slaughter of the Jews of Europe by the Nazis and their collaborators during the Second World War. Two-thirds of European Jewry perished between 1939 and 1945.

On coming to power in 1933, the Nazis began to actively persecute the Jews of Germany with the introduction of discriminatory legislation which was accompanied by vicious antisemitic propaganda. With the outbreak of the Second World War, the process escalated. Nazi conquests meant that every Jew in occupied Europe was under the threat of death.

Other groups besides the Jews fell victim to Nazi racial policies. Poles, Slavs, Soviet prisoners of war, Roma and Sinti (gypsies), were all murdered in vast numbers. And Hitler's political opponents, communists and trade unionists, Jehovah's Witnesses and homosexuals were also brutally done to death in Nazi concentration camps.

_____

*This definition has been abridged, specifically the third paragraph has not been included. No other changes have been made. The complete definition is available at iwm.org.uk/history/the-holocaust#.

GENOCIDE DEFINITION

L1

In 1948, the United Nations defined genocide as any of the following acts committed with intent to destroy, in whole or in part, a national, ethnic, racial, or religious group, including

- killing members of the group

- causing serious bodily or mental harm to members of the group

- deliberately inflicting on the group conditions of life calculated to bring about its physical destruction in whole or in part

- imposing measures intended to prevent births within the group

- forcibly transferring children of the group to another group

HEYDRICH'S INSTRUCTIONS, NOVEMBER 1938

Secret

Copy of Most Urgent telegram from Munich, of November 10, 1938, 1:20 A.M.

To
All Headquarters and Stations of the State Police
All districts and Sub-districts of the SD [Security Service]

Urgent! For immediate attention of Chief or his deputy!

Re: *Measures against Jews tonight*

Following the attempt on the life of Secretary of the Legation vom Rath in Paris, demonstrations against the Jews are to be expected in all parts of the Reich in the course of the coming night, November 9/10, 1938. The instructions below are to be applied in dealing with these events:

1. The Chiefs of the State Police, or their deputies, must immediately upon receipt of this telegram contact, by telephone, the political leaders in their areas *Gauleiter* or *Kreisleiter*—who have jurisdiction in their districts and arrange a joint meeting with the inspector or commander of the Order Police to discuss the arrangements for the demonstrations. At these discussions the political leaders will be informed that the German Police has received instructions, detailed below, from the *Reichsfuehrer* SS and the Chief of the German Police, with which the political leadership is requested to coordinate its own measures:

   a. Only such measures are to be taken as do not endanger German lives or property (i.e., synagogues are to be burned down only where there is no danger of fire in neighboring buildings).

   b. Places of business and apartments belonging to Jews may be destroyed but not looted. The police is instructed to supervise the observance of this order and to arrest looters.

   c. In commercial streets particular care is to be taken that non-Jewish businesses are completely protected against damage.

   d. Foreign citizens even if they are Jews are not to be molested.

2. On the assumption that the guidelines detailed under para. 1 are observed, the demonstrations are not to be prevented by the Police, which is only to supervise the observance of the guidelines.

3. On receipt of this telegram Police will seize all archives to be found in all synagogues and offices of the Jewish communities so as to prevent their destruction during the demonstrations. This refers only to material of historical value, not to contemporary tax records, etc. The archives are to be handed over to the locally responsible officers of the SD.

4. The control of the measures of the Security Police concerning the demonstrations against the Jews is vested in the organs of the State Police, unless inspectors of the Security Police have given their own instructions. Officials of the Criminal Police, members of the SD, of the Reserves and the SS in general may be used to carry out the measures taken by the Security Police.

5. As soon as the course of events during the night permits the release of the officials required, as many Jews in all districts, especially the rich, as can be accommodated in existing prisons are to be arrested. For the time being only healthy male Jews, who are not too old, are to be detained. After the detentions have been carried out the appropriate concentration camps are to be contacted immediately for the prompt accommodation of the Jews in the camps. Special care is to be taken that the Jews arrested in accordance with these instructions are not ill-treated....

signed Heydrich,

SS *Gruppenfuehrer*

LETTER BY MARGARETE DREXLER TO THE GESTAPO

Mannheim, 24 November 1938
Margarete Drexler, Landau Pfalz Suedring St. 10

To the Secret State Police Landau (Pfalz) The sum of 900 Marks* in cash was confiscated from me in the course of the action of 10 November. I herewith request to act for the return of my money, as I need it urgently for me and my child's livelihood. I hope that my request will be granted, as my husband died as a result of his injuries during the war—he fought and died for his fatherland with extreme courage—and I am left without any income. Until recent years you could have found a photo of my husband on the wall next to the picture of Generalfeldmarschall von Hindenburg in the canteen of the 23 Infantry regiment in Landau. This was done to honour his high military performance. His medals and decorations prove that he fought with great courage and honour. He received: The Iron Cross First Class, The Iron Cross Second Class, The Military Order of Merit Fourth Class with swords. The Military Order of Sanitation 2 class with a blue-white ribbon. This ribbon is usually bestowed only upon recipients of the Max Joseph Order, which accepts only members of the nobility. I can only hope that as a widow of such a man, so honoured by his country, my request for the return of my property will not be in vain.

With German greetings,
(signed) Frau Margarete Drexler Widow of reserve staff surgeon Dr. Hermann Drexler
Presently in Mannheim, 11 Kant St.

Enclosed: 6 photos of medals and decorations.

In 1938, 2.49 Marks = $1.00 U.S.

[NOTE: Margarete Drexler was deported to France in October 1940 with the other Jews of the Pfalz area. She died in the Gurs camp. The date of her death is unknown.]

Reprinted with permission from Yad Vashem Archives O.51/81. All rights reserved.

DESCRIPTION OF THE RIOT IN DINSLAKEN
Yitzhak S. Herz

...I recognized a Jewish face. In a few words the stranger explained to me: "I am the president of the Jewish community of Duesseldorf. I spent the night in the waiting-room of the Gelsenkirchen Railway Station. I have only one request—let me take refuge in the orphanage for a short while. While I was traveling to Dinslaken I heard in the train that anti-Semitic riots had broken out everywhere, and that many Jews had been arrested. Synagogues everywhere are burning!"

With anxiety I listened to the man's story; suddenly he said with a trembling voice: "No, I won't come in! I can't be safe in your house! We are all lost!" With these words he disappeared into the dark fog which cast a veil over the morning. I never saw him again.

In spite of this Job's message I forced myself not to show any sign of emotion. Only thus could I avoid a state of panic among the children and tutors. Nonetheless I was of the opinion that the young students should be prepared to brave the storm of the approaching catastrophe. About 7:30 A.M. I ordered 46 people, among them 32 children, into the dining hall of the institution and told them the following in a simple and brief address: "As you know, last night a Herr vom Rath, a member of the German Embassy in Paris, was assassinated. The Jews are held responsible for this murder. The high tension in the political field is now being directed against the Jews, and during the next few hours there will certainly be anti-Semitic excesses. This will happen even in our town. It is my feeling and my impression that we German Jews have never experienced such calamities since the Middle Ages. Be strong! Trust in God! I am sure we will withstand even these hard times"....

After breakfast the pupils were sent to the large study-hall of the institution. The teacher in charge tried to keep them busy. At 9:30 A.M. the bell at the main gate rang persistently. I opened the door: about 50 men stormed into the house, many of them with their coat- or jacket-collars turned up. At first they rushed into the dining room, which fortunately was empty, and there they began their work of destruction, which was carried out with the utmost precision. The frightened and fearful cries of the children resounded through the building. In a stentorian voice I shouted: "Children, go out into the street immediately!" This advice was certainly contrary to the orders of the Gestapo. I thought, however, that in the street, in a public place, we might be in less danger than inside the house. The children immediately ran down a small staircase at the back, most of them without hat or coat despite the cold and wet weather. We tried to reach the next street crossing, which was close to Dinslaken's Town Hall, where I intended to ask for police protection. About ten policemen were stationed here, reason enough for a sensation-seeking mob to await the next development. This was not very long in coming; the senior police officer, Freihahn, shouted at us: "Jews do not get protection from us! Vacate the area together with your children as quickly as possible!" Freihahn then chased us back to a side street in the direction of the backyard of the orphanage. As I was unable to hand over the key of the back gate, the policeman drew his bayonet and forced open the door. I then said to Freihahn: "The best thing is to kill me and the children, then our ordeal will be over quickly!" The officer responded to my "suggestion" merely with cynical laughter. Freihahn then drove all of us to the wet lawn of the orphanage garden. He gave us strict orders not to leave the place under any circumstances.

Facing the back of the building, we were able to watch how everything in the house was being systematically destroyed under the supervision of the men of law and order, the police. At short intervals we could hear the crunching of glass or the hammering against wood as windows and doors were broken. Books, chairs, beds, tables, linen, chests, parts of a piano, a radiogram, and maps were thrown through apertures in the wall, which a short while ago had been windows or doors.

In the meantime the mob standing around the building had grown to several hundred. Among these people I recognized some familiar faces, suppliers of the orphanage or tradespeople, who only a day or a week earlier had been happy to deal with us as customers. This time they were passive, watching the destruction without much emotion.

At 10:15 A.M. we heard the wailing of sirens! We noticed a heavy cloud of smoke billowing upward. It was obvious from the direction it was coming from that the Nazis had set the synagogue on fire. Very soon we saw smoke-clouds rising up, mixed with sparks of fire. Later I noticed that some Jewish houses, close to the synagogue, had also been set alight under the expert guidance of the fire-brigade. Its presence was a necessity, since the firemen had to save the homes of the non-Jewish neighborhood....

In the schoolyard we had to wait for some time. Several Jews, who had escaped the previous arrest and deportation to concentration camps, joined our gathering. Many of them, mostly women, were shabbily dressed. They told me that the brown hordes had driven them out of their homes, ordered them to leave everything behind and come at once, under Nazi guard, to the schoolyard. A stormtrooper in charge commanded some bystanders to leave the schoolyard "since there is no point in even looking at such scum!"

In the meantime our "family" had increased to 90, all of whom were placed in a small hall in the school. Nobody was allowed to leave the place. Men considered physically fit were called for duty. Only those over 60, among them people of 75 years of age, were allowed to stay. Very soon we learned that the entire Jewish male population under 60 had already been transferred to the concentration camp at Dachau....

I learned very soon from a policeman, who in his heart was still an anti-Nazi, that most of the Jewish men had been beaten up by members of the SA before being transported to Dachau. They were kicked, slapped in the face, and subjected to all sorts of humiliation. Many of those exposed to this type of ill-treatment had served in the German army during World War I. One of them, a Mr. Hugo B.C., had once worn with pride the Iron Cross First Class (the German equivalent of the Victoria Cross), which he had been awarded for bravery....

MAGDEBURG, GERMANY, NOVEMBER 10, 1938

Yad Vashem Photo Archive (135GO1)

SIEGEN, GERMANY, NOVEMBER 10, 1938

Et derrière:
LE JUIF

About Photo

An Antisemitic Propaganda
Poster from France (5299/9)

Yad Vashem Photo Archive

"Antisemitism had become suddenly very rampant...."

– H. Henry Sinason, Jewish Survivor

Preparing to Use This Lesson

Below is information to keep in mind when using this lesson. In some cases, the points elaborate on general suggestions listed in the "Teaching about the Holocaust" section in the Introduction to this resource, and are specific to the content of the lesson. This material is intended to help teachers consider the complexities of teaching the Holocaust and to deliver accurate and sensitive instruction.

- Antisemitism did not begin when Adolf Hitler came to power in January 1933. Antisemitism had long been entrenched in Germany and other European countries, and Jews for many centuries had been victims of widespread hatred and suspicion. By studying the roots of antisemitism, and its different forms, students will better understand the historical context about the rise of racial antisemitic ideology in Nazi Germany.

- When discussing stereotypes with students, there is always the risk of introducing them to generalizations that they did not know before. Special care should be taken when debriefing this lesson to reinforce the idea that while stereotypes and myths are easy to believe that does not make them true. It is also important to create an environment where students feel comfortable asking questions about the origins of specific stereotypes and why certain stereotypes continue to be believed. When discussing these issues with students, be cautious of the effect this discussion might have on them.

- This lesson has been designed to help teachers translate abstract ideas (e.g., antisemitism, propaganda, stereotypes, scapegoating) into active learning experiences, thereby creating a framework for processing and organizing information that otherwise might be difficult for students to understand. For some students it will be difficult to comprehend circumstances that are outside their immediate environment or experiences for which they have little or no previous background. There is also the possibility that students will be introduced to the concept of hatred against the cultural group to which they belong.

- Propaganda is an effective tool that has been used by both tyrants and democracies. Throughout this lesson, reinforce the idea that propaganda is manipulative and no one is immune to it.

- Some students may be uncomfortable with some of the subject matter associated with antisemitism and should be given opportunities to discuss their thoughts and feelings about the topic. Within the context of that conversation, it is important to stress that while antisemitism was a fundamental part of Christianity for centuries, it was also a product of world events and history. It is important, whenever possible, to accentuate the humanitarian aspect of Christianity as evidenced in many of the individuals identified as "Righteous Among the Nations." Information about the "Righteous Among the Nations" can be found in Lesson 7: Rescuers and Non-Jewish Resistance.

ANTISEMITISM

About This Lesson

 120–180 minutes

❖ **INTRODUCTION** This lesson provides an opportunity for students to learn about the origins of antisemitism. Students will also learn about prewar Jewish life in Germany and antisemitism in Nazi ideology and its similarities and differences from pre-Nazi antisemitism. Students will also examine propaganda methods that were used to exploit antisemitic attitudes among the German people and to create an atmosphere of terror.

This two-part lesson has material appropriate for history, social studies, civics, English/language arts, ethics, religion, and art classes. Instructional strategies used in the lesson include large-group discussion, brainstorming, reading skills, small-group work, understanding chronology of events, interpreting visual history testimony, analyzing political cartoons, analyzing photographs, critical thinking, and journaling.

❖ **OBJECTIVES** After completing this lesson, students will be able to:

- Define antisemitism and trace its origins.

- Explain how pre-Nazi antisemitism and Nazi racial ideology are similar and different.

- Discuss both the content and the messages in clips of visual history testimony.

- Describe propaganda methods.

- Give examples of propaganda methods that the Nazis used to exploit antisemitic attitudes among the German people and to isolate Jews from the rest of the population.

- Identify historical and contemporary examples of antisemitism, propaganda, and stereotyping.

RESOURCES & TESTIMONIES

All of the resources used in this lesson can be found in this guide at the end of this lesson and at echoesandreflections.org.

Visual history testimonies are available on the website or on the DVD that accompanies this resource guide.

Teachers are urged to review the lesson procedures to identify other materials and technology needed to implement the lesson.

❖ **KEY WORDS & PHRASES**

antisemitism	*Der Stürmer*	Nazi ideology
Aryan	discrimination	prejudice
Bar Mitzvah	hate group	propaganda
blood libel	Hitler Youth	racism
boycott	Judaism	*Rassenkunde*
cantor	*kippah*	scapegoat
caricature	kosher	stereotype
Chanukah	Ku Klux Klan	Storm Troopers
Christianity	*menorah*	swastika
dehumanization	Nazi	Zionism

❖ ACADEMIC STANDARDS The materials in this lesson address the following national education standards:

Common Core State Standards

- Reading Standards for Informational Text 6–12

- Writing Standards 6–12

- Speaking and Listening Standards 6–12

- Reading Standards for Literacy in History/Social Studies 6–12

- Writing Standards for Literacy in History/Social Studies 6–12

A complete analysis of how this lesson addresses Common Core State Standards by grade level and specific skills is available on the Echoes and Reflections website.

National Curriculum Standards for Social Studies

❶ Culture

❷ Time, Continuity, and Change

❹ Individual Development and Identity

❺ Individuals, Groups, and Institutions

❻ Power, Authority, and Governance

❿ Civic Ideals and Practices

Procedures

Part 1: Prewar Jewish Life and Nazi Antisemitism

1. Begin this lesson by showing students the map *Jewish Communities in Europe before the Nazis Rise to Power*. Provide time for students to share their observations and to consider the importance of demographic data when studying historical events; how can such data help us address questions or be integrated into a coherent understanding of an event?

2. Direct students' attention to Germany and note the Jewish population as well as the percentage of the total population that Jews represented. Ask students if they have any knowledge regarding Jewish life in Germany prior to the Holocaust and if so, what have they learned. Follow by asking students to consider what life might have been like for Jews in Germany prior to Hitler's rise to power.

3. Tell students that they will now watch three clips of testimony from individuals who experienced life in Germany prior to the rise of the Nazi Party. After introducing students to John Graham, H. Henry Sinason, and Margaret Lambert, show the first three clips from Part 1 of Visual History Testimony: *Antisemitism*.

> **TESTIMONY VIEWING**
>
> About the Interviewees
>
> John Graham was born on May 22, 1920, in Berlin, Germany. He did not experience life in the ghettos or concentration camps. In 1939, he fled to Kitchener Camp, a refugee camp in

continued on page 47

Richborough, England. His interview was conducted in the United Kingdom. When the war began, John was nineteen years old.

H. Henry Sinason was born on August 26, 1925, in Berlin, Germany. He did not experience life in the ghettos or concentration camps. In 1939, Henry, along with his brother, fled to France to live with their uncle. After the Nazis entered France, both Henry and his brother were sent to live in an orphanage and later fled to the United States. His interview was conducted in the United States. When the war began, Henry was fourteen years old.

Margaret Lambert was born on April 12, 1914, in Laupheim, Germany. She did not experience life in the ghettos or concentration camps. In 1937, Margaret fled from Germany to the home of a family friend living in the United States. Her interview was conducted in the United States. When the war began, Margaret was twenty-five years old.

For additional information about John Graham, H. Henry Sinason, and Margaret Lambert, see their Biographical Profiles available on the website.

4. After students have listened to the testimony, ask them if they heard anything in the testimony that supported or differed from what they imagined life was like for Jews in Germany before 1933. Additional questions for discussion might include:

   • In his testimony, how does John Graham describe his feelings toward Germany before the war?

   • H. Henry Sinason mentions that his father considered himself German first and Jewish second. What does this lead you to believe about how many Jews might have identified with their country during this time period?

   • After listening to Margaret Lambert's testimony, what is your sense of what the relationship between Jews and non-Jews was like before the war?

5. Before showing the next clips of testimony, ask students if they are familiar with the terms "stereotype" and "antisemitism" and to share their understanding of what the terms mean. Continue by asking them if based on what they know or have heard about the Holocaust, whether the attitudes and actions against Jews and the laws legislated against them in Nazi Germany were a new phenomenon or part of a continuum of antisemitism throughout history.

6. Introduce students to Henry Laurant and Judith Becker and then show the next three clips from Part 1 of Visual History Testimony: *Antisemitism* and discuss the following questions:

   • Describe how H. Henry Sinason says that his friends have changed. Who does he believe is responsible for their change in attitude and behavior?

   • Henry Laurant makes it a point to discuss his father's occupation and position in the community. What did the vandalism signal for Henry's father? How does Henry's testimony add to your understanding of what was happening in Germany during this time period?

   • In her testimony, Judith Becker speaks about a course on racism that was taught in schools. What was the irony that Judith describes? Why do you think the Nazis wanted to target young people with their racial ideology?

   • From listening to these testimonies, what do you learn about how the atmosphere in Germany was changing?

About the Interviewees

Henry Laurant was born on May 28, 1924, in Königsberg, Germany. He was sent on the *Kindertransport* to the United Kingdom where he stayed for the duration of the war. His interview was conducted in the United States. When the war began, Henry was fifteen years old.

Judith Becker was born on September 8, 1928, in Stettin, Germany. She was forced to live in the Radom ghetto and later imprisoned in the Majdanek, Auschwitz I, Taucha, Wieliczka, Krakau-Plaszow, Malchow, and Mauthausen concentration camps. Judith was also a prisoner in the Auschwitz-Birkenau extermination camp. Her interview was conducted in Israel. When the war began, Judith was ten years old.

For additional information about Henry Laurant and Judith Becker, see their Biographical Profiles available on the website.

7. Review important information about stereotypes with students:

   A **stereotype** is an oversimplified generalization about a person or group of people without regard for individual differences. Even seemingly positive stereotypes that link a person or group to a specific positive trait (e.g., Asian Americans are good in math; African Americans are good in sports) can have negative consequences because they ignore an individual's interests and abilities. Explain to students that while all stereotypes are hurtful because they group people into one category, some stereotypes are particularly dangerous because they express very negative things about a group of people (e.g., violent, greedy, sly). Such stereotypes perpetuate hateful attitudes and hurt individuals and entire communities. There is also the danger that targets of such stereotypes may begin to believe they are true.

8. Elicit from students examples of how a group to which they belong is stereotyped. Have students discuss why they think people believe and perpetuate stereotypes and why stereotypes are dangerous.

9. Display the definition of antisemitism; read and discuss together.

10. Prepare students for reading the *Summary of Antisemitism* handout by reviewing key terms and phrases as necessary. Distribute the text and have students study it as a whole group, in small groups, or individually. Instruct students to identify and underline or highlight examples of stereotypes or accusations made against Jews in the selection.

11. After reading the handout, conduct a class discussion based on some or all of the questions below.

   • What examples of stereotypes or accusations against Jews were discussed in the text? [Optional: Chart responses on the board or on chart paper.]

   • In what way did Nazi ideology create a new form of antisemitism?

   • What does the term "scapegoat" mean?

   • What are some situations when people may be likely to scapegoat a group of people?

   • Can you name groups of people in the United States who have been unfairly blamed for circumstances or events? (e.g., immigrants blamed for unemployment, Japanese Americans blamed for bombing of Pearl Harbor)

   • Why do you think many people didn't question or protest what they were being told about Jews?

- How is antisemitism similar to or different from scapegoating?

12. Ask students to consider whether antisemitism was only a problem of the past or if it remains an area of concern today. Have them support their thinking and, if possible, give contemporary examples of antisemitism at the local, national, or international level. Share with students that the Anti-Defamation League (ADL) identifies both criminal and non-criminal acts of harassment and intimidation, including distribution of hate propaganda, threats, and slurs, and compiles the information into its annual publication, *Audit of Anti-Semitic Incidents*. The full report of antisemitic incidents for the past year is available on the website in the Additional Resources section of the Lesson Components. Information about ADL can be found at the beginning of this guide and on the Echoes and Reflections website.

13. Provide students with the *Not in Our Town* handout and review together. Follow with a discussion using some or all of the questions below.

- What is a hate group?
- Why do you think some people choose to join hate groups?
- How do you think people are recruited to join hate groups?
- How, if at all, is the ideology of hate groups today similar to Nazi racial ideology?
- What is meant by the term "ally"?
- What specifically did the people of Billings, Montana do to show that they were allies to those who had become targets of antisemitism and other forms of bigotry?
- What risks did the people of Billings take when they decided to take action against what was happening in their community?
- What are some of the possible risks that a person takes when he or she decides to become an ally?

14. Explain to students that following the 1995 broadcast of the film *Not in Our Town,* which told the story about the events in Billings, Montana, many other communities joined the "Not in Our Town" campaign. The campaign (www.niot.org), which continues today, includes such events as public statements by community leaders promising that the community will stand together against prejudice and hate toward any group or individual, educational programs, workshops and conferences, contests, and online programs.

15. Distribute a sticky note to each student. Have each student write a response to one of the following questions which have been posted on the board and "post" the response under the appropriate question prior to leaving class:

- What specifically did you learn about antisemitism that you didn't know before studying the topic in class?
- Which of the testimonies that you watched today do you think you will remember and why?
- Why do you think the story of what happened in Billings, Montana still resonates for people twenty years later?

Part 2: Nazi Antisemitic Ideology and Propaganda

1. Begin this lesson by having students brainstorm the meaning of the word "ideology" and share what they think constitutes an ideology (e.g., a pattern of beliefs; a way of thinking; a system

of ideas that organizes one's goals, expectations, and actions).

2. Distribute the *Nazi Ideology* handout and have students individually, in pairs, or in small groups cite textual evidence to support their responses to the following questions:

   • How did the Nazi ideology depict Jews?

   • Compare and contrast this text to *Summary of Antisemitism* reviewed earlier. What new ideas appear in Hitler's writings? What ideas reflect continuity with previous antisemitic thinking?

   • How do you think these ideas might have influenced people in Germany who were exposed to them?

3. Ask students to think about the term "propaganda" and share what they understand it to mean. [Optional: Have a volunteer read the definition of propaganda found in the Glossary.] Continue by having students post what they see as the distinction between "propaganda" and "ideology" (i.e., ideology is a system of ideas and principles on which a political or economic theory is based; propaganda is a tool or method used to disseminate such a system of ideas).

4. Introduce students to Esther Clifford and H. Henry Sinason, if his testimony was not shown earlier. Show students Part 2 of Visual History Testimony: *Antisemitism* and discuss the following questions:

   • H. Henry Sinason discusses how many of his former friends became part of the Hitler Youth movement. Why do you think the children were receptive to joining such a movement?

   • What changes does Henry describe? What is the process he describes? What do you think influenced this process of change?

   • What were some of the visual images that Esther Clifford talks about seeing on her way to school? What effect did seeing such things have on her?

About *Der Stürmer* *Der Stürmer* is probably the most infamous antisemitic newspaper in history. For twenty-two years, beginning in May 1923, every weekly issue denounced Jews in crude, vicious, and vivid ways. The paper's publisher and editor was Julius Streicher, a virulent antisemite and senior member of the Nazi Party. Streicher's goal was to capture the attention of the masses; therefore, he wrote in a way that the masses could understand, in a style that was simple and easy to comprehend. By 1925, Streicher realized that a cartoon or photograph could be absorbed even faster than a simply written article. He hired the cartoonist Philipp Rupprecht (pen name Fips), who went on to draw thousands of vivid and revolting anti-Jewish caricatures for *Der Stürmer*.

TESTIMONY VIEWING

About the Interviewee

Esther Clifford was born on December 5, 1920, in Munich, Germany. She did not experience life in the ghettos or concentration camps. After escaping deportation to Poland, Esther hid in the homes of family members. Later, Esther fled to England. Her interview was conducted in the United States. When the war began, Esther was eighteen years old.

For additional information about Esther Clifford, see her Biographical Profile available on the website.

5. On the board or on chart paper, write the heading "How does propaganda work?" and then write the following list:

   • Repeats the same information over and over

   • Often twists and exploits the truth

   • Appeals to people's emotions

   • Gives the illusion that most people agree with the message

   • Talks to people in their own language

   • Uses accessible media (e.g., newspaper, radio)

6. Have students suggest examples of propaganda that they have seen and explain which of the techniques listed above was/were used. They might want to consider advertisements, political campaigns, social movements, and so forth in their examples.

7. Continue the discussion about propaganda by asking the following:

   • What are the possible effects of propaganda?

   • Can one become critical toward propaganda? Why or why not?

8. Display and review together as a whole group some of the examples of Nazi propaganda. Have students consider some or all of the questions below, depending on which document they are analyzing.

   • What statement is this photograph or caricature making?

   • How is the example exploiting the already existing antisemitic attitudes in Germany?

   • How is the example attempting to further isolate Jews from the rest of the population?

   • Which of the propaganda methods (listed on the board or on chart paper) apply to this photograph or caricature?

   • What is the irony of the photograph of the German woman reading the sign saying to beware of Jewish propaganda?

   • In what ways do the caricatures and photographs depict the ideas expressed in Nazi ideology?

   • Why did the Nazis use a variety of methods to spread their ideology?

9. After reviewing several examples, have a general discussion using the following questions:

   • How would you characterize Nazi propaganda?

   • Do you think that some people recognized that what they were seeing and hearing was propaganda? If they did, why do you think they still believed it?

   • Why do you think that many of the German people did not see Nazi propaganda as negative? (e.g., it was pro-Aryan so it reinforced their self-concept)

   • How can a person be tempted to believe in propaganda?

   • What is dehumanization?

NOTE 2.8

In some cases, at the bottom of the document there is an explanation. Allow time for students to analyze what they are seeing before providing them with this information.

L2

- What are some examples of ways that the Nazis dehumanized Jews in their propaganda?

- How did the dehumanization of Jews make them an easy target for abuse?

- What other groups of people have been dehumanized in history? What was the purpose or goal behind such dehumanization? What methods were used? What has been the result?

10. Close the lesson by having students discuss specific examples of national and international events that demonstrate that antisemitism and propaganda are still part of contemporary society.

Reflect and Respond

Either in class or as homework, have students reflect and respond to one or more of the topics below or have them develop a topic that has meaning for them based on the material covered in the lesson.

- Some people thought that after the Holocaust, antisemitism would disappear, which it did not. How can you explain that? Why do you think it did not disappear? What have you learned of the history of antisemitism that might explain why the Holocaust did not end antisemitism?

- Do you recognize propaganda in your life and society? Do you feel that you are influenced by it? If so, how? If not, how do you protect yourself from its influence?

- Think about the dangers in stereotyping. Why are stereotypes so easy to believe and perpetuate? How can you combat stereotypes in your daily life? What would be the value of doing so?

- Many of the testimonies in this lesson related stories of hurtful, neglectful, and/or abusive behavior toward children who could not defend themselves. Who in a society is responsible for the care of children? What should those entrusted with this responsibility do to ensure that all children are emotionally and physically safe?

Making Connections

The additional activities and projects listed below can be integrated directly into the lesson or can be used to extend the lesson once it has been completed. The topics lend themselves to students' continued study of the Holocaust as well as opportunities for students to make meaningful connections to other people and events, including relevant contemporary issues. These activities may include instructional strategies and techniques and/or address academic standards in addition to those that were identified for the lesson.

1. Visit IWitness (iwitness.usc.edu) for activities specific to Lesson 2: Antisemitism.

2. Assign students a research project that explores modern-day antisemitism and hate groups. The following questions can guide the research:
   - What organized groups use antisemitism to advance their goals?
   - How have these groups made use of Nazi ideology?
   - What other groups of people do hate groups target?
   - What activities of these hate groups are banned by law? What activities are legal?
   - Who joins hate groups?

- How are young people lured into joining hate groups?

- What role does the Internet play in spreading the message of hate groups?

- What recent events have served to increase the intensity and broaden the scope of modern antisemitism?

The class might be divided into small groups, each one responsible for a particular aspect of the whole topic: e.g., origins of antisemitism in the United States, hate groups, the escalation of antisemitism. Research may be presented in written, oral, or in visual form (e.g., video). Encourage students to use the Anti-Defamation League's website (adl.org) and the Southern Poverty Law Center's website (splcenter.org) in their research.

3. Divide the class in half. Provide time for groups to prepare an argument for debate. Have one group argue that the United States government should prohibit the activities of groups and individuals that promote hatred, as in Germany where the dissemination of racist and antisemitic material is illegal. Have the other group argue that the First Amendment must be upheld.

4. The antisemitic children's book *The Poisonous Mushroom* (*Der Giftpilz* in German) was written by Ernst Hiemer and published by Julius Streicher who also published the antisemitic newspaper *Der Stürmer*. Instruct students to gather relevant information from multiple print and digital sources about how children's books like *The Poisonous Mushroom* were used to promote Nazi ideology and prepare a PowerPoint or cloud-based presentation (e.g., Prezi), a written report, or decide on another format to present their work. Their presentations should include examples of children's books published during the time period, information about how people responded to the books if possible, as well as their interpretations of the books and what they learned about propaganda from studying them.

5. Have students answer the following question in an explanatory text or in a multimedia presentation: At what point does political discourse become propaganda? To begin, students should identify specific examples of politicians attempting to sway voters to vote for them or to agree with them on a particular issue. This can be accomplished by listening to or reading speeches or transcripts from community forums made by national, state, or local politicians. This investigation should be followed by an argument for why the techniques do or do not fit the definition of propaganda. Which techniques, if any, are the same as those of propaganda? If they are different, how are they different? What safeguards, if any, are in place to prevent political discourse from becoming propaganda? The text or presentation should end with a concluding statement that answers the research question based on the evidence compiled.

6. Using online resources have students research and prepare a graphic that shows the Jewish experience in the United States at roughly the same time as the Nazis were coming to power in Germany. The graphic might include information on various regions of the country where Jews lived or the countries from which they emigrated. Include data about the attitude toward Jews based on polling data compiled at the time. Encourage students to consider the implications of their findings on whether the United States would intervene in the events that were to unfold in Europe.

JEWISH COMMUNITIES IN EUROPE BEFORE THE NAZIS RISE TO POWER

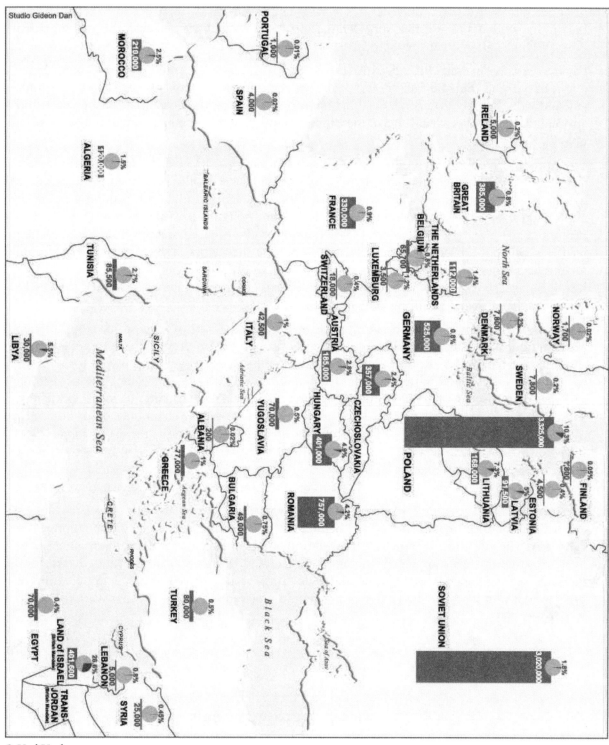

© Yad Vashem

ANTISEMITISM DEFINITION

Antisemitism is the term for hatred of Jews as a group or a concept. Hatred of Jews has existed since ancient times, and in the nineteenth century it was being influenced by modern scientific ways of thinking. The word "antisemitism" was coined in Germany by political activist Wilhelm Marr to represent this newer way of thinking. "Semitism" supposedly expressed all things Jewish, since at the time national groups were frequently defined by their language and the traditional language of Jews is Hebrew, which is a Semitic language. Of course there is no such thing as "Semitism" and all speakers of Semitic languages never belonged to the same national or ethnic groups.

Antisemitism may take the form of religious teachings that proclaim the inferiority of Jews, their supposedly evil nature, or other negative ideas about Jews. It may include political efforts to isolate, oppress, or otherwise injure them. It may also include prejudiced or other stereotyped views about Jews derived from racial or other ideologies.

SUMMARY OF ANTISEMITISM

L2

Antisemitism is the term used for hatred of Jews as a group or Jews as a concept. It is an archaic term conceived in the latter part of the nineteenth century when the social sciences were trying to develop "scientific" terms to match those of the pure sciences. In practice, however, the hatred of Jews has deep roots in history. As far back as ancient times, Jews were often seen as outsiders and a stubborn people who were unwilling to assimilate, primarily because of their religious beliefs.

With the beginning of Christianity, there was an inherent clash between Judaism and Christianity. Christianity grew out of Judaism, but at the same time was competing with it. Early Church fathers believed that the Jews had failed in their role in the world and that Christians had inherited it. In addition, although the Romans crucified Jesus, the blame was put on all Jews everywhere and forever (a false blame that was condemned by the Catholic Church in the 1960s). Jews were also said to be in league with the devil, which both dehumanized and demonized them. For these reasons, not only were Jews seen as outsiders, but they were also regarded as a people who should be eternally punished.

By the Middle Ages, Jews were living in Europe not as an integrated part of society, but as outsiders and on the sufferance of local rulers. Popular antisemitism prevailed partly to win favor with the ruling Romans. Jews could live only where the rulers allowed them and practice only certain trades and professions that generally were shunned by the rest of the population. As a result, Jews often engaged in trade and banking, which led to negative stereotypes that Jews care only for money and engage in shady business practices. When crisis struck, primarily the massive death caused by the "Black Death" in the 1300s, Jews were falsely accused of having caused the sickness by poisoning the wells—they were made the scapegoats for the tragedy. Other accusations included the patently false blood libel—the belief that Jews use the blood of Christians for ritual purposes. As a result of these many layers of anti-Jewish stereotypes, Jews were frequently massacred, expelled, or forcibly converted to Christianity.

By the nineteenth century, a constellation of antisemitic stereotypes was deeply rooted in the Western World. Nevertheless, under the influence of the Enlightenment and modern thought, the process of giving Jews equal rights unfolded in much of Europe. As Jews integrated more, there were some in the general society who applauded these changes and hoped that by assimilating, the allegedly bad characteristics of Jews would disappear. There was a paradox that even among the greatest champions of Jewish rights, there were those who still had many antisemitic beliefs, and Jews frequently faced social discrimination even where they had been granted legal equality.

Especially as the modern nations of Europe took shape, there was heated discussion about whether or not Jews, who were often viewed as a separate group or nation, could really be a part of the broader nation. In light of all the antisemitic stereotypes attributed to them, many people believed Jews were simply not capable of being part of "the nation."

New stereotypes also arose at this time. It was said that Jewish elders plotted to take over the world. A fabricated record of the supposed Jewish conspiracy was published as *The Protocols of the Elders of Zion,* which nevertheless a great many people believed was true and many still believe is accurate today. Jews were also accused of being unpatriotic, despite much evidence to the contrary.

Most significantly during the last third of the nineteenth century, racism as a pseudoscience first surfaced. Racism grew out of the emerging sciences of biology, genetics, and anthropology, and it held that human civilization could be best understood through biology. Moreover, it held that different national and ethnic groups were defined by their biological characteristics, and some groups were superior to others. With the long history of antisemitism as the background, Jews were seen by many racial thinkers as the worst race—strong, yet very dangerous. In other words, all the negative stereotypes Jews supposedly had were now explained as being the result of Jewish biology, or in language of the time, "Jewish blood." With earlier forms of antisemitism Jews could escape hatred, at least in theory, by converting to Christianity or shedding their alleged bad characteristics by assimilating. As soon as anti-Jewish prejudice was linked to racism, Jews could do nothing to change themselves or the hatred directed toward them.

Adolf Hitler and the Nazi Party did not invent antisemitism, but it was central to their ideology. They embraced a racial ideology that stated the Germans were the master race in the world. Their goal was to make Germany a superpower by conquering lands of supposedly lesser people and restructuring society according to racial principles. For the Nazis, the Jews were the racial archenemy. They saw them as a demonic force that aspired to dominate the world, and they believed that the Jews' victory would spell the end of the world. The Nazis believed that Jews were behind Bolshevism (Communism), exploitative capitalism, and democracy, all of which supposedly threatened mankind. Nazi ideology also argued that Christianity had been weakened by Jewish ideas, such as that all human beings are created in the image of God. In short they blamed Jews for all of humanity's shortfalls and troubles. Not only did they believe that Jews had no place in a racially restructured Europe, they felt that they must put an end to the "Jewish menace" lest the Jews destroy them.

One would think after the Holocaust antisemitism would have disappeared. Unfortunately it has continued to exist. Today a constellation of antisemitic stereotypes and motifs still may be found, some elements with older ideas and some with newer variations, chief among them hatred of Jews linked to a demonic image of Israel and Zionism.

The Protocols of the Elders of Zion

In 1903, a newspaper in Czarist Russia published a false document that allegedly described a secret action plan by which "the Jews" were plotting to take over the world. Although the Russian secret police quickly proved the document to be a forgery, *The Protocols* was distributed across Europe. The first version in German came out in 1911, in Berlin. In 1937, a court in Switzerland declared this myth of global Jewish conspiracy to be groundless. This finding, however, did not stop the dissemination of *The Protocols* worldwide, including throughout the United States, or its translation into dozens of languages. For instance, in the 1920s, the famous American car manufacturer Henry Ford financed the translation of *The Protocols of the Elders of Zion* into English. No other antisemitic text has been—and continues to be—so widely distributed.

NOT IN OUR TOWN

L2

In the mid-1980s, some hate groups declared the northwestern part of the United States to be their "homeland." These hate groups were becoming more and more violent in the region. In 1986, the Aryan Nations organization declared its intention to make the region a place where only whites and Christians could own property, vote, conduct business, bear arms, and hold public office. Incidents of harassment and violence against "minority" groups became more and more common. It was not long before Billings, a city in southern Montana, found itself the target of a series of hateful incidents. Billings, with a population of approximately 104,000 people, is the largest city in Montana and the commercial, shipping, and processing center of a region that produces cattle, wheat, and sugar beets. Billings is the gateway to Yellowstone National Park, the Crow Indian Reservation, and the Little Bighorn Battlefield National Monument.

In 1993, Ku Klux Klan flyers were distributed around Billings, tombstones in the Jewish cemetery were overturned; the home of a Native American family was spray-painted with swastikas; members of an African-American church were intimidated, and bricks were thrown through windows of homes that displayed *menorahs* for the Jewish holiday of Chanukah.

Rather than accept what was happening in their community, people decided to take a stand against hate. Those who were not targets became allies to those who were. City officials and law enforcement officers made strong statements against the activities. The Painters Union formed a work force to paint over the graffiti. Religious and community leaders sponsored human rights activities. The local newspaper printed full-page *menorahs* for display in homes and businesses throughout the town. Most of the 10,000 people who decided to display the *menorahs* were not Jewish; they displayed the symbols to show that they were unwilling to accept prejudice and hate in their community. In a show of support, people attended religious services at an African-American church where the congregation was being harassed and intimidated by members of hate groups.

Actions by the people of Billings, Montana became a model for other communities around the country who also spoke out against hate. The motto for such community actions became known as "Not in Our Town."

Adapted with permission from *Anti-Bias Study Guide,* Elementary/Intermediate Level (New York: Anti-Defamation League, 2000), 257. All rights reserved.

NAZI IDEOLOGY

Excerpts from Adolf Hitler's *Mein Kampf*

...To what an extent the whole existence of this people is based on a continuous lie is shown incomparably by *The Protocols of the Elders of Zion,* so infinitely hated by the Jews. They are based on a forgery, the Frankfurter *Zeitung* [German newspaper] moans and screams once every week: the best proof that they are authentic... For once this book has become the common property of a people, the Jewish menace may be considered as broken.

Hence today I believe that I am acting in accordance with the will of the Almighty creator: by defending myself against the Jew, I am fighting for the work of the Lord.

With satanic joy in his face, the black-haired Jewish youth lurks in wait for the unsuspecting girl whom he defiles with his blood, thus stealing her from her people. With every means he tries to destroy the racial foundations of the people he has set out to subjugate.

For a racially pure people which is conscious of its blood can never be enslaved by the Jew. In this world he will forever be master over bastards and bastards alone. And so he tries systematically to lower the racial level by a continuous poisoning of individuals.

Culturally, he contaminates art, literature, the theater, makes a mockery of natural feeling, overthrows all concepts of beauty and sublimity, of the noble and the good, and instead drags men down into the sphere of his own base nature.

Excerpt from Adolf Hitler's *Zweites Buch* (Second Book)

Because of the lack of productive capacities of its own the Jewish people cannot carry out the construction of a state, viewed in a territorial sense, but as a support of its own existence it needs the work and creative activities of other nations. Thus the existence of the Jew himself becomes a parasitical one within the lives of other peoples. Hence the ultimate goal of the Jewish struggle for existence is the enslavement of productively active peoples.

Excerpt from a speech by Adolf Hitler in the Reichstag, January 30, 1939

Today I will once more be a prophet: If the international Jewish financiers in and outside Europe should succeed in plunging the nations once more into a world war, then the result will not be the Bolshevization of the earth, and thus the victory of Jewry, but the annihilation of the Jewish race in Europe!

Reprinted with permission from Yitzhak Arad, Yisrael Gutman, Abraham Margaliot, eds., *Documents on the Holocaust, Selected Sources on the Destruction of the Jews of Germany and Austria, Poland, and the Soviet Union* (Jerusalem: Yad Vashem, 1981), 22–27; 134–135. All rights reserved.

NAZI PROPAGANDA: CHILDREN'S BOOK COVER

The cover of a book entitled *Der Giftpilz (The Poisonous Mushroom)*. Inside the book, the comparison to the mushroom is explained when a mother tells her child, "Just as it is difficult to distinguish between a poisonous mushroom and an edible mushroom, it is difficult to distinguish between a good Jew and a lying, thieving Jew."

NAZI PROPAGANDA: CARICATURE OF A JEW WITH ARYAN CHILDREN

„Hier, Kleiner, haſt du etwas ganz Süßes! Aber dafür müßt ihr beide mit mir gehen..."

Taken from the children's book, *The Poisonous Mushroom*, the caption in this picture reads: "Here my little one, you get something very sweet, but as a reward you both must come with me." This caricature portrays an elderly Jew trying to tempt small children with candy. It relies on one of the basic fears of all parents and the common instruction to little children not to take candy from a stranger. There are links made between "a stranger," "danger," "poison," and "a Jew." The Jew is portrayed as a dark, evil, threatening, manipulative stranger, as opposed to the innocent, pure, naïve Aryan children.

NAZI PROPAGANDA: WOMAN AND CHILDREN LOOKING AT CRUCIFIX

L2

„Wenn ihr ein Kreuz seht, dann denkt an den grauenhaften Mord der Juden auf Golgatha…"

Yad Vashem Photo Archive (1599/232)

Taken from the children's book, *The Poisonous Mushroom*, the caption in this picture reads: "Whenever you see a crucifix, think of the horrible murder of Jesus by the Jews." The Nazis used this common belief among Christians to further alienate Jews. Nazi ideology, however, was against all religions and viewed Christianity as a transferred form of Judaism. Some Aryan symbols appear in this picture such as the bright hair, the connection to nature, children, and the continuity of the race.

NAZI PROPAGANDA: SCHOOL CHILDREN AND NAZI IDEOLOGY

„Die Judennase ist an ihrer Spitze gebogen. Sie sieht aus wie ein Sechser..."

Taken from the children's book, *The Poisonous Mushroom*, the inscription in this picture reads: "The Jewish nose is wide at the end and looks like the number six..." The number six is connected to Satan and this explanation of the "Jewish nose" gives it a devilish meaning. Even though the message of this caricature is of a mythological nature, it is presented as truth in that it is being taught by a respectable Aryan teacher in a normal class. It can also refer to a situation in 1930s Germany when special instructors came to classrooms to explain Nazi racial ideology to the students.

NAZI PROPAGANDA: COMPARISON OF JEW AND ARYAN

The Jew in this caricature is portrayed as ugly, greedy, and controlling the media and stock exchange (the newspaper in his pocket with the title "Burse"). His eyes are made to look suspicious. Overall he is to be seen as unproductive, exploitive, unstable, and evil. By contrast, the German or Aryan is portrayed as hard-working, strong, stable, and honest. He is tall, in good physical shape, and has a direct look in his eyes.

Masses parade with Nazi flags in honor of the dead on Reichsparteitag.

Yad Vashem Photo Archive (3922/83)

A woman reads a boycott sign posted in the window of a Jewish-owned department store in Berlin, April 1, 1933. The sign reads: "Germans defend yourselves against Jewish atrocity propaganda, buy only at German shops!"

About Photo

A Ceremony for the Annual
Nazi Party Rally, Germany,
1935 (3922/116)

Yad Vashem Photo Archive

"With the rise of Nazism, nothing Jews had done for their country made any difference...."

– Alfred Gottschalk, Jewish Survivor

Preparing to Use This Lesson

Below is information to keep in mind when using this lesson. In some cases, the points elaborate on general suggestions listed in the "Teaching about the Holocaust" section in the Introduction to this resource, and are specific to the content of the lesson. This material is intended to help teachers consider the complexities of teaching the Holocaust and to deliver accurate and sensitive instruction.

- Studying about the rise of the Nazi Party in Germany inherently requires students to reflect on the importance of preserving and protecting democratic values and institutions and to consider the role of a responsible citizen in that process. Students may have the impression that the Holocaust was inevitable. Whenever possible, help students recognize that the Holocaust took place because individuals, groups, and nations made decisions to act or not to act. Begin to set the stage for this understanding in this lesson. The Weimar Republic was a fragile democracy. This unstable democracy paved a path for the Nazi Party. However, it must be made absolutely clear to students that the German people did not have to vote for the Nazis in the 1932 election; this was a choice they made.

- Students learn about Nazi concentration camps in this lesson. The Nazis initially built these camps to control and subdue any opposition from within Germany. Over time, the Nazi camp system branched out to many kinds of camps and their story is the story of millions that Nazi Germany incarcerated, abused, and exploited. The concentration camp system was not established as part of the "Final Solution"; however, as the policy of murder took hold, the concentration camps played a role in it. The story of the "Final Solution" is addressed in Lesson 5.

- When using the "Pyramid of Hate" to study the Holocaust, caution students not to think that there was a methodical progression from one stage to the next, ultimately resulting in genocide. The atmosphere of the German state was chaotic, and there was an experimental nature to the Nazis' actions. Not only is it important to keep that in mind when trying to understand Nazism, but also when trying to understand the Jewish and other victims' reactions to German policies.

Lesson 3 NAZI GERMANY

About This Lesson

 180–270 minutes

❖ **INTRODUCTION** The purpose of this lesson is for students to learn about the Weimar Republic's fragile democracy between 1918 and 1933 and to examine historical events that allowed for the complete breakdown of democracy in Germany between 1933 and 1939, which led to the unfolding of anti-Jewish policies. Students will also investigate primary source materials in order to understand how legislation, terror, and propaganda isolated German Jewry from German society. Students also have an opportunity to consider the role and responsibility of the individual in interrupting hate and the escalation of violence.

This three-part lesson has material appropriate for history, social studies, civics, Holocaust studies, and English/language arts classes. Instructional strategies used in the lesson include large-group discussion, small-group work, analyzing maps, reading for information, understanding chronology of events, comparing and contrasting information, interpreting visual history testimony, analyzing primary source documents, critical thinking, and journaling.

❖ **OBJECTIVES** After completing this lesson, students will be able to:

- Describe the features of the Weimar Republic.
- Summarize the key provisions in the Treaty of Versailles.
- Explain how the failure of the Weimar Republic played a role in the rise of the Nazis to power.
- Identify historical events that allowed for a dramatic change in social policies in Germany between 1933 and 1939.
- Interpret primary source materials—including clips of visual history testimony—that represent a range of Jewish experiences and responses to Nazi-German state policies.
- Analyze the role and responsibility of the individual in interrupting the escalation of hate and violence.

❖ **KEY WORDS & PHRASES**

antisemitism	dehumanization	*Kristallnacht Pogrom*
Aryan	democracy	Magen David
boycott	discrimination	nationalism
Bund	"Hatikvah"	Nazi
bystander	Hitler Youth	Nuremberg Laws
Communist	"Horst Wessel" song	prejudice
concentration camp	kosher	Reichstag

RESOURCES & TESTIMONIES

All of the resources used in this lesson can be found in this guide at the end of this lesson and at echoesandreflections.org.

Visual history testimonies are available on the website or on the DVD that accompanies this resource guide.

Teachers are urged to review the lesson procedures to identify other materials and technology needed to implement the lesson.

scapegoat   stereotype   Weimar Republic
Sinti-Roma   totalitarian
Socialist   Treaty of Versailles

❖ ACADEMIC STANDARDS The materials in this lesson address the following national education standards:

Common Core State Standards

- Reading Standards for Informational Text 6–12

- Writing Standards 6–12

- Speaking and Listening Standards 6–12

- Reading Standards for Literacy in History/Social Studies 6–12

- Writing Standards for Literacy in History/Social Studies 6–12

A complete analysis of how this lesson addresses Common Core State Standards by grade level and specific skills is available on the Echoes and Reflections website.

National Curriculum Standards for Social Studies

❶ Culture

❷ Time, Continuity, and Change

❸ People, Places, and Environments

❹ Individual Development and Identity

❺ Individuals, Groups, and Institutions

❻ Power, Authority, and Governance

❼ Production, Distribution, and Consumption

❾ Global Connections

❿ Civic Ideals and Practices

Procedures

Part 1: Weimar Republic and Rise of the Nazi Party

1. Begin this lesson by having students think about the word "democracy." Using a web format, chart student responses to the sentence stem "Democracy is…"on the board or on chart paper.

2. Provide students with an introduction to Alfred Caro and Frank Shurman and then show Part 1 of Visual History Testimony: *Nazi Germany*.

TESTIMONY VIEWING

About the Interviewees

Alfred Caro was born on July 27, 1911, in Samter, Germany (today Szamotuly, Poland). He was imprisoned in the Sachsenhausen concentration camp and later fled to France. After the Nazis

continued on page 71

entered France, Alfred fled to Columbia. His interview was conducted in the United States. When the war began, Alfred was twenty-eight years old.

Frank Shurman was born on January 8, 1915, in Hildesheim, Germany. He was imprisoned in the Buchenwald concentration camp and later fled to Kitchener Camp, a refugee camp in Richborough, England. His interview was conducted in the United States. When the war began, Frank was twenty-four years old.

_____

For additional information about Alfred Caro and Frank Shurman, see their Biographical Profiles available on the website.

Follow with a discussion using the questions below.

- In his testimony, how does Alfred Caro characterize the Weimar Republic?
- What example does Frank Shurman share to illustrate the "insecure situation" that Germany was facing in the early 1920s? How does Frank indicate that Hitler took advantage of the situation?
- Based on what you heard from Alfred and Frank, how confident do you think the German people were with the status of the government?

3. Distribute *The Weimar Republic and the Rise of the Nazi Party*. After reading the text together, have a discussion using some or all of the following questions:

- Do you think that the Nazis' rise to power was inevitable based on what you read? Support your answer with examples from the text.
- According to the text, why was the democracy of Germany so fragile? How does information in the text compare to what Alfred Caro and Frank Shurman shared in their testimonies?
- Considering what was taking place in Germany at the time (e.g., unemployment), how might the German people have viewed what the Nazis were offering as positive steps toward solving the problems the country was facing? Identify one specific point from the Nazi Party's platform that could have been perceived as solving the problems facing Germany, and explain why it might have been appealing.
- Can you also see the dangers in what the Nazis offered? Identify a specific point in the Nazi Party's platform that is particularly dangerous in your opinion, and explain why you chose that particular point.
- What are the characteristics of a democracy?
- Do you think that democracy, in general, is fragile? Explain your thinking.
- How does democracy benefit the individual?
- How does democracy benefit society?
- How can a democracy be affected by individuals and society?
- What are some ways that a democracy protects itself so as to avoid becoming a totalitarian state?

4. Show students the maps of Europe before and after 1919 and the Treaty of Versailles and have them identify how the borders of Europe changed after 1919. Have students refer back to the text and summarize the provisions of the Treaty of Versailles in addition to the change in borders.

Part 2: Anti-Jewish Policy

1. Begin this part of the lesson by introducing students to Julia Lentini, Herman Cohn, and Margaret Lambert and then show the first three clips of Part 2 of Visual History Testimony: *Nazi Germany* and discussing the following questions:

    *   Julia Lentini describes wanting to join the Hitler Youth along with her friends. What made the Hitler Youth attractive to her? What are some possible reasons why her parents wouldn't let her join?

    *   What are some of the specific ways that Herman Cohn says his life changed after the Nuremberg Laws were adopted? Herman says that things were much harder for children than for their parents. Why did he feel this way—what specific examples does he share to support his assertion?

    *   How does Margaret Lambert say things changed in Germany after 1933? How did her personal relationships change? What kinds of things was she forced to give up?

TESTIMONY VIEWING

About the Interviewees

Julia Lentini was born on April 15, 1926, in Eisern, Germany. She was imprisoned in the concentration camp of Schlieben and the Auschwitz-Birkenau extermination camp. Her interview was conducted in the United States. When the war began, Julia was thirteen years old.

Herman Cohn was born on September 8, 1921, in Essen, Germany. He did not experience life in the ghettos or concentration camps. In early 1939, Herman fled to the Netherlands. Toward the end of 1939, he was reunited with his parents and they immigrated to the United States. His interview was conducted in the United States. When the war began, Herman was seventeen years old.

Margaret Lambert was born on April 12, 1914, in Laupheim, Germany. She did not experience life in the ghettos or concentration camps. In 1937, she fled from Germany to the home of a family friend living in the United States. Her interview was conducted in the United States. When the war began, Margaret was twenty-five years old.

For additional information about Julia Lentini, Herman Cohn, and Margaret Lambert, see their Biographical Profiles available on the website.

2. Provide each student with a copy of the activity *What Rights Are Most Important to Me?* Have students take a few minutes to rank the choices in order of importance from 1 (most important) to 9 (least important).

3. Divide the class into small groups and have students share how they ranked the rights on the handout and the rationale behind their decisions. [Optional: Have groups come to consensus on how the choices should be ranked. If it is not possible for group members to come to consensus, have them analyze why consensus is not possible.]

4. Distribute the *Nazi Germany and Anti-Jewish Policy* handout. Explain to students that this is a timeline of official Nazi actions against the Jews in Germany beginning in 1933 when Adolf Hitler and the Nazi Party gained control of Germany. After students have reviewed the timeline of anti-Jewish policy, discuss the following questions:

    *   What is the purpose of laws?

    *   Looking at the chronological list of laws and decrees included on the handout, why could

this be called a "build up of anti-Jewish policies"?

- What spheres of life do the laws and decrees affect? Into what groups could you divide them? Which belong to which sphere?

- Where does the idea of race appear in the decrees and laws?

- How do you think a Jewish person might react to all of these restrictions and laws?

- How do you think a German might react to these policies?

- What would you imagine the overall atmosphere in Germany to be during this time?

- What other laws, if any, do you know about that have dehumanized people? (e.g., Jim Crow Laws; apartheid in South Africa)

5. Introduce students to Esther Clifford and show the fourth clip from Part 2 of Visual History Testimony: *Nazi Germany* and discuss the following questions:

- After listening to Esther Clifford's testimony, what picture do you begin to create in your mind about her experiences during the *Kristallnacht Pogrom*? What does she say she saw and felt?

- What does Esther say in her testimony that supports that the *Kristallnacht Pogrom* was a government-sponsored terrorist action against the Jews of Germany and Austria?

- Do you think that the *Kristallnacht Pogrom* reflected a turning point for Jews in Germany? On what have you based your response?

6. Show students *Graz, Austria, November 9/10, 1938*. Ask them to describe what they see in the photograph. Follow by asking students to consider the following:

- What questions come to mind as you look at this photograph?

- In what context was this photograph taken? Why is it important to know the context for a photograph?

- Focus on one person in the photograph. What do you think this person was thinking when this photograph was taken?

- In your opinion, did the person that you are focusing on have a role and responsibility for this event? Explain your answer.

- What would you title this photograph and why?

- What is someone called who stands by and watches something happen without offering assistance? (i.e., bystander)

- Would you say that most of the people in this photograph were "bystanders"? Explain your answer.

7. Provide students with background information on the concentration camps established beginning in the 1930s by having them read the *Concentration Camps* handout. Ask students to consider the following questions:

- Who do you think the concentration camps influenced and how?

NOTE 2.4

During the Weimar Republic, there were "German Jews," whereas after 1933 there were "Jews" and there were "Germans." They had a different quality of life and were viewed as two separate groups.

TESTIMONY VIEWING

About the Interviewee

Esther Clifford was born on December 5, 1920, in Munich, Germany. She did not experience life in the ghettos or concentration camps. After escaping deportation to Poland, Esther hid in the homes of family members. Later, Esther fled to England. Her interview was conducted in the United States. When the war began, Esther was eighteen years old.

———

For additional information about Esther Clifford, see her Biographical Profile available on the website.

NOTE 2.6

Additional testimony, photographs, and other primary source documents about the *Kristallnacht Pogrom* can be found in Lesson 1: Studying the Holocaust and on IWitness.

- How do you think the use of concentrations camps may have furthered the Nazis' goals for German Society before the war?

8. Conclude this part of the lesson by having students summarize how Germany had changed for Jews and for Germans in the six-year period from 1933 to 1939.

Reflect and Respond

Either in class or as homework, have students reflect and respond to one or more of the topics below or have them develop a topic that has meaning for them based on the material covered in the lesson.

- In 1821, Heinrich Heine wrote, "Where one burns books, one will, in the end, burn people." Consider what Heine meant by this statement. In your opinion, what is the danger of burning books? How, if at all, does burning books jeopardize human life? [Note: Heinrich Heine was a noted German author who converted to Christianity from Judaism in the nineteenth century. According to the Nuremberg Laws, Heine would have been considered a Jew; therefore, his books were also burned and forbidden.]

- Write a journal entry from the point of view of a fictional person living in Nazi Germany during the years 1933–1939. In addition to telling things like your name, age, town, and occupation, give your thoughts about what is happening to the Jews in Germany at the time.

- Desecrating or destroying places of worship is an all-too common form of violence in both historical and contemporary times—in the United States, the bombing of Atlanta's oldest synagogue in the late 1950s, burning down African-American churches across the South in the mid-1990s, and vandalizing mosques in the Midwest following 9/11—are but a few examples. Why do you think places of worship are so often the targets of hate?

Part 3: Pyramid of Hate

1. Introduce students to Alfred Gottschalk, Ellen Brandt, and Esther Clifford if her testimony was not shown earlier, and then show Part 3 of Visual History Testimony: *Nazi Germany* and discuss the following:

- What was the turning point for Esther Clifford's family? Where did they want to go and how did they try to accomplish their goal?

- According to Esther, how did countries around the world respond to Jews trying to leave Germany?

- What evidence is presented in Esther's testimony that supports the idea that the Nazis were set on destroying the economic life of Jews?

TESTIMONY VIEWING

About the Interviewees

Alfred Gottschalk was born on March 7, 1930, in Oberwesel, Germany. He did not experience life in the ghettos or concentration camps. In 1939, Alfred, along with his mother, fled to the United States. His

continued on page 75

- Discuss the significance of Alfred Gottschalk's statement "nothing Jews had done for their country made any difference."

- How did Ellen Brandt respond to what was happening around her in Germany at the time? How does she say she changed?

- According to these testimonies, in what ways did the daily routines of German Jews change during the years 1933–1939?

2. Show students the *Pyramid of Hate*. Review each part of the pyramid by having students refer to the Glossary for the definition of each term used and by presenting examples for each section (e.g., scapegoating–blaming immigrants for lack of jobs).

3. After reviewing each part of the pyramid, have students consider how prejudiced attitudes might, if left unchecked, eventually lead to violence. Have students follow an example from something they learned in this lesson through each part of the pyramid.

4. Divide the class into groups of four or five students. Provide each group with a piece of chart paper, markers, and sticky notes. Have each group select a recorder. Instruct the recorder to draw a large pyramid on the chart paper and divide it into the four sections, labeling each section.

5. Have group members work together to identify examples for each part of the pyramid from the visual history testimony that they have watched and from the handouts in Lessons 2 and 3: *Summary of Antisemitism* and *Nazi Germany and Anti-Jewish Policy,* write them on the sticky notes, and affix them to the chart paper (e.g., Jews dismissed from civil service would be placed on the "Discrimination" section). Not all events need be used, but students should be encouraged to have at least four examples for each category. Students may not agree on the placement of events and should be encouraged to share their thought processes in arriving at consensus.

6. After completing the pyramids, have groups post them around the room. Review the placement of events as a whole group, discussing how students determined what each action exemplified. After reviewing the pyramids, have a discussion using some or all of the following questions:

- Which parts of the pyramid primarily reflect acts by individuals?

- Which parts of the pyramid reflect state-sponsored acts that need government support to continue?

- Did the events on this pyramid always follow an upward progression or were there instances when the actions would represent an earlier segment of the pyramid? (e.g., violent acts followed by acts of discrimination and then back to violent acts again) What are some possible explanations for why this might have happened?

- Explain how the *Kristallnacht Pogrom* represented an escalation of anti-Jewish acts.

- What does the pyramid of hate explain about Nazi anti-Jewish

About the Interviewees

continued from page 74

interview was conducted in the United States. When the war began, Alfred was nine years old.

Ellen Brandt was born on May 10, 1922, in Mannheim, Germany. She did not experience life in the ghettos or concentration camps. In 1938, Ellen, along with her parents, fled to the United States. Her interview was conducted in the United States. When the war began, Ellen was seventeen years old.

For additional information about Alfred Gottschalk and Ellen Brandt, see their Biographical Profiles available on the website.

NOTE 3.6

An additional activity for use with the *Pyramid of Hate* can be found on the website in the Additional Resources section of the Lesson Components.

L3

attitudes and policies and their development? What other factors should also be taken into account? (e.g., material covered in Lesson 2: Antisemitism)

7. Raise the issue of personal responsibility by introducing the following quotation by Reverend Martin Niemoller, a German Protestant minister who survived Sachsenhausen and Dachau concentration camps where he was sent because of his outspoken criticism of the Nazi government in Germany.

> "In Germany, the Nazis came for the Communists, and I didn't speak up because I was not a Communist. Then they came for the Jews and I didn't speak up because I was not a Jew. Then they came for the trade unionists, and I didn't speak up because I was not a trade unionist. Then they came for the Catholics, and I didn't speak up because I was a Protestant. Then they came for me... and by that time there was no one left to speak up. "

8. Ask students to consider the role of the individual in the events that surround him or her, using Reverend Niemoller's words as a catalyst for the discussion.

- Why do you think Reverend Niemoller did not "speak up" when Hitler's government began its persecution of various groups in Germany?

- Why do you think it was difficult to oppose the government's actions?

- At what point in the escalation of anti-Jewish policies in Nazi Germany did non-Jews have a responsibility to interrupt what they saw happening?

- What actions could they have taken?

- Do you think it is difficult for individuals to do these kinds of things? Why or why not?

- What is the cost to the individual who does not act to interrupt injustice?

- What is the harm to the victims?

- What is the harm to society as a whole?

- Thinking about the key events that you have learned about in this lesson (and Lesson 2), what, in your opinion, is the power of peer pressure?

Reflect and Respond

Either in class or as homework, have students reflect and respond to one or more of the topics below or have them develop a topic that has meaning for them based on the material covered in the lesson.

- Ellen Brandt shares in her testimony that as a response to what was happening in her life during the 1930s, she became both

NOTE 3.7

Multiple versions of this quotation exist as Niemoller himself was not consistent in the wording. It is often written in poem form as well. A version of the poem, titled "They Came For," can be found in the Additional Resources section of the Lesson Components.

L3

politically active and intensely religious. Write about a time or event in your life that you feel has helped to shape your identity or influenced how you view yourself.

- Some historians point out that the majority of Germans were indifferent to the plight of Jews. Their attitude was not rooted in hatred, but rather in complete apathy. Why might it have been that so many people simply didn't care what happened to their former colleagues, neighbors, and, in some cases, friends? Do you see examples of apathy in your school, community, country? Why do you think people become apathetic toward problems that others may be facing?

- Write about a time when you spoke out against a rule or policy that you believed to be unfair. What was the situation? What caused you to act? How did others view your actions? How did the situation end? How did you feel about what you had done?

Making Connections

The additional activities and projects listed below can be integrated directly into the lesson or can be used to extend the lesson once it has been completed. The topics lend themselves to students' continued study of the Holocaust as well as opportunities for students to make meaningful connections to other people and events, including relevant contemporary issues. These activities may include instructional strategies and techniques and/or address academic standards in addition to those that were identified for the lesson.

1. Visit IWitness (iwitness.usc.edu) fc   ·ities specific to Lesson 3: Nazi Germany.

2. After conducting research on an   ~ted by the Nazis (e.g., homosexuals, Sinti-
   Roma, Jehovah's Witnesses, peo   ···al dissidents), have students prepare
   a written, oral, or multimedia r   ¹·ould consult multiple sources
   of information presented in d¹   ⁻esearch.

3. Share a copy of Reverend M⸗   ⸗n with students
   (available in poem form ir   n Components).
   Review the historical cont   vents taking place
   in their time and "updat⸗   ſar situation taking
   place in their school, cc   e students post their
   work on the class wiki   ɔics raised.

4. Have students use ⸗   aphic that shows the
   immigration of Ger⸗   aphic might include the
   number of Jews wh   ie United States, Canada,
   Latin American cc   e; quota systems that were
   in place in vario·   Germany and Austria, etc.
   Students should

5. Dr. Seuss, bor   il cartoons for the New York
   daily newspa⸗   ſ. In the cartoons, he expressed
   his support for the   slow-to-act American political
   bureaucracy and organizau⸗   ¹ to the war. Have students select
   one or more of these political ca⸗   ıd online or in *Dr. Seuss Goes to*
   War (New Press, 2001) and determine ι⸗   of view or purpose in creating the
   cartoon; analyze both the message and the meaı⸗   ⸗comment on the overall effectiveness
   of the cartoon.

6. Survivors in both Lessons 2 and 3 describe the verbal and physical harassment they suffered at the hands of the *Hitlerjugend* (Hitler Youth). To help students better understand the

history and purpose of the Hitler Youth, provide an opportunity for them to gather relevant information from multiple print and digital sources about this organization and present their findings in a form of their choice (written, oral, visual). Encourage students to explore Susan Campbell Baroletti's *Hitler Youth: Growing Up in Hitler's Shadow* (Scholastic, 2005) for diaries, letters, oral histories, and historical photos from youth who followed the Nazi Party.

The class might be divided into small groups, each responsible for a particular aspect of the whole topic. Suggested questions for research are outlined below, but students should be encouraged to develop their own questions as well.

- When was the Hitler Youth started and by whom?

- What was the original purpose of the Hitler Youth?

- How did the Hitler Youth change over time?

- Who was expected to participate in the *Hitlerjugend* and at what age?

- How many boys belonged to the Hitler Youth at any one time?

- What were some of the activities that boys would participate in as members of the Hitler Youth?

- What messages were conveyed to the members of the Hitler Youth? How were these messages reinforced in the classroom?

- What were the goals and activities of the League of German Girls (*Bund Deutscher Mädel*), the female counterpart to the Hitler Youth?

- What role did propaganda play in shaping the beliefs, thinking, and actions of German youth?

THE WEIMAR REPUBLIC AND THE RISE OF THE NAZI PARTY

The Putsch: Nazi Party members arresting city councilmen, Munich, Germany. Yad Vashem Photo Archive (4254/80)

The Weimar Republic refers to the German government that was formed at Weimar, a town in the eastern part of the country, in February 1919, after Germany's defeat in World War I. The new republic emerged following a revolution, resulting in the abdication of Wilhelm II in November 1918. The Weimar Republic's constitution safeguarded basic democratic human rights, such as freedom of speech and religion and even equality for women, including their right to vote in public elections (which had not yet been given to French and English women).

The Republic was often perceived by Germans as having been forced upon them by the victors of World War I. Many German citizens remained deeply sympathetic to the Kaiser who was forced to resign, and to the leadership of the Second Reich, who had not signed the Treaty of Versailles. The treaty offended many sectors of the German nation mainly because of the following conditions:

A. Germany had to admit to being guilty for the war and for all the damage it had caused.
B. Germany had to pay reparations to compensate the victorious powers.
C. Germany was forced to give up 13 percent of its territory and six million of its inhabitants to France, Belgium, and Poland.
D. Germany was severely restricted in rebuilding and establishing its military force.

As a result of these conditions and the need to cope with the resentment it created in Germany, the "stabbed in the back" myth arose. According to this myth, Germany had not been defeated on the battlefield but rather had been betrayed by the Communists, Socialists, and Jews.

The Weimar Republic had to contend with many economic, political, and social problems. The German soldiers who came back from the war faced high unemployment. Many Germans were simply starving. Germany's heavy debts made it very difficult for the economy to recover and for new jobs to be created. One of the most serious problems was that of hyperinflation. The value of the German currency plummeted from 60 marks to the dollar in 1921 to 4.2 billion marks to the dollar at the end of 1923. For a time people were paid twice a day. The image that expresses this best is that of people filling wheelbarrows with currency and trying to buy anything they could before the currency lost more value.

Among other ways, the political crisis was expressed in frequent elections: 10 in 14 years. Three major revolution attempts also occurred in the first years of the Weimar Republic. In 1919, the Communists tried to overthrow the democratic republic, and in 1920 and 1923, there were attempts by right-wing nationalists, including Adolf Hitler, to seize power.

In 1922, Foreign Minister Walter Rathenau, who was a Jew and strongly identified with the Weimar Republic, was assassinated.

The New York stock market crash of 1929 deeply affected Germany—German banks collapsed and inflation rose. Six million Germans were unemployed in 1932, and the country, like most other nations, entered a serious and drawn-out economic depression.

In light of this situation, many Germans believed that the Nazis were the only ones who could solve Germany's problems and stop the "Communist menace." German president Paul von Hindenburg, who had opposed offering Adolf Hitler the leadership of Germany, was persuaded in January 1933 to appoint him chancellor. The government under Hitler was a coalition in which the Nazi Party was the dominant member with over one-third of the seats in the Reichstag (the German Parliament). Four weeks later, the Reichstag building was set on fire. Hitler blamed the fire on the Communists and used it as an excuse to pass new laws "for the protection of the German people." This was the start of the Nazi dictatorship and the process of remaking German society in the Nazis' image. Over time media and culture came under control of the Nazis, democratic freedoms were abolished, and the Nazi Party replaced or overtook other previously existing organizations and institutions throughout the country.

Selections from "The Program of the National-Socialist (Nazi) German Workers Party"

written 1920

1. We demand the uniting of all Germans within one Greater Germany, on the basis of the right to self-determination of nations.

2. We demand equal rights for the German people (*Volk*) with respect to other nations, and the annulment of the peace treaty of Versailles and St. Germain.

3. We demand land and soil (Colonies) to feed our People and settle our excess population.

4. Only Nationals (*Volksgenossen*) can be Citizens of the State. Only persons of German blood can be Nationals, regardless of religious affiliation. No Jew can therefore be a German National.

5. Any person who is not a Citizen will be able to live in Germany only as a guest and must be subject to legislation for Aliens.

6. Only a Citizen is entitled to decide the leadership and laws of the State. We therefore demand that only Citizens may hold public office, regardless of whether it is a national, state or local office.

7. We demand that the State make it its duty to provide opportunities of employment first of all for its own Citizens. If it is not possible to maintain the entire population of the State, then foreign nationals (non-Citizens) are to be expelled from the Reich.

8. Any further immigration of non-Germans is to be prevented. We demand that all non-Germans who entered Germany after August 2, 1914, be forced to leave the Reich without delay.

9. We demand the nationalization of all enterprises (already) converted into corporations (trusts).

10. We demand profit-sharing in large enterprises.

11. We demand the large-scale development of old-age pension schemes.

12. We demand the creation and maintenance of a sound middle class; the immediate communalization of the large department stores, which are to be leased at low rates to small tradesmen. We demand the most careful consideration for the owners of small businesses in orders placed by national, state, or community authorities.

13. We demand ruthless battle against those who harm the common good by their activities. Persons committing base crimes against the People, usurers, profiteers, etc., are to be punished by death without regard to religion or race.

14. We demand the replacement of Roman Law, which serves a materialistic World Order, by German Law.

15. The State must raise the level of national health by means of mother-and-child care, the banning of juvenile labor, achievements of physical fitness through legislation for compulsory gymnastics and sports, and maximum support for all organizations providing physical training for young people.

16. We demand the abolition of hireling troops and the creation of a national army.

17. We demand laws to fight against *deliberate* political lies and their dissemination by the press. In order to make it possible to create a German press we demand:

    a) All editors and editorial employees of newspapers appearing in the German language must be German by race;

    b) Non-German newspapers require express permission from the State for their publication. They may not be printed in the German language;

    c) Any financial participation in a German newspaper or influence on such a paper is to be forbidden by law to non-Germans and the penalty for any breach of this law will be the closing of the newspaper in question, as well as the immediate expulsion from the Reich of the non-Germans involved.

    d) Newspapers which violate the public interest are to be banned.

18. We demand laws against trends in art and literature which have a destructive effect on our national life, and the suppression of performances that offend against the above requirements.

19. To carry out all the above we demand:

    • The creation of a strong central authority in the Reich.

    • Unquestioned authority by the political central Parliament over the entire Reich and over its organizations in general.

    • The establishment of trade and professional organizations to enforce the Reich's basic laws in the individual states.

The Party leadership promises to take an uncompromising stand, at the cost of their own lives if need be, on the enforcement of the above points.

Reprinted with permission from Yitzhak Arad, Yisrael Gutman, Abraham Margaliot, eds., *Documents on the Holocaust, Selected Sources on the Destruction of the Jews of Germany and Austria, Poland and the Soviet Union* (Jerusalem: Yad Vashem, 1981), 15–18. All rights reserved.

EUROPE BEFORE 1919 AND THE TREATY OF VERSAILLES

Germany

Austria-Hungary

| 0 | miles | 250 |
| 0 | kilometers | 400 |

© 2005, Florida Center for Instructional Technology

L3

© 2005, Florida Center for Instructional Technology

WHAT RIGHTS ARE MOST IMPORTANT TO ME?

Directions: Rank the following in order of importance to you, with #1 being most important and #9 being least important.

_____   Date/Marry whomever you choose?

_____   Go to a public school close to home?

_____   Live in a neighborhood of your choice?

_____   Swim and play in a public swimming pool or park?

_____   Eat what you want, according to taste, culture, and religious custom?

_____   Be able to own a pet?

_____   Leave your house whenever you choose?

_____   Shop at stores and businesses of your choosing?

_____   Vote?

SA soldier near a Jewish-owned store on the day of the boycott, Germany. Yad Vashem Photo Archive (1652/11)

The Nazi Party rose to power with an antisemitic racial ideology. However, the anti-Jewish campaign was not conducted according to a blueprint, rather it evolved. Before the outbreak of the war, political and economic factors, as well as public opinion both inside and outside Germany influenced the evolution of Nazi anti-Jewish laws and measures.

The main purpose of the anti-Jewish policy between 1933 and 1938 according to the racial theory was to isolate German Jewry from German society and ultimately encourage them to leave their homeland. Through 1938 and into 1939, more and more force was used to push Jews out of German territory.

In addition to the fact that the laws and decrees were issued chronologically, they should also be understood for how they affected different spheres of life. They affected personal status, the interaction of Jews with general society, and their economic situation. The restrictions affected individuals and the Jewish community as a whole. Jews were not only limited by the flurry of laws and decrees, they also frequently felt deeply humiliated by them.

Build Up of Anti-Jewish Policy (1933–1938)

1933–1934: marked by boycotts against Jews and the exclusion of Jews from all government-related jobs, including serving as judges and teachers.

1935: marked by the Nuremberg Laws which classified Jews according to racial criteria and deprived them of German citizenship.

1937–1938: marked by increasing anti-Jewish violence, confiscation of Jewish property, and the forbidding of Jewish ownership of businesses. The culmination of violence was the *Kristallnacht Pogrom* in November 1938.

Anti-Jewish Policy by Year

Hitler begin power

1933

- All non-"Aryans" were dismissed from holding government jobs. This regulation applied to public school teachers, university professors, doctors, lawyers, engineers, etc.—all Jews who held government positions of any kind. Non-"Aryans" were defined as Jews, the children of Jews, and the grandchildren of Jews.

- A general boycott of all Jewish-owned businesses was proclaimed. Officially it lasted for one day, but actually it continued for much longer in many localities.

- Membership in the Reich Chamber of Culture was prohibited. This meant that Jews could not hold jobs in radio, in the theaters, or sell paintings or sculptures.
- Mass bonfires were ignited throughout Germany. Books written by Jews and anti-Nazis were burned.
- Jews were prohibited from owning land.
- Jewish lawyers and judges were barred from their professions.
- Jewish doctors were barred from treating "Aryan" patients.
- Jews were prohibited from producing kosher meat.

1935

- The Reichstag adopted the Nuremberg Laws, which defined Jews by racial criteria and determined that Jews could no longer be citizens of Germany.
- Marriage and intimate relations between Jews and those of "Aryan" blood were declared criminal acts.
- German females under the age of 45 were prohibited from being employed by Jews.
- Jews were forbidden to wave the Reich's flag or to display the flag's colors.

1936

- Hitler temporarily relaxed the antisemitic propaganda and other measures against Jews in order to avoid criticism by foreign visitors attending the Summer Olympic Games in Berlin.

1937

- "Aryanization," the confiscation of Jewish businesses and property, intensified greatly.

1938

- The Reich Supreme Court declared that being a Jew was cause for dismissal from a job.
- The Nuremberg Laws were extended to Austria after the *Anschluss,* the annexation of Austria.
- All Jews had to add the names "Israel" and "Sarah" to their identification papers, and passports were marked with the red letter J, for *Jude* (Jew).
- Jews could no longer attend plays and concerts, own phones, or have drivers' licenses, car registrations, etc.
- *Kristallnacht Pogrom:* approximately 1,400 synagogues were burned and 7,000 stores owned by Jews and hundreds of homes were damaged and looted.
- 30,000 Jews, most of them leaders in the Jewish communities, were sent to concentration camps. Many were offered the opportunity to leave the camps provided they could prove they had arranged their emigration from Germany.
- Very few Jewish children remained in German schools.
- All Jewish shops were ordered to close by December 31, 1938.
- Jews had to abide by curfews.

Between 1933 and the autumn of 1938, nearly 150,000 Jews managed to leave Nazi Germany. This number represented approximately 30 percent of the total Jewish population. In order for Jews to legally emigrate from Germany, they were required to have German passports and visas permitting them to enter another country and a long list of other official documents. In addition, most countries had quotas that limited the number of immigrants allowed to enter and required that those entering were able to support themselves, which posed a particular problem since the German authorities severely restricted the amount of money emigrating Jews could take with them. In short, leaving Nazi Germany and finding a place of refuge was extremely difficult. After the *Kristallnacht Pogrom*, a panicked exit of the remaining German Jews began. Despite all the difficulties involved, until October 1941—as long as the German authorities allowed Jews to leave—nearly 60 percent managed to do so. Ironically, many of the Jews who fled Germany went to other European countries that were occupied by the Nazis months or a few years later.

literally 1,000s of Nürnberg laws

© USHMM (04372)

ECHOES and REFLECTIONS
Leaders in Holocaust Education

Pick 1 person to be
- What thinking about
worry?
See?
Concern?

What missing?
How would this be different today?
Where fire hoses?

CONCENTRATION CAMPS

The first concentration camps were established in Nazi Germany after Hitler came to power in 1933. In the first few years of the regime, the concentration camps were instruments of terror, control, and punishment, used for the incarceration of political dissidents; later, people defined by the Nazis as "asocial elements"—including the homeless, beggars, Sinti-Roma, and hardened criminals—were also taken there. Beginning in the summer of 1938, many Jews were held in these camps. The number of incarcerated Jews in Germany itself reached its peak following the *Kristallnacht Pogrom*.

After the war broke out, the Nazi camp system branched out to many kinds of camps, and Jews, local resistance activists, and civilians whom the Nazis wanted to punish were incarcerated in them and generally were exploited as forced laborers. The cruel regime, lack of sufficient food, general conditions in the camps, brutal forced labor, and episodes of outright murder all led to a high death rate in most of the camps. The concentration camp system was not established as part of the "Final Solution," but as the policy of murder took hold, they too played a role in it.

About Photos

Top: SA members guarding inmates who are standing in line in the camp in Oranienburg, Germany, 1933. Yad Vashem Photo Archive (4613/38)

Middle: Inmates at a roll-call, Dachau, Germany, 1938. Yad Vashem Photo Archive (3EO1)

Bottom: A group of prisoners at a roll-call, Dachau, Germany, 1938. Bundesarchiv, Bild 152-21-06/ Friedrich Franz Bauer/CC-BY-SA

PYRAMID OF HATE

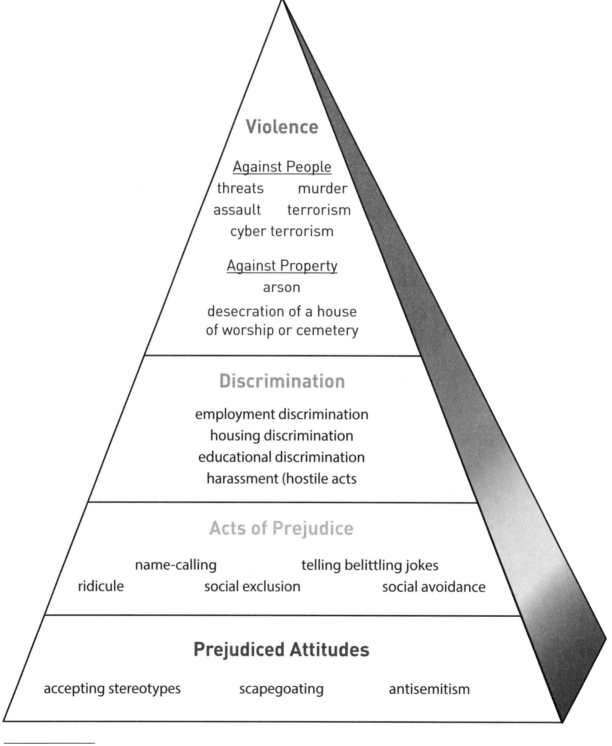

Violence

<u>Against People</u>
threats   murder
assault   terrorism
cyber terrorism

<u>Against Property</u>
arson
desecration of a house
of worship or cemetery

Discrimination

employment discrimination
housing discrimination
educational discrimination
harassment (hostile acts

Acts of Prejudice

name-calling   telling belittling jokes
ridicule   social exclusion   social avoidance

Prejudiced Attitudes

accepting stereotypes   scapegoating   antisemitism

Adapted with permission from *Anti-Bias Study Guide*, Elementary Level (NY: Anti-Defamation League, 2000): 223. All rights reserved.

About Photo

Street Scene in the Ghetto,
Lodz, Poland (1027/1)

Yad Vashem Photo Archive

"It was the beginning of the end...."

– Ellis Lewin, Jewish Survivor

Preparing to Use This Lesson

Below is information to keep in mind when using this lesson. In some cases, the points elaborate on general suggestions listed in the "Teaching about the Holocaust" section in the **Introduction** to this resource, and are specific to the content of the lesson. This material is intended to help teachers consider the complexities of teaching the Holocaust and to deliver accurate and sensitive instruction.

- During the transitional phase from the beginning of World War II before the "Final Solution" was planned and before extermination camps were built, ghettos were established. This was done in order to isolate Jews from the rest of the population, pending the formulation of a more definitive solution to the so-called "Jewish problem." At this stage a detailed blueprint for carrying out mass murder did not yet exist; rather, death was a side effect of the starvation, disease, and overcrowding in the ghettos. For instance, more than 80,000 Jews died in the Warsaw ghetto alone. Though there was no plan, there was a wish to solve the so-called "Jewish problem" in some rapid and radical way. It was only in 1941, with the invasion of the Soviet Union, that the Nazis began murdering Jews in a systematic mass fashion, and a project for murdering all Jews only coalesced during the course of the year and into 1942.

- Students often ask why more Jews did not escape from the ghettos. It is important for students to remember the extenuating circumstances that made it nearly impossible for the vast majority of Jews to flee.

  - While *we* know the ultimate fate of Jews during the Holocaust, Jews themselves did not know (especially during the early years of World War II when the first ghettos were established) that later they would be shot, sent to extermination camps, or worked to death, especially while German policies of persecution were still evolving and the Germans continuously employed many different means to camouflage their actions.

  - The physical conditions in the ghettos meant that the energies of the Jews were sapped just trying to stay alive.

  - The Holocaust created a world of "choiceless choices." Every action had a consequence, which, in many cases, became a matter of life and death. For instance, while many Jews may have wished they could escape, they felt a strong responsibility to take care of family members living with them, especially young children and elderly parents. Escape would have meant abandoning these people.

  - The Germans also commonly imposed collective punishment on those who were left behind; so that prospective escapees understood that their actions could endanger the lives of others.

  - Even if there was a way to escape, frequently there was no place to go. Non-Jews living outside the ghetto walls were mostly reluctant to help them, since hiding Jews was cause for severe punishment, even death. It is also important to keep in mind that even prior to the beginning of World War II, Jews who attempted to emigrate from Nazi-dominated Europe faced tremendous obstacles when they sought to leave, due to the world depression, immigration quotas, strict policies toward refugees, and far too often, anti-Jewish attitudes, as well. Overall, most Jews in Europe were trapped at that time.

THE GHETTOS

About This Lesson

 180–270 minutes

❖ **INTRODUCTION** This lesson provides students with an opportunity to learn about the ghettos established throughout Nazi Europe and understand that the ghettos were one phase in the continuum of Nazi racial policies that sought to solve the so-called "Jewish problem." Students will also learn about the conditions in most ghettos and how those conditions severely limited Jewish life and led to feelings of humiliation and loss of dignity. Using several primary sources, students will have an opportunity to learn that despite severe overcrowding, starvation, diseases, and grief, Jews still did their utmost to conduct their lives and retain their human dignity.

This two-part lesson has material appropriate for history, social studies, Holocaust studies, and English/language arts classes. Instructional strategies used in the lesson include large-group discussion, small-group work, interpreting visual history testimony, brainstorming, reading for comprehension and information, comparing and contrasting sources, map skills, analyzing primary source material, interpreting poetry, and journaling.

❖ **OBJECTIVES** After completing this lesson, students will be able to:

- Explain the aims of the Nazis in establishing ghettos.
- Name countries in Eastern and Central Europe where the Nazis established ghettos.
- Describe what life was like for Jews imprisoned in ghettos, with particular emphasis on the Lodz ghetto.
- Identify ways that Jews forced to live in ghettos attempted to maintain their dignity and preserve some of their previous ways of life.
- Interpret primary source documents—including clips of visual history testimony—that represent the experiences of those forced to live in the Lodz ghetto.
- Analyze various ways that individuals respond to unjust actions and the possible reasons behind those responses.

RESOURCES & TESTIMONIES

All of the resources used in this lesson can be found in this guide at the end of this lesson and at echoesandreflections.org.

Visual history testimonies are available on the website or on the DVD that accompanies this resource guide.

Teachers are urged to review the lesson procedures to identify other materials and technology needed to implement the lesson.

L4

❖ **KEY WORDS & PHRASES**

Aktion	"Final Solution of the	Lodz ghetto	*Ressortes*
Auschwitz-Birkenau	Jewish Question"	Nazi ideology	Sonderkommando
Chelmno	Gentile	occupation	Warsaw ghetto
concentration camp	ghetto	propaganda	Zionist
death march	Holocaust	Purim	
Einsatzgruppen	*Judenrat*	refugee	
extermination camp	liquidated	Reich	

❖ ACADEMIC STANDARDS The materials in this lesson address the following national education standards:

Common Core State Standards

- Reading Standards for Informational Text 6–12
- Reading Standards for Literature 6–12
- Speaking and Listening Standards 6–12
- Writing Standards 6–12
- Reading Standards for Literacy in History/Social Studies 6–12
- Writing Standards for Literacy in History/Social Studies 6–12

A complete analysis of how this lesson addresses Common Core State Standards by grade level and specific skills is available on the Echoes and Reflections website.

National Curriculum Standards for Social Studies

❶ Culture

❷ Time, Continuity, and Change

❹ Individual Development and Identity

❺ Individuals, Groups, and Institutions

❻ Power, Authority, and Governance

❿ Civic Ideals and Practices

Procedures

Part 1: Life in the Ghettos

NOTE 1.1

Throughout history, a ghetto referred to a street or city section where only Jews lived. The word ghetto was first used in Venice in 1516, as part of the phrase "Gèto Nuovo," meaning "New Foundry." This referred to the closed Jewish section of the city, which had originally been the site of a foundry. During World War II, the Jews of Eastern Europe were forced to leave their homes and move to ghettos where they were essentially held as prisoners.

1. Write the word "ghetto" on the board. Have students share what they know about the word and record their responses. Follow this discussion by sharing the history of the word.

2. Introduce students to Ellis Lewin and Joseph Morton and then show Part 1 of Visual History Testimony: *The Ghettos*. As students watch the two clips of testimony, encourage them to listen for specific examples of how ghettos during the Holocaust were different from their understanding of what is referred to as a "ghetto" today.

TESTIMONY VIEWING

About the Interviewees

Ellis Lewin was born on May 22, 1932, in Lodz, Poland. He was forced to live in the Lodz ghetto and later imprisoned in the Augsburg, Dachau, München-Allach, and Kaufbeuren concentration camps. Ellis was also a prisoner in the Auschwitz-Birkenau extermination camp. His interview was conducted in the United States. When the war began, Ellis was seven years old.

continued on page 95

Joseph Morton was born on July 11, 1924, in Lodz, Poland. He was forced to live in the Lodz ghetto and later imprisoned in the Kaufering, Auschwitz, Mühldorf, Dachau, München-Allach, and Landshut concentration camps. His interview was conducted in the United States. When the war began, Joseph was fifteen years old.

_____

For additional information about Ellis Lewin and Joseph Morton, see their Biographical Profiles available on the website.

Discuss the testimonies using the questions below.

- In their testimonies, Ellis Lewin and Joseph Morton share some of their early feelings and experiences in the ghetto. How does Ellis say his life changed after being forced into the ghetto? What does Joseph share about his observations of life in the ghetto?

- Based on the testimonies you just watched, how were ghettos during the Holocaust different from your understanding of what a ghetto is today?

- What images have begun to emerge for you about ghetto life after listening to these two testimonies?

- How do you think Ellis and Joseph felt sharing these memories? How did you feel listening to them?

3. Ask a volunteer to explain (or draw) what Joseph said about the bridge in the Lodz ghetto. Share information about the bridge and show the photograph *Jews Crossing the Bridge in the Lodz Ghetto*. Ask students to discuss what they think the Jews crossing the bridge were feeling as they looked down upon the scene below.

4. Explain to students that Nazi ideology called for expanding the rule of Germany. After conquering Poland in September 1939 (after already controlling Austria and parts of Czechoslovakia), Germany sought to dominate the whole world along with its partners, and arrange it in a "new order" based on Nazi racial ideology. According to the Nazi racial view, the populations living in Poland were deemed to be Slavs, who were considered inferior and therefore treated as such.

5. Distribute *The Ghettos* handout; have students read the text individually or as a whole group. [Optional: Teachers may want to pose several of the questions listed in procedure #6 below prior to reading the material.]

6. Have a whole-class discussion based on the questions below. Encourage students to cite evidence from the text to support their answers whenever possible.

Questions about Nazi ideology:

- What were the Nazis' intentions in closing Jews in the ghettos?

NOTE 1.3

The two separate physical areas that comprised the Lodz ghetto were separated by a bridge that spanned trolley tracks in the city of Lodz. Since Jews were not permitted to use the trolleys and had to be completely sequestered and isolated, the German occupiers built a bridge over the tracks to connect the two parts of the ghetto. Because the bridge was narrow, Jews often had to wait long periods of time to get from one side of the bridge to the other.

NOTE 1.6

The first several questions address Nazi ideology and the second group of questions ask students to consider Jewish responses to the ghettos. It is important that students have sufficient time to explore both perspectives.

- The Germans wanted to concentrate Jews living in the countryside into the larger cities, and establish ghettos in the vicinity of railroad junctions. What do you think was the purpose of concentrating Jews together in certain central locations? Why did the Germans want to establish ghettos near railway transports?

- Heydrich writes, "For the time being, the first step toward the final goal is the concentration of the Jews...." What do you think Heydrich meant by "for the time being"? What do you think Heydrich meant by "the final goal"?

- Why did the Germans establish a Jewish Council, or *Judenrat,* in each ghetto?

- What are some possible reasons why the Germans themselves didn't govern the ghettos?

- How might the establishment of a *Judenrat* have given Jews in the ghetto a false sense of security?

Questions about Jewish responses:

- Share the following statement made by Chaim A. Kaplan, a teacher from the Warsaw ghetto: "Ghetto life does not flow— rather it is stagnant and frozen. Around us—are walls! We have no space, we have no freedom of movement and action." What is the main feeling that emerges from hearing this passage?

- Identify some of the dilemmas that Jews faced on a daily basis in the ghettos.

- What were some ways that Jews attempted to keep their dignity and sanity in the ghettos?

- How does this description of ghetto life compare to the descriptions of ghetto life presented in the testimonies at the beginning of this lesson?

- Discuss the difference between physical and economic segregation.

- When people describe a neighborhood today as a "ghetto," how is it different from the Nazi ghettos? Are there any similarities?

7. Show students the *Ghettos in Europe* map. Ask students to consider the following questions after studying the map:

- In which countries were the ghettos located? (Poland, Latvia, Lithuania, Czechoslovakia, Romania, Hungary, Soviet Union)

- Looking at this map, how many ghettos would you estimate were established across Eastern and Central Europe?

- Why do you think that there were no ghettos in Western Europe?

- What other observations do you have after looking at this map?

8. Explain to students that the next part of the lesson will concentrate on one ghetto in particular, the Lodz ghetto in Poland. Tell students that in addition to learning background information on this particular ghetto, they will also analyze primary source documents

NOTE 1.7

According to the latest findings on ghettos, the Nazis established approximately 1,000 ghettos throughout Eastern and Central Europe. These ghettos had both commonalities and differences.

and watch first-person visual history testimonies from survivors of the Lodz ghetto. These sources will provide a glimpse into what life was like for Jews living in ghettos between 1940 and 1944.

9. Distribute a copy of *The Lodz Ghetto* to each student and read together as a whole class. Follow with a discussion using the questions below. Have students cite evidence from the text to support their answers.

   • Why did the Nazis completely seal the Lodz ghetto?

   • Why did Chaim Rumkowski encourage the people in the Lodz ghetto to work and produce war supplies for the Nazi troops?

   • What was the reasoning behind having children work in the workshops?

   • Why were the city inhabitants hostile to Jews in the Lodz ghetto?

10. Divide the class into small groups and give each group a copy of the following documents: *Lodz Ghetto, 1941, Poem by an Unknown Girl,* and *Poem by Avraham Koplowicz.* Provide background information on the photograph. Have group members discuss the photograph and poems using the following questions:

   • What specifically do you see in the photograph?

   • What do you think is happening in the photograph?

   • What are you able to determine about life in the Lodz ghetto from studying this photograph? How, if at all, is what you have already learned about the Lodz ghetto influencing your answer? Do you think you would have come to similar conclusions had you seen this photograph without background on the Lodz ghetto?

   • Do you think knowing who took this particular photograph and under what circumstances influenced your reaction or response to it? Is it possible that your response might have been different if you hadn't known who the photographer was, or if you had assumed it was taken by the Nazis? Discuss your answer.

   • How would you describe the tone of each of the poems? Identify how specific words or phrases have an impact on the meaning and tone of each poem.

   • What is the significance of time in both poems? Which poem talks about the past and which talks about the future?

   • What is Avraham Koplowicz's dream? Do you think the dream Avraham describes is figurative or literal? What words or lines in the poem have influenced your answer?

   • Does it appear from reading these poems that both these children believed that they would survive the ghetto? Support your response with specific words, phrases, or lines from the poems.

   • What are your feelings as you look at the photograph and read the poems from the Lodz ghetto?

NOTE 1.10

This 1941 photograph by Mendel Grossman (1917–1945) is of a child leaving a soup kitchen with a pot of soup. Mendel Grossman, a Jew who took more than 10,000 photographs in the Lodz ghetto, recorded for posterity the horrors of the ghetto. He took advantage of his job in the ghetto statistics department—for which he was authorized to have a camera—to document ghetto life. Grossman's photos, unlike most of the surviving photos of the Holocaust, were not taken by the Germans, who usually took photos for purposes of anti-Jewish propaganda. When the ghetto was liquidated, he was deported to the Königs Wusterhausen labor camp, where he secretly continued taking photographs. In April 1945, Grossman collapsed on a death march, still clutching his camera. After the war, the negatives of pictures he had hidden in the ghetto were discovered. Some of the photographs were published in the book *My Secret Camera: Life in the Lodz Ghetto* (Gulliver Books, 2000).

Part 2: The Role of the Ghettos

1. Begin this part of the lesson by explaining to students that the role of the ghetto was to control and confine Jews and that the situation in the ghetto led to Jews being weakened as well. Based on what they learned about the ghettos in Part 1 of this lesson, have them share examples of what they already know about specific ways that the Nazis attempted to control and confine Jews in the ghettos.

2. Instruct students to divide a piece of paper into three columns and label the columns "control," "confine," and "weaken." Introduce students to Leo Berkenwald, Milton Belfer, and George Shainfarber and then show the first three clips from Part 2 of Visual History Testimony: *The Ghettos*. Have students complete the chart with specific examples they hear in the testimonies about what life was like in the Lodz ghetto.

TESTIMONY VIEWING

About the Interviewees

Leo Berkenwald was born on August 31, 1923, in Lodz, Poland. He was forced to live in the Lodz ghetto and later imprisoned in the Dörnhau, Auschwitz, and Eule concentration camps. His interview was conducted in the United States. When the war began, Leo was sixteen years old.

Milton Belfer was born on August 24, 1922, in Lodz, Poland. He was forced to live in the Lodz ghetto and later imprisoned in the Auschwitz, Siegmar-Schönau, and Hohenstein-Ernsttahl concentration camps. His interview was conducted in the United States. When the war began, Milton was seventeen years old.

George Shainfarber was born on January 4, 1927, in Lodz, Poland. He was forced to live in the Lodz ghetto and was also imprisoned in the Auschwitz-Birkenau extermination camp. His interview was conducted in the United States. When the war began, George was twelve years old.

For additional information about Leo Berkenwald, Milton Belfer, and George Shainfarber, see their Biographical Profiles available on the website.

3. Have students review their charts with a partner, sharing the examples that they wrote down for each of the three categories. Encourage students to discuss differences and similarities in their answers and also consider how some of the experiences that the survivors discussed might fit into more than one category. Follow with a discussion using the following questions:

- Leo Berkenwald lived within the confines of what would eventually become the Lodz ghetto. Even though he was still living in the same city, how did his life change once the ghetto was created?

NOTE 2.2

This lesson uses the Lodz ghetto as a way to tell a larger story. While each ghetto was unique, this lesson uses Lodz as a prism to try and understand the ghettos in general and something of the mentality of the people who would confine human beings in such an inhumane manner. What happened in Lodz and the decisions made by people who established the ghetto shed light on larger decisions that were being made elsewhere, even though the Lodz ghetto had its own uniqueness and special historical circumstances.

- What does Milton Belfer's testimony add to your understanding of life in the ghetto? What does Leo's add?

- What role did food play in George Shainfarber's experience in the ghetto?

4. Show students *Diary Entry from the Lodz Ghetto* and read the entry together. Have students identify examples from Josef's diary entry that also illustrate how the Nazis controlled, confined, and ultimately weakened Jews forced to live in the ghetto.

5. Ask students what they have learned thus far in this lesson about what life was like for children in the Lodz ghetto and cite how they learned the information (e.g., testimony, photograph, poems, informational text). Introduce students to Eva Safferman (and Ellis Lewin and George Shainfarber if their testimonies were not shown earlier), and then show the next three clips from Part 2 of Visual History Testimony: *The Ghettos*. Follow with a discussion using the questions below.

- What are some specific things that you learned about what life was like for children in the ghettos from Eva Safferman, Ellis Lewin, and George Shainfarber?

- Would you describe their behavior as uncharacteristic for most children? Why or why not?

- What were some of the ways in which families and neighbors tried to cope with circumstances in the ghetto?

6. Explain to students that one of the diaries discovered after the city of Lodz was liberated on January 19, 1945 was the diary of a teenager named Dawid Sierakowiak. Distribute *Excerpts from The Diary of Dawid Sierakowiak* and read the background information. Read as many of the entries as possible.

7. Have a discussion using some or all of the questions below. Whenever possible, students should use specific examples from the primary sources they have investigated in this lesson to support their answers.

- What do you learn from reading diary entries and listening to testimonies that is different from what you learn from a handout like *The Ghettos*? How are both types of information useful and necessary when studying a topic like the ghettos?

- What does Josef Zelkowicz mean when he asks "Do you have any children at all in the ghetto?" What are some examples from the testimonies that illustrate that children felt they could not afford to be children?

- How do excerpts in Dawid Sierakowiak's diary substantiate what you heard in the testimonies?

- What does Dawid mean when he says "Oh, my dear school! Damn the times when I complained about getting up in the morning and about tests. If only I could have them back!" Have you ever had a similar feeling about something?

- What did school mean in the ghetto?

NOTE 2.5

To learn more about what life was like for children in the ghettos, see Lesson 6: Jewish Resistance and Lesson 10: The Children.

TESTIMONY VIEWING

About the Interviewee

Eva Safferman was born on April 15, 1928, in Lodz, Poland. She was forced to live in the Lodz ghetto and imprisoned in the Hamburg-Sasel, Auschwitz I, and Bergen-Belsen concentration camps. Eva was also a prisoner in the Auschwitz-Birkenau extermination camp. Her interview was conducted in the United States. When the war began, Eva was eleven years old.

For additional information about Eva Safferman, see her Biographical Profile available on the website.

NOTE 2.6

If time is limited, the following excerpts are recommended: September 3, 1939; September 10, 1939; October 24, 1939; April 27, 1941; May 2, 1941; May 16, 1941; April 4, 1943; April 15, 1943.

- What does going to school represent for Dawid?

- What are some things that young people you know might take for granted that young people in the ghetto learned to cherish?

- What do you think Dawid means when he writes, "Humiliation inflicted by force does not humiliate"? Do you agree with him? Explain your thinking or give an example to illustrate why you do or do not agree with Dawid's statement.

- Dawid writes, "long live humor." How does he show in his diary that he had a sense of humor? How do you think it is possible for people to keep a sense of humor during unthinkably difficult times?

- There are also examples of hope and optimism in Dawid's diary entries. Point out an example. Explain where Dawid began to lose hope.

- In his testimony, Ellis Lewin says he believes that the children who were physically able to survive did so because "they didn't know any better." What do you think Ellis means by this? Do you agree or disagree with him? Why or why not?

NOTE 2.8

To learn more about cultural and spiritual resistance in the ghettos, see Lesson 6: Jewish Resistance.

8. End this lesson by having students complete an "Exit Slip", whereby they reflect on the information they have learned in this lesson and express their thoughts about this new information. In a paragraph, have students respond to the prompt below and submit prior to the next class period. If the "Exit Slips" are submitted electronically, the teacher may wish to post on the class website, blog, or wiki for others to see.

Prompt: In his testimony, Ellis Lewin states that arriving in the Lodz ghetto was "the beginning of the end." After learning about the Lodz ghetto through both primary and secondary sources, explain what Ellis meant by this statement not only for him and his family but more broadly for the Jews of Europe. Provide specific examples to support your response.

Reflect and Respond

Either in class or as homework, have students reflect and respond to one or more of the topics below or have them develop a topic that has meaning for them based on the material covered in the lesson.

- The establishment of ghettos marked the end of freedom of movement for Jews. Write about what freedom means to you in your life and what you think it would mean to lose it.

- In very challenging times, the importance of remaining hopeful and the persistent belief that one's situation will improve is crucial. However, this outlook and attitude is difficult to maintain over a long period of time. Do you believe there is a certain point when people begin to lose hope? If so, what do you think that point is? Do you think it is the same for everyone? Has the loss of hope ever happened to you? Have you witnessed it in others? How does a person restore hope?

- In his testimony, Ellis Lewin talks about what he sees as the only things that have the power to hurt children—losing the comfort of family, being beaten, and being hungry. Do you agree with Ellis's assessment? Are there other things that you would add to this list? Do you think that the things that have the power to hurt children are different from those that can hurt adults?

Making Connections

The additional activities and projects listed below can be integrated directly into the lesson or can be used to extend the lesson once it has been completed. The topics lend themselves to students' continued study of the Holocaust as well as opportunities for students to make meaningful connections to other people and events, including relevant contemporary issues. These activities may include instructional strategies and techniques and/or address academic standards in addition to those that were identified for the lesson.

1. Visit IWitness (iwitness.usc.edu) for activities specific to Lesson 4: The Ghettos.

2. Using information from the **Timeline** available on the website, have students align events happening in Europe and other parts of the world to Dawid Sierakowiak's diary entries in an overlapping timeline that is presented in a format of their choice. Encourage students to read additional entries of *The Diary of Dawid Sierakowiak* (Oxford University Press, 1996) to complete this assignment.

3. In this lesson, students have examined three types of primary sources in addition to visual history testimony: diaries, poems, and a photograph. Review the potential value of these kinds of sources, and consider how each adds to our knowledge and understanding of the ghettos, in general, and the Lodz ghetto, in particular. Introduce students to another kind of primary source—artifacts—by showing them the *Monopoly Game from Theresienstadt* available on the website in the **Additional Resources** section of the **Lesson Components**. Ask students to study the artifact and consider the questions below. Encourage students to review the definition of Theresienstadt in the **Glossary** on the website.

    - Even though you did not learn about Theresienstadt in this lesson, what knowledge do you have about ghettos in general that you can apply to your examination of this artifact?

    - What do you see on the Monopoly board that provides you with insight into what life was like in Theresienstadt?

    - What kind of game is Monopoly? (e.g., a game of chance, a game of power and control)

    - What is the irony of children in Theresienstadt playing Monopoly?

    - Why do you think the adults in Theresienstadt made this game for the children?

    Have students research print or digital sources and identify an artifact from one of the ghettos. After studying the artifact, instruct students to report their observations using the following guiding questions:

    - What was the artifact that you investigated and what ghetto was it from? Was there any information available about the artifact; if so, what information was supplied?

    - What can be learned about ghetto life by studying this artifact?

    - Reflect on the experience of locating and studying an artifact. How was the experience different from studying secondary sources? How, if at all, was it different from studying other types of primary sources?

4. Introduce students to Theresienstadt by having them review the definition in the **Glossary** available on the website. Explain that although most of the Jews of Theresienstadt were deported and murdered, many of the drawings and poems did survive the war and some can be found in the book, *I Never Saw Another Butterfly* (Schocken Books, 1993). Introduce students to one of the poems from this collection, Pavel Friedman's "The Butterfly," available on the website in the **Additional Resources** section of the **Lesson Components.** Have students read the poem aloud several times and then discuss the following questions:

   - What is the tone of this poem? Identify how specific words or phrases have an impact on the meaning and tone of the poem.

   - Why do you think the poet said the butterfly "wished to kiss the world good-bye"?

   - What has the poet found to love in the ghetto?

   - What is the significance of the line, "Only I never saw another butterfly"?

   - Do you think the poet is hopeful that he will one day leave the ghetto or is he resigned to his fate to remain "penned up," or worse? Explain how you reached your decision.

   - Study the painting by Liz Elsby that is paired with this poem. Describe specific techniques that the artist uses in the painting and why you think she chose those techniques when creating a painting to accompany the poem. In your opinion, is this painting a good representation of the poem? Why or why not?

   - If you were creating a piece of art to accompany "The Butterfly," what would it look like? What medium would you use? If you were setting the poem to music, what would the music sound like? [**Optional:** Have students create their own piece of art or set the poem to music.]

5. Have students research the role that music played in the lives of Jews forced to live in the ghettos. In particular, have students research one of the following ghettos: Kovno, Vilna, or Lodz. Among other sources, encourage students to refer to Yad Vashem's *Heartstrings* exhibition (available on the website in the **Additional Resources** section of the **Lesson Components**). Have students prepare and share an oral or multimedia report on their findings.

JEWS CROSSING THE BRIDGE IN THE LODZ GHETTO

THE GHETTOS

Invasion of Poland

In September 1939, the Germans invaded Poland. Poland lost its independence, and its citizens were subjected to severe oppression. Schools were closed, all political activity was banned, and many members of the Polish elite, intellectuals, political leaders, and clerics, were sent to concentration camps or murdered immediately. Jews were subjected to violence, humiliation, dispossession, and arbitrary kidnappings for forced labor by German soldiers who abused Jews in the streets, paying special attention to religious Jews. Many thousands of Poles and Jews were murdered in the first months of the occupation, not yet as a policy of systematic mass murder, but an expression of the brutal nature of the occupying forces.

On September 21, 1939, just after the German conquest of Poland, Reinhard Heydrich, Nazi head of the SIPO (security police) and SD (security service) issued an order to the commanders in occupied Poland. The first, immediate stage called for several practical measures, including deporting Jews from western and central Poland and concentrating them in the vicinity of railroad junctions and forming *Judenrate* (councils of elders or Jewish councils) that would be responsible for these actions.

Establishment of Ghettos

Guided by ideological principles and striving to establish a "New Order" in Europe based mainly on racial doctrine, Nazi Germany separated Jews from the rest of the population by establishing ghettos. A ghetto was a section of the city in which Jews were confined and restricted to live behind walls, fences, or barbed wire. The Germans wanted to isolate Jews and completely disconnect them from the world around them, from Jews in other places, and from everyday life. This gave

Jews rounded up for forced labor, Przemysl, Poland, October 1939. Yad Vashem Photo Archive (5323)

them great control over the Jews. Soon after the ghettos began to be established, the Nazis tried to remove the Jews from their midst through population transfer. At first they sought to drive Jews into Soviet territory, but when that strategy proved unworkable, the Nazis developed a plan to send the Jews to the island of Madagascar. This plan also proved

> SECRET
>
> Berlin: September 21, 1939
> To: Chiefs of all Einsatzgruppen of the Security Police
> Subject: Jewish question in the occupied territory
>
> I refer to the conference held in Berlin today.... For the time being, the first step toward the final goal is the concentration of the Jews from the countryside into the larger cities. This is to be carried out with all speed....
>
> In each Jewish community a council of Jewish Elders is to be set up.... The councils of Elders are to be informed of the dates and deadlines.... They are then to be made personally responsible for the departure of the Jews from the countryside.... For general reasons of security, the concentration of Jews in the cities will probably necessitate orders altogether barring Jews from certain sections of the cities, or, for example, forbidding them to leave the ghetto....

impractical. Only later, once the Nazis began to implement a policy of systematic mass murder of Jews through deportation to extermination camps, were the Jews who had been concentrated in the ghettos deported and murdered. A minority of Jews was also deported from the ghettos to a myriad of labor camps to be exploited as slave labor. As such, ghettos were a means to an end and not an end in and of themselves.

Ghettos were set up almost exclusively in Eastern Europe for two main reasons. First, in many Eastern European cities, as opposed to Western Europe, there already was a large Jewish district and so confining all Jews to those districts made the process of establishing ghettoes more practical. Second, because of perceived cultural and "racial" differences (Western Europeans were seen by the Nazis as being on a higher racial level); the Nazis refrained from antagonizing Western Europeans and did not concentrate Jews in ghettos in Western Europe.

Relatively little time was generally allotted for moving into the ghettos. Jewish families who in some cases had lived in their homes for decades had to gather their belongings and find shelter in a defined area that was extremely crowded. Motor vehicles were not available, and even horse-drawn carts were rare; therefore, many people moved their belongings in baby carriages or on their backs. Jews had to painfully decide what to take with them to the ghetto although they had no information about how long they would have to stay or what life would be like there.

In the ghettos, the *Judenrate* were held fully responsible for compliance with German policy. Members of the *Judenrate* were exposed to German abuse and many were murdered for not obeying German orders. The *Judenrate* were required to act as municipal authorities and to provide a full range of services that Jewish communities had not provided in the past. The *Judenrate* were not only responsible for re-establishing systems of education, culture, and religious services in the ghettos and maintaining health and welfare institutions; they also had to arrange for garbage removal and postal services. Of course, the German authorities did not allocate resources for these purposes, and this put the *Judenrate* in an extremely difficult situation. They had to provide community services to a needy population without any infrastructure or financial resources. Therefore, members of the *Judenrate* were constantly forced to contend with moral dilemmas and make crucial decisions in unprecedented situations. As restrictions, shortages, hunger, and diseases worsened in the ghettos, the dilemmas of the members of the *Judenrate* became increasingly more extreme. The most difficult dilemma came when the German authorities demanded that the *Judenrate* supply lists of Jews to be deported from the ghettos, often to death camps.

Conditions in the Ghettos

Conditions in the ghettos were influenced by many factors, among them whether the ghetto was hermetically sealed or was open to some extent; the size of the ghetto and its location, since ghettos in the countryside often had access to more food; and the personality of the Nazis who were in charge of the ghetto. In many ghettos, a large number of Jews died of starvation or various epidemics that raged due to the harsh conditions. Lack of medication presented a constant dilemma in the ghettos.

Two Starving Women on a Rickshaw, Warsaw Ghetto, Poland, September 19, 1941. Yad Vashem Photo Archive (2536/85)

Doctors faced with shortages of medication had to decide which patients to treat.

In the shadow of chaos and terror, many Jews attempted to retain their humanity and operate relief organizations just as they had done before World War II broke out. Despite the deteriorating conditions and extreme deprivation, a refugee aid network was established in many places. For example, children gathered in special kitchens, where, in addition to receiving food, they were kept busy with educational activities. Frequently, relief center staff recruited unemployed but highly educated people to work with youth in the ghetto. In most cases, the relief centers had to figure out how best to distribute their limited resources, which raised many moral dilemmas.

Commonly the Jewish family unit underwent a major change during the ghetto period. The prewar situation, in which the father of the family had been the main breadwinner, was altered unrecognizably because the father could no longer work in the ghetto, or was absent because he had been killed or sent to a labor camp. As a result, the women and children had to share in the financial burden. In ghettos where it was still possible to sneak through the barriers and reach the world outside, many small children became smugglers, clandestinely bringing back food for their families. Smuggling was very dangerous: a Jew found outside the ghetto walls was generally killed immediately. Starving parents, therefore, confronted an awful dilemma.

Life in the Ghettos

Education was outlawed by the Germans in many of the ghettos; schools were closed and learning was punishable by death. Despite this prohibition, in some ghettos an underground educational system was set up by the Jews, though many young people had to help support the family and could not afford to sit in class. In addition to the underground educational system, some *Judenrate* set up vocational school systems in ghettos where this was permitted. The idea was to enlarge the ghetto labor force and to give youth a practical means of earning a living during the war.

Cultural activity took place within some ghettos and the extent varied from ghetto to ghetto. Some of the activities were secret, held at the initiative of underground organizations; they included literary evenings, gatherings to mark the anniversary of a Jewish artist, and concerts. Jewish authors, directors, and poets produced works in the ghettos, and there were secret libraries. Some of the cultural activities were based on works written before the war (in the Theresienstadt ghetto, for instance, works by Shakespeare, Moliere, and Chekhov were presented, while theaters in Warsaw staged Yiddish classics by S. An-ski, Sholem Asch, and Sholem Aleichem, among other things); others drew on the situation in the ghetto. The cultural activities helped people temporarily forget the worries of ghetto life and were a source of encouragement. However, there was also criticism; some people argued that these events were inappropriate in a place where so many people were dying every day.

Ultimately, once the Germans developed a plan for the "Final Solution of the Jewish Question," they embarked on a process of closing down and liquidating the ghettos, deporting most of the Jews who remained alive. The vast majority of Jews deported from the ghettos were murdered in the extermination camps; only a small percentage were taken to concentration and forced labor camps in the late stages of the war. By the end of the war when Europe was liberated, except in Budapest, not a single ghetto, neither in its entirety, nor in part, remained.

The Library, Theresienstadt, Czechoslovakia. Yad Vashem Photo Archive (2977/471)

GHETTOS IN EUROPE

© Yad Vashem

THE LODZ GHETTO

Lodz is the second largest city in Poland, known for its textile industry. Before the war, Jews played an influential role in this industry. Lodz was occupied by the German army (Wehrmacht) in September 1939. As part of western Poland, Lodz was annexed to the Reich, and named Litzmannstadt for the German general who had conquered the city in World War I. The Nazis reserved this part of Poland for settlement by Germans, most of whom had lived for generations in the Baltic countries. By the end of 1939, tens of thousands of Jews and Poles had been deported from the area, and Germans were settled there. However, for administrative and logistical reasons, population transfers were halted at the beginning of 1940.

Earlier than most Jewish communities in Poland, the Jews of Lodz suffered from exceptionally brutal persecution, eviction from their homes, and deportation. As early as May 1940, the ghetto was established, and 164,000 Jews were incarcerated in it. The Lodz ghetto was one of the first ghettos to be established and it became the second largest ghetto in the occupied Polish territories. The Lodz ghetto was completely sealed off and detached from the outside world. Since many of the residents of Lodz were of German origin and identified with Germany and the Nazis, Jews there faced a hostile environment. The hostility of their neighbors and the strict closure of the ghetto made it almost impossible to smuggle food into the ghetto, which compelled the Jews to live on the meager ration of food allotted to them by the Germans.

The *Judenrat* in Lodz was led by Mordechai Chaim Rumkowski. Before the war, Rumkowski had been a junior member of the Jewish community administration in Lodz. Like many other Jewish leaders during the Holocaust, Rumkowski found himself in an impossible position between obeying German orders and trying to help Jews grapple with the hardships of ghetto existence. The German authorities created this tension on purpose, hoping the anger and the frustration of the local Jewish population would be spent on Jewish leaders and not the German authorities.

Mordechai Chaim Rumkowski, Chief of the Judenrat (center), among Jewish policemen, Lodz, Poland. Yad Vashem Photo Archive (36CO9)

It appears that Rumkowski often displayed delusions of grandeur and his behavior bordered on dictatorial since he perceived himself to be the only one who could successfully navigate the Lodz Jewish community through troubled times. Although he believed that he could be the savior of the ghetto, in the end, he too was murdered along with most of Lodz Jewry.

By the end of 1942, some 204,800 people had passed through the Lodz ghetto.

The large number of Jews in the ghetto, the total isolation in a hostile environment, the strict supervision imposed by the Germans, the acute hunger, and the difficulties in obtaining the most basic resources necessary to live made it very difficult to survive in the Lodz ghetto.

The struggle for survival was a daily, up-hill battle.

Rumkowski thought that the only possible way to keep people alive in the ghetto was to open factories and workshops so that the German authorities would consider the Jews valuable and allow them to live; his hope was they would live long enough to be liberated. This policy came to be known as "salvation through labor." Jews forced to work in these factories and workshops manufactured textile products for the Germans. Conditions in the labor workshops were harsh. The factory floors were small and congested, lighting and ventilation were poor, and most work was done by hand for lack of appropriate machinery. Production quotas were set beyond the workers' abilities. Workers were "remunerated" for their efforts with a portion of soup each day and a slice of bread. Despite Rumkowski's efforts to obtain increased food rations from the Germans, the daily portions did not suffice, and more than 43,000 Jews starved to death.

In the first years of the ghetto's existence, the chairman of the *Judenrat* ran an education system with the enrollment of 15,000 children, from preschool to high school; even matriculation exams were given in the ghetto. Regular studies ceased in October 1941. Once children were enrolled in the workshops (to protect them from being deported to death), some managed to continue studying at their place of work. Over 7,000 young people continued to study in this way. However, most of the children, as Josef Zelkowicz mentions, were too busy lining up at the soup kitchens and on the bread lines, carrying around a pot, which Zelkowicz calls "the symbol of the ghetto," just in case some food was being given out somewhere. In the ghetto, there were also some cultural and religious activities, which were often felt to be no more than a sad reminder of what life had been.

Excerpts From Rumkowski's Speech of September 4, 1942:

"[...] The ghetto has been struck a hard blow. They demand what is most dear to it - children and old people [...] I never imagined that my own hands would be forced to make this sacrifice on the altar. In my old age, I am forced to stretch out my hands and to beg: "Brothers and sisters, give them to me! - Fathers and mothers, give me your children..." (Bitter weeping shakes the assembled public) [...]

There are many people in this ghetto who suffer from tuberculosis, whose days or perhaps weeks are numbered. I do not know, perhaps this is a satanic plan, and perhaps not, but I cannot stop myself from proposing it: "Give me these sick people, and perhaps it will be possible to save the healthy in their place." I know how precious each one of the sick is in his home, and particularly among Jews. But at a time of such decrees, one must weigh up and measure who should be saved, who can be saved and who may be saved.

Common sense requires us to know that those must be saved who can be saved and who have a chance of being saved and not those whom there is no chance to save in any case [....]"

In 1942, the first *Aktion* against the Jews of Lodz took place. Rumkowski adhered to his concept of work as a means of survival, and—presented with the dilemma of who to deport—made the fatal decision to deport children under the age of ten, as well as the sick and the old, because they did not work. He convened the entire ghetto in an open field and addressed them. The *Aktion* associated with this event came to be known as the "Children's *Aktion*" or *Sperre* (from the German word for curfew), and is an extreme manifestation of the dilemmas leaders of *Judenrate* faced.

During the Children's *Aktion,* approximately 20,000 very young Jewish children, elderly, and sick were deported over a number of days. Included among them was Dawid Sierakowiak's mother (see *Excerpts from The Diary of Dawid Sierakowiak,* September 5, 1942). They were taken to the Chelmno extermination camp where they were murdered in gas vans.

The ghetto continued to exist for two more years, and work was the focal point of ghetto life. The populace was desperately hungry and food could be obtained only through work. The Lodz ghetto was the last remaining ghetto in Poland, and it was only liquidated in August 1944. Most of the remaining inhabitants were transported to Auschwitz, where the majority was murdered, Rumkowski among them. During the four years of its existence, Jews in the Lodz ghetto attempted, despite the severe hardships, to preserve some of their previous ways of life and imbue their daily lives in the arbitrary and hopeless ghetto reality with meaning.

Rumkowski's idea—which was shared by other *Judenrat* heads—of work as a means of survival, turned out to be erroneous. Within the circumstances of the "Final Solution" all Jews were targeted for murder, and the speech quoted above manifests how impossible it was to fathom this reality at the time and how tragic the dilemmas of the *Judenrate* really were.

Children Celebrating Purim in the Ghetto, Lodz, Poland. Yad Vashem Photo Archive (4062/194)

In the summer of 1944, an unknown Jew was sent from the Lodz ghetto to Auschwitz. Upon his arrival at the camp, he entrusted his diary, which he carried on his last journey, to a member of the Sonderkommando, Zalman Loewenthal. Loewenthal hid the diary, but also felt a historical obligation to add some of his own comments in the margins. The writer of the diary blamed Rumkowski for the catastrophe that had befallen the Jews of Lodz, and Loewenthal added in his own hand that the accusatory finger should be pointed at the Germans—they were the ones who were truly responsible for the murder of the Jews. All three of these individuals, the writer of the diary, Zalman Loewenthal, and Mordechai Chaim Rumkowski, perished in Auschwitz.

About Photos

From left to right: Jews rounded up in the ghetto, apparently prior to deportation, Lodz, Poland (4062/448); Jews pushing a "Scheisskommando" cart, Lodz, Poland (4062/153).

Yad Vashem Photo Archive

LODZ GHETTO, 1941

Yad Vashem Photo Archive (4062/36)

POEM BY AN UNKNOWN GIRL

Childhood, precious days,

Alas, how few they were!

I will remember them as if in a fog.

Only in dreams at night can I

Identify days long gone.

Brief, brief is the happiness of a person in

this world of ours.

This poem was written by an unknown girl who was left alone in the Lodz ghetto with her brother. Their fate is unknown, but it must be assumed that both brother and sister perished in the Holocaust. Reprinted with permission from *Anonymous Diary*, 0.33/1032, Yad Vashem Archives, 2. All rights reserved.

About Photo Deportation of Jewish children from orphanage in Marysin to Kulmhof extermination camp, Lodz ghetto, 1942.

POEM BY AVRAHAM KOPLOWICZ

When I grow up and reach the age of 20

I'll set out to see the enchanting world.

I'll take a seat in a bird with a motor;

I'll rise and soar high into space.

I'll fly, sail, hover

Over the lonely faraway world.

I'll soar over rivers and oceans

Skyward shall I ascend and blossom,

A cloud my sister, the wind my brother.

This poem was written by Avraham Koplowicz, a child in the Lodz ghetto. Avraham was born in 1930. In the ghetto he worked in a shoemaker's workshop. He was taken to Auschwitz-Birkenau with his mother and father in 1944. Avraham was murdered in Auschwitz at the age of fourteen. Reprinted with permission from Avraham Koplowicz, 0.48/47.B.1, Yad Vashem Archives. All rights reserved.

Echoes and Reflections Teacher's Resource Guide **113**

DIARY ENTRY FROM THE LODZ GHETTO

"...Do you have any children at all in the ghetto? This species is steadily approaching extinction even before it develops in order to produce at the machine. A child, if fortunate enough to avoid death, immediately becomes a full-fledged grown-up. There are no children in the ghetto; there are only small Jews up to the age of ten, who do not work but queue at the soup kitchens [and] the bread lines, and...small Jews aged ten and over who already work—still beardless and unmarried, but already working.

It is difficult, if only because it's the burden of this small Jew has to report to work by seven o'clock, he has to wake up at six o'clock, and for this small Jew every extra hour of wakefulness means another hour of hunger pangs all day long.

And if hunger has not yet caused their legs to swell, because they do not have to carry a large body as do their parents' legs, they nevertheless have twisted, bent spines; sunken chests; lifeless and turgid eyes, their gazes turned somewhere far away, alien and cold, like today's sky..."

Excerpted from Josef Zelkowicz, *In Those Terrible Days* (Jerusalem: Yad Vashem, 2002), 186–188.

EXCERPTS FROM *THE DIARY OF DAWID SIERAKOWIAK*

Background

In early 1940, in the city of Lódź, Poland, Gentiles were evicted by the German occupiers from the slum area of the Baluty district and forced to make way for the hundreds of thousands of Jews who were soon concentrated into the district from other parts of the city, elsewhere in Poland, and the rest of conquered Europe. The Germans sealed off the area's perimeter and renamed it "Getto Litzmannstadt" ("Lódź ghetto"). Among those forced to relocate there was the local lower middle class family of Majlech and Sara Sierakowiak and their two children, Dawid and Natalia. One by one, each of their lives was extinguished in the Holocaust.

Dawid Sierakowiak, courtesy of Ghetto Fighters House Archives

Dawid began his diary while at a Zionist youth camp in southern Poland prior to the German invasion of Poland in 1939. He continued his daily entries until shortly before he died of hunger and exhaustion ("ghetto disease") on August 8, 1943, some two weeks after his eighteenth birthday. He was an inspiring young intellectual, brave, dark-humored, astonishingly aware politically, and an outstanding student at the top of his class. He had studied Latin, Hebrew, English, German, and French. His classmates elected him president of the ghetto *gymnasium* student council.

Dawid's notebooks were found after the war by a man returning to his apartment at 20 Wawelska Street, the Sierakowiaks' address in the ghetto. According to the man's words, "a whole pile of notebooks filled with notes was lying on a stove. Someone must have been using them for firewood because some of them were torn up. They contained stories, poems and other notes."

In the end, only five notebooks of at least seven Dawid wrote survived. Today, two of them are housed at the Jewish Historical Institute in Warsaw, and the other three reside in the archives of the United States Holocaust Memorial Museum in Washington, DC. Dawid's diary has been published in six languages and is considered one of the richest accounts of daily Jewish life written from within the German-perpetrated war against the Jews.

Excerpts

[1939]

Sunday, September 3. Lódź. An alarm at half past twelve at night. I curse as much as I can. In the street it's cold, dark, nasty. In the shelter we want to amuse ourselves a little, but as usual the females raise an uproar, shrieking that it's no joke, this is war. We leave for the street. Bombs and cold are better than old women. This should always be kept in mind. Long live humor; down with hysteria!...

[The next day there is] the first big air raid on Lódź. Twelve planes in triangles of three break through the defense lines and start bombing the city. We stand in front of the entry to our buildings' yard and watch the sky in spite of the danger....

Suddenly the planes turn in our direction, forcing us to fight our curiosity and hide in terror in the stairwell…and just when it seems that we will be bombed at any moment, they leave us in peace to breathe a sigh of relief. The planes finally disappear, which we announce in the shelter to the terrified, nerve-racked, crying women, some holding small babies in their arms. Truly a moving sight.

…

Wednesday, September 6. Łódź. God, what's going on! Panic, mass exodus, defeatism. The city, deserted by the police and all other state institutions, is waiting in terror for the anticipated arrival of the German troops. What happened? People run from one place to another finding no comfort: they move their worn bits of furniture around in terror and confusion, without any real purpose….

At home I meet our neighbor Mr. Grabiński, who has come back from downtown and tells about the great panic and anxiety that has taken hold of the people there. Crowds of residents are leaving their homes and setting off on a danger-filled trek into an unknown future. In the streets crying, sobbing, wailing.

I go to sleep, but a loud conversation wakes me at five in the morning. A neighbor, Grodzeński, is sitting there with his crying wife, telling us to leave. Where? Go where? Why? Nobody knows. To flee, flee farther and farther, trek, wade, cry, forget, run away…just run away as far as possible from the danger…. Father loses his head; he doesn't know what to do…finally the decision: stay put. Whatever will be will be.

…

Sunday, September 10. Łódź. …Tomorrow is the first day of school. Who knows how our dear school has been? My friends are going there tomorrow to find out what's cooking, while I have to stay home. I have to! My parents say that they are not going to lose me yet. Oh, my dear school!… Damn the times when I complained about getting up in the morning and about tests. If only I could have them back!

…

Monday, September 18. Łódź. …I am finally going to school tomorrow. Coeducational classes! There are great girls there, they say. Only let our education be normal. We are supposed to receive certificates of "immunity" so we won't be seized for work.

…

Tuesday, September 19. Łódź. I rode to school in a clean uniform (I came back on foot, however, and will go on foot every time now because there is no money to go by streetcar). At the gate I met two boys from our class….

…

Sunday, September 24. Łódź. The streets of Łódź feel eerie. Although richly decorated with Nazi flags, they are gray and sad. Dozens of [regulations], [public notices], and so on have been posted…. A person has to wait in line for bread for five or six hours, only to go away empty-handed 50 percent of the time. They are still seizing people for forced labor. Nothing seems to go well.

Wednesday, October 4. Lódź. I didn't escape the sad fate of my countrymen who are being seized for work. As luck would have it, some older people talked me into going to school by way of Wólczańska Street, a slightly shorter route. As I walked along there yesterday I could see almost nothing but swastikas on all the buildings along the street, as well as a lot of German cars and a great number of soldiers and Lódź Germans with swastikas on their arms. I somehow made it through and today, thus emboldened, I went the same way. Then,…some student from the German [school] ran up to me with a big stick in his hand and shouted [in German]: "Come work! You can't go to school!" I did not resist because I knew that no papers could help me here. He took me to a square where over a dozen Jews were already at work picking up leaves! The sadistic youngster badly wanted to make me climb over a 2-meter-high fence, but seeing that I couldn't do it, he gave up and went away.

The work at the square was supervised by a single soldier, also with a big stick. Using rude words, he told me to fill puddles with sand. I have never been so humiliated in my life as when I looked through the gate to the square and saw the happy, smiling mugs of passersby laughing at our misfortune. Oh, you stupid, abysmally stupid, foolish blockheads! It's our oppressors who should be ashamed, not us.

Humiliation inflicted by force does not humiliate. But anger and helpless rage tear a man apart when he is forced to do such stupid, shameful, abusive work. Only one response remains: revenge!

[1941]

Sunday, April 6. Lódź.* I'm beginning a new notebook of my diary, and thus dare to express the wish that it will become the start of a new, brighter and better period in my life than the one I covered in the preceding notebook. That seems just another pipe dream, though. In spite of a gorgeous (and expensive) holiday food ration, the situation remains as tragic as before. There's no hope for improvement.

No notebooks covering 1940 or the first four months of 1941 have been recovered. During that time, the Sierakowiak family, along with all the Jews remaining in Lódź, were forced into the area designated by the Germans as the Litzmannstadt (Lódź) ghetto.

Wednesday, April 9. Lódź. The weather is still nasty. It's cold, and raining almost incessantly; absolutely no sign of the sun. It looks like there won't be any spring this year. I just hope that such weather won't have a tragic effect on the harvests.

This week I wrote an article about the plight of school youths for a newspaper organized by the textile workers' association (Communists). I handed it in today, but it seems to me that before anything comes of it (there are enormous technical problems), the article will be out of date.

…

Sunday, April 27. Lódź. The first day of school. The trip to Marysin is quite long, but the worst thing about it is the awful mud from the incessant rain. I must cross all kinds of fields, and my shoes are in terrible shape. They are beginning to "go," but any repair is out of the question. I suppose I'll soon have to rush to school barefoot.

Friday, May 2. Lódź. …We continue to receive whole loaves of bread for our food rations, but now they check the weight carefully and, if needed, deduct or add the amount that the loaf's short. In any case, the loaf distribution system is no good. The portion of bread I receive won't feed me for more than two or three days; after that my stomach's empty, and all I can think of is the next loaf of bread.

...

Sunday, May 11. Lódź. It's raining constantly, and it absolutely won't get warm this year. I feel awful and look worse and worse. I hear that it's hard to recognize me.

...

Friday, May 16. Lódź. I have been examined by a doctor at school. She was terrified at how thin I am. She immediately gave me a referral for X rays. Perhaps I will now be able to get a double portion of soup in school. In fact, five such soups would be even better, but the two will do me some good, too. In any case, one soup is nothing.

The checkup has left me frightened and worried. Lung disease is the latest hit in ghetto fashion; it sweeps people away as much as dysentery or typhus. As for the food, it's worse and worse everywhere. It's been a week since there were any potatoes.

...

Saturday, July 19. Lódź. All day long I had nothing to eat but water (soup) in the kitchen. It's more and more difficult for me to go on starving. In the past I was able to not eat all day and still hold on somehow, but now I'm an empty pot. I was so weakened by the lack of soup at school that I thought I would collapse.

[1942]

Monday, May 25. Lódź. There are no vegetables in the June ration, not even potatoes. Now Rumkowski won't have to bother himself that people have eaten their potatoes too early; we won't even have a chance to see them this time. The situation is worsening, and there is no hope for the end.

They keep relocating Jews from small neighboring towns...into the ghetto, while the deportations from the ghetto have been stopped. Even that chance for getting out of the ghetto has been taken away. Death is striking left and right. A person becomes thin (an "hourglass") and pale in the face, then comes the swelling, a few days in bed or in the hospital, and that's it. The person was living the person is dead; we live and die like cattle.

...

Saturday, September 5. Lódź. My most Sacred, beloved, worn-out, blessed, cherished Mother has fallen victim to the bloodthirsty German Nazi beast!!! And totally innocently, solely because of the evil hearts of two Czech Jews, the doctors who came to examine us....

...[T]wo doctors, two nurses, several firemen, and policemen entered our building completely unexpectedly. They had lists with the names of the tenants in every apartment. A frantic, unexpected examination began. The doctors...started an extremely thorough examination of every tenant, and fished out a great many of the "sick and unable to work," and the ones whom they described as [in German] "questionable reserve." My unfortunate dearest mother was among the latter.... The shabby old doctor who examined her...kept shaking his head, saying to his comrade in Czech,

"Very weak, very weak."…

…My mother has been caught, and I doubt very much that anything will save her.

…My poor mother, who always feared everything, yet invariably continued to believe in God, showed them, in spite of extreme nervousness, complete presence of mind. With fatalism and with heartbreaking, maddening logic, she spoke to us about her fate. She kind of admitted that I was right when I told her that she had given her life by lending and giving away provisions, but she admitted it with such a bitter smile that I could see she didn't regret her conduct at all, and, although she loved her life so greatly, for her there are values even more important than life, like God, family, etc. She kissed each one of us good-bye, took a bag with her bread and a few potatoes that I forced on her, and left quickly to her horrible fate. I couldn't muster the willpower to look through the window after her or to cry. I walked around, talked, and finally sat as though I had turned to stone. Every other moment, nervous spasms took hold of my heart, hands, mouth, and throat, so that I thought my heart was breaking. It didn't break, though, and it let me eat, think, speak, and go to sleep.

…Meanwhile, if Mom had only left home, nothing would have happened to her. And so, someone else's baby has been saved in our home, while my mother has been taken. [My sister] Nadzia screamed, cried, suffered spasms, but these days it doesn't move anyone. I am speechless and close to madness.

[1943]

Sunday, April 4. Łódź. My state of mind is worsening every day. The fever persists, and I look like a complete "death notice." I can't bring my irritated skin back to normal, either.

In politics there's still nothing new. The war is extending infinitely, and here I am with no more strength. Everyone in the ghetto is sick. TB is spreading unbelievably, and there is a great number of other infectious and noninfectious diseases. Nadzia has noticed symptoms of scabies on her body again. If things continue like this, I will go crazy. Oh, this horrible, endless hopelessness. No chance or hope for life.

…

Thursday, April 15. Łódź. …I am completely sick, and I have a high fever. I bought a Bayer medication for the flu, fever, and cold, for Nadzia and me. Nadzia stays in bed, and I think she will remain there for another day or two.

Mrs. Deutsch came to see me today…. I think she is the most devoted friend I have in the ghetto, or anywhere else for that matter.

In the evening I had to prepare food and cook supper, which exhausted me totally. In politics there's absolutely nothing new. Again, out of impatience I feel myself beginning to fall into melancholy. There is really no way out of this for us.

Here the last of Dawid Sierakowiak's surviving notebooks breaks off. He died four months later of tuberculosis, starvation, and exhaustion, the syndrome known as "ghetto disease."

Selections reprinted by permission of the publisher from *The Diary of Dawid Sierakowiak: Five Notebooks from the Lodz Ghetto*, ed. Alan Adelson, trans. Kamil Turowski (New York: Oxford University Press, Inc., 1996). © 1996 by the Jewish Heritage Project and Kamil Turowski.

About Photo

USSR, German Schupo Policeman Aims His Rifle at a Woman Carrying a Child

"When you marched out...you never knew who would come back..."

– Itka Zygmuntowicz, Jewish Survivor

Preparing to Use This Lesson

Below is information to keep in mind when using this lesson. In some cases, the points elaborate on general suggestions listed in the "Teaching about the Holocaust" section in the Introduction to this resource, and are specific to the content of the lesson. This material is intended to help teachers consider the complexities of teaching the Holocaust and to deliver accurate and sensitive instruction.

- Students' information about the Nazi extermination camps is often in the form of dates, place names, and numbers. While it is important for students to realize that millions of Jews died at the hands of the Nazis in the extermination camps, it is equally important that they see the victims of the Holocaust as individuals. They were mothers, fathers, sons, daughters, and grandparents; young and old; tradesmen, teachers, students, scientists, and doctors. They were artists, musicians, and poets. Reflecting on the Holocaust as a human story will make it more meaningful in students' lives and will make them more likely to take the messages that can be learned from it to heart.

- In this lesson, students learn about the amazing struggle for survival of Jews imprisoned in the extermination camps. It is important that students realize, however, that the vast majority of Jews who arrived at the Nazi extermination camps were murdered. Only a few were chosen to work and of those, very few survived the harsh conditions, the beatings, the lack of food, extreme weather, and forced labor.

- The "Final Solution" is the story of Jews in the time of the Nazis. In this lesson, students learn about the extermination camps where most Jews were murdered. This is not to minimize the suffering of other groups and millions of individuals at the hands of the Nazis. The uniqueness of the Jewish fate is that the Nazis strived to murder all Jews and succeeded in murdering one-third. No other group was considered subhuman according to Nazi ideology and therefore deserving to be extinguished.

- The six extermination camps were located in occupied Poland. There were several important reasons for this: Poland had the largest population of Jews before the war, and Poland was considered a location where the Nazis could do as they pleased, without any concern for the Poles, who were considered inferior. In addition, Poland was far from the eyes of the Western Allies, yet it had a well-developed system of trains that made transporting Jews from all over Europe to Poland feasible. Even though these camps were on Polish soil, the Poles were not responsible for initiating the camps nor for the policies carried out in them. These were Nazi German extermination camps in Poland.

- This lesson contains very difficult and complex subject matter. Teachers are encouraged to be sensitive to students' reactions and to assure them that experiencing a range of emotions—anger, sadness, outrage, melancholy—are all natural responses to this kind of material, and that they should feel free to express and discuss those feelings with others. Caution should be exercised in using graphic images.

About This Lesson

 270–360 minutes

❖ **INTRODUCTION** The purpose of this lesson is for students to learn about one of humanity's darkest chapters—the systematic mass murder of the Jews that came to be known as the "Final Solution of the Jewish Question." This includes learning about the Einsatzgruppen (mobile killing squads), the Nazi extermination camps, and the perpetrators and collaborators who took part in the murder. This lesson also provides an opportunity for students to learn how Jews attempted to maintain their humanity in the camps despite the inhumane conditions and brutal treatment they faced.

This two-part lesson has material appropriate for history, social studies, ethics, Holocaust studies, English/language arts, and art classes. Instructional strategies used in this lesson include large-group discussion, small-group work, reading for information, interpreting visual history testimony, art, poetry, and artifacts, brainstorming, oral presentation, comparing and contrasting information, and journaling.

❖ **OBJECTIVES** After completing this lesson, students will be able to:

- Explain the purpose of the mobile killing squads and extermination camps in Nazi Europe.

- Name the six extermination camps in Nazi-occupied Poland.

- Summarize the role of Nazi ideology in the location of the extermination camps.

- Describe the living conditions for people imprisoned in the extermination camps.

- Interpret a variety of primary sources—visual history testimony, artifacts, artwork—used to document conditions of life and death in the camps.

- Identify specific ways that Jews imprisoned in the extermination camps attempted to maintain their humanity.

- Identify ways that individuals and groups act responsibly or evade responsibility.

❖ **KEY WORDS & PHRASES**

antisemitism	Bergen-Belsen	crematoria
Appell	Chelmno	Dachau
Auschwitz-Birkenau	collaborator	dehumanization
Babi Yar	Communist	Einsatzgruppen
Belzec	concentration camp	European Jewry

RESOURCES & TESTIMONIES

All of the resources used in this lesson can be found in this guide at the end of this lesson and at echoesandreflections.org.

Visual history testimonies are available on the website or on the DVD that accompanies this resource guide.

Teachers are urged to review the lesson procedures to identify other materials and technology needed to implement the lesson.

L5

extermination camp	Majdanek	Sinti-Roma
"Final Solution of the Jewish Question"	Nazi ideology	Sobibor
	perpetrator	SS
genocide	Reich	Theresienstadt
Holocaust	selection	Treblinka

❖ ACADEMIC STANDARDS The materials in this lesson address the following national education standards:

Common Core State Standards

- Reading Standards for Informational Text 6–12

- Reading Standards for Literature 6–12

- Speaking and Listening Standards 6–12

- Writing Standards 6–12

- Reading Standards for Literacy in History/Social Studies 6–12

- Writing Standards for Literacy in History/Social Studies 6–12

A complete analysis of how this lesson addresses Common Core State Standards by grade level and specific skills is available on the Echoes and Reflections website.

National Curriculum Standards for Social Studies

❶ Culture

❷ Time, Continuity, and Change

❸ People, Places, and Environments

❹ Individual Development and Identity

❺ Individuals, Groups, and Institutions

❻ Power, Authority, and Governance

❾ Global Connections

❿ Civic Ideals and Practices

Procedures

Part 1: The Victims

1. Help students develop a framework for studying the "Final Solution" by using the K-W-L strategy. Have students create a graphic organizer with three columns labeled "K" (What I Know), "W" (What I Want to Learn), and "L" (What I Learned). Instruct students to list what they know about the "Final Solution" and the extermination camps in the first column and what they would like to learn about this topic in the second column. Tell students that as they listen to the testimonies and participate in the activities that follow, they should go back to the chart and add information to the "L" column.

2. Introduce students to Ellis Lewin and Abraham Bomba and then show the first two clips of Part 1 of Visual History Testimony: *The "Final Solution."* Discuss the testimony using the questions below.

   - What are your feelings after hearing these testimonies?

- Both Ellis Lewin and Abraham Bomba talk about the sounds that they remember hearing upon arriving at the extermination camps of Auschwitz and Treblinka, respectively. What are some of the sounds they describe?

- How does Ellis describe the pace at which things moved when the train arrived at Auschwitz? Why does he think the Germans moved things at such a rapid pace?

- Why didn't Ellis's father want Ellis to hang on to him?

- What were the last words Ellis remembers his father saying to his mother?

- What is Ellis's last image of his mother?

- How many people does Abraham say were on each train going to Treblinka?

- What is the significance of the description that Abraham shares about the people being forced to undress?

- Abraham explains that out of 18,000 people, only five were taken out to work. How was it that he was one of the five?

- In what ways are these two testimonies similar? In what ways are they different?

- After watching these two testimonies, is there anything that you can add to your K-W-L chart? If so, what are you able to add?

3. Distribute *Excerpt from Night* and have volunteers read the material aloud. Follow with a discussion using the following questions:

- In addition to being forcibly torn away from the rest of their family, what else did Elie Wiesel and his father "leave behind"?

- In this excerpt from Elie Wiesel's *Night,* how did the Nazis dehumanize Jews?

- Why do you think the older men did not want the younger men to revolt?

- Why were Elie Wiesel and his father told to lie about their ages?

- Choose one moment identified in the excerpt that you think was a defining moment or a turning point in Elie Wiesel's life. How did this moment change his perception of the world, relationships, life, other people, and even himself?

- How is Elie Wiesel's account of arriving at Auschwitz similar to the account given in Ellis Lewin's testimony? What is the value of having both of these accounts available?

About the Author

Elie Wiesel was born in Sighet, Romania in 1928, to an ultra-Orthodox Jewish Hasidic family. In 1944, Elie Wiesel was deported to Auschwitz where he was imprisoned for a short time. From there he was sent to the Buchenwald concentration camp. After liberation in 1945, Elie Wiesel went to Paris where he eventually became a

continued on page 126

TESTIMONY VIEWING

About the Interviewees

Ellis Lewin was born on May 22, 1932, in Lodz, Poland. He was forced to live in the Lodz ghetto and later incarcerated in the Augsburg, Dachau, München-Allach, and Kaufbeuren concentration camps. Ellis was also imprisoned in the Auschwitz-Birkenau extermination camp. His interview was conducted in the United States. When the war began, Ellis was seven years old.

Abraham Bomba was born on June 9, 1913, in Beuthen, Germany. He was incarcerated in the Czestochowa ghetto and later imprisoned in the concentration camps of Treblinka I and Tschenstochau and the Treblinka extermination camp. His interview was conducted in the United States. When the war began, Abraham was twenty-six years old.

_____

For additional information about Ellis Lewin and Abraham Bomba, see their Biographical Profiles available on the website.

About the Author

continued from page 125

journalist. During an interview with the distinguished French writer, Francois Mauriac, he was persuaded to write about his experiences in the camps. The result was his internationally acclaimed memoir, *Night (La Nuit),* which has since been translated into more than thirty languages. In this book, Wiesel summarizes his experiences as a concentration camp prisoner. Wiesel went on to publish more than sixty books of fiction and non-fiction. Wiesel has exerted an influence on world leaders regarding commemoration of the Holocaust—he perceives his role as that of society's conscience, which must be alert to wickedness and injustice. Elie Wiesel was awarded the Nobel Peace Prize in 1986.

NOTE 1.4

Prepare questions in advance on the board or on a handout.

About the Poet

Dan Pagis was born in 1930, in Bukovina, Romania. He spent three of his adolescent years in a Nazi concentration camp in the Ukraine before arriving in Palestine, in 1946. He became one of the most vibrant voices in modern Israeli poetry and is considered a major world poet of his generation. Dan Pagis died in Jerusalem in 1986.

About the Artist

Zinovii Tolkatchev was born in 1903, in the town of Shchedrin in Belorussia. As an official artist of the Red Army he joined with Soviet forces in Majdanek, shortly after its liberation (1944) and immediately after that with the forces that liberated Auschwitz (1945). During this period, Tolkatchev drew the series: *Majdanek, Auschwitz,* and *Flowers of Auschwitz.* Zinovii Tolkatchev died in Kiev in 1977.

4. Distribute a copy of the handouts: *Poems from a Camp Survivor* and *Appell, 1944.* Divide the class into small groups and assign each group one of the poems or the piece of art. Working in their small groups, have students discuss the questions below that pertain to the piece they have been assigned. After completing the small-group assignment, have groups share their observations and analysis with the rest of the class. Encourage students to listen for any differences in how groups with the same document interpreted the words or images.

- What is the biblical story of Cain and Abel?

- Why do you think Dan Pagis choose Adam, Eve, and their sons for the poem "Written in Pencil in the Sealed Railway-Car"? What is the role of each one of them?

- Eve appears to be attempting to convey a message to Cain. What might that message be?

- Read "Written in Pencil" several times. What is the feeling that you get reading this poem?

- What is the significance of the fact that Dan Pagis specifies that the letter written in the sealed railway car was written in pencil?

- What do you think Pagis was trying to say with the line, "No, no: they definitely were human beings" in the poem "Testimony"?

- What do you think Pagis was trying to convey with the lines, "I was a shade. A different creator made me"?

- Why do you think Dan Pagis titled this poem "Testimony"?

- What do you notice in *Appell, 1944*? What message(s) do you think the artist was trying to convey?

- How do you feel looking at this piece of art?

- How is studying a piece of art (e.g., a painting or a drawing) different from studying a photograph?

- What feelings emerge from all of these works? What do you learn about the artists through their works?

- What is communicated through poems and art that cannot be communicated in a textbook?

5. Introduce students to Itka Zygmuntowicz and show the third clip of testimony from Part 1 of Visual History Testimony: *The "Final Solution."* Have students reflect on Itka's testimony using the following questions:

   • What does Itka mean when she says she "felt the bitter taste of slavery"? What is the significance of her saying, "I understood what my forefathers—what the Jews in Egypt— must have felt like"?

   • What reason does Itka give for "writing a poem in her head"?

   • What did Itka say "writing the poem" helped her realize?

6. Ask students what an artifact is and what kinds of things are considered artifacts. Have students consider how, like diaries, photographs, government documents, etc., artifacts are primary sources. Ask them to brainstorm a list of items that might be considered artifacts to a historian (e.g., tools, jewelry, postcards, manuscripts) and explain what might be learned about people, institutions, or cultures from studying artifacts.

7. Distribute the handout *Life in the Shadow of Death* and review the material with students. Follow with a discussion using the questions below.

   • Which of the items on this handout would you identify as artifacts and why? If you did not identify the photograph as an artifact, why didn't you?

   • How do these seemingly simple items (e.g., a comb) take on additional meaning when studied within the context of the Holocaust?

   • What do we learn from studying the comb? The prayer book? The photograph of Annie Fisk Levinger?

   • How do these items help us understand what some inmates in the extermination camps were thinking?

   • Why do you think this handout is titled "Life in the Shadow of Death"?

8. Distribute *Excerpt from Man's Search for Meaning* and read the selection together. Ask students to share their thoughts about the selection and then continue with a discussion using the questions below as a guide.

   • How does Viktor Frankl explain transcending his experience in the camp? What does Frankl want us to understand when he says: "I did not know whether my wife was alive, and I had no means of finding out […], but at that moment it ceased to matter. There was no need for me to know; nothing could touch the strength of my love, my thoughts, and the image of my beloved"?

   • After listening to Itka Zygmuntowicz's earlier testimony, studying the artifacts/photograph, and reading the selection from Viktor Frankl, what do you think made it possible for people to cope with life in a world that dehumanized them and denied their existence?

TESTIMONY VIEWING

About the Interviewee

Itka Zygmuntowicz was born on April 15, 1926, in Ciechanow, Poland. She was forced to live in the Nowe Miasto ghetto and later incarcerated in the concentration camps of Ravensbrück and Malchow. Itka was also imprisoned in the Auschwitz-Birkenau extermination camp. Her interview was conducted in the United States. When the war began, Itka was thirteen years old.

For additional information about Itka Zygmuntowicz, see her Biographical Profile available on the website.

L5

- Why is important for those studying the Holocaust to understand how Jews struggled for life and dignity in a world of dehumanization?

9. Have students review the K-W-L charts that they developed earlier and share what they added to the "L" column. Encourage students to add additional questions to the "W" column, reinforcing the idea that learning about a complex topic like the Holocaust often results in more questions. Remind students to continue using the chart for Part 2 of this lesson as more of the questions that they identified in the "W" column may be answered.

Part 2: The Perpetrators

TESTIMONY VIEWING

About the Interviewee

Nathan Offen was born on December 15, 1922, in Cracow, Poland. He was forced to live in the Cracow ghetto and was also incarcerated in the Gusen, Krakau-Plaszow, and Wieliczka concentration camps. His interview was conducted in the United States. When the war began, Nathan was sixteen years old.

For additional information about Nathan Offen, see his Biographical Profile available on the website.

1. Introduce students to Nathan Offen and Itka Zygmuntowicz, if she was not introduced earlier, and then show students Part 2 of Visual History Testimony: *The "Final Solution"* and discuss the following questions:

- After listening to Itka Zygmuntowicz, what image emerges for you regarding what life was like in the extermination camps?

- What are some examples of daily humiliation and intimidation that camp prisoners had to endure?

- What experience does Nathan Offen share in his testimony?

- Nathan continues to show emotion while he recounts experiences in his testimony. Why do you think after so many years he continues to convey such great emotion?

- What are some of your emotions as you listen to these testimonies?

- What do you learn from hearing the survivors talk about their experiences that is different from what you learn from textbooks?

2. Explain to students that many people ask the question "How was it humanly possible?" when studying the Holocaust. Ask them to think about this seemingly simple, yet complex, question in light of the survivor testimony they just watched.

3. Review the definition of *perpetrator* available in the **Glossary** on the website.

NOTE 2.4

Due to the sensitive nature of this material, it is recommended that the teacher read Franz Stangl's responses to the interview questions.

4. Distribute *Interview with Franz Stangl*. After reading the interview together, use some or all of the questions below in a whole-group discussion.

- How would you characterize Stangl's ability to see human beings as cargo or cattle?

- Why do you think he is unable to make the connection between the children who arrive on transports and his own children? Do you think there should be a connection? Explain your thinking.

- Do you think Stangl had a choice in the decisions he made? Explain why or why not.

- How does Stangl explain working for the system?

- Are there any emotions expressed in the interview? If so, what are they? If not, how might this lack of emotion be explained?

- In the past, some regarded perpetrators such as Stangl as "human beasts." Today, we realize that they were human beings. What were the possible reasons for people to regard the perpetrators as "beasts"? What purpose did it serve?

- Revisit the Dan Pagis poem, "Testimony," and consider what the poet may have been trying to convey to his readers with the line, "No, no, they definitely were human beings."

- Think about the earlier question, "How was it humanly possible?" What, if anything, can you add to your thinking about this question in light of the Franz Stangl interview?

5. Divide the class into four groups and distribute the student handout, *The "Final Solution."* Assign one section of the handout to each group. Have group members read their section of the handout together and prepare an oral presentation for the rest of the class on the material. Instruct each group to also develop one or two discussion questions based on its section of the reading material.

6. Have each group present its material to the class. After all groups have made their presentations, have a whole-group discussion using the discussion questions that the groups developed and/or the suggested questions below.

- In what way did the invasion of the Soviet Union reflect the basic tenets of Nazi ideology?

- What was the difference between a concentration camp and an extermination camp?

- Why were the extermination camps located in Poland? What role did Nazi ideology play in this decision?

- In what ways did the Nazis apply modern technology to the mass murder of the people in the camps?

- How do we understand the word "modern" in the context of the Holocaust? What does modern mean to you? Does this term always imply enlightenment and humanity? Why or why not?

- The Nazis used deception in the extermination camps. What do you think was their purpose in using deception?

- As noted in the reading, "hundreds of thousands of people were involved, either directly or indirectly, in implementing the 'Final Solution.'" In your opinion, were any of these people exempt from responsibility? Explain your thinking.

7. Display the map of the Nazi camps and sites of mass execution and have students identify which camps the survivors talked about in their testimonies. Allow time for students to make additional observations based on the map.

8. Show students the photographs from Auschwitz-Birkenau. Provide students an opportunity to study and discuss their thoughts and feelings about each photograph using the questions below.

NOTE 2.8
Explain to students that all of the photographs are from *The Auschwitz Album.* With the exception of three photographs smuggled out by the Sonderkommando, this is the only surviving visual evidence of the process leading to mass murder at Auschwitz-Birkenau. A link to *The Auschwitz Album* is available on the website under the Additional Resources section of the Lesson Components. Included at the site are the photographs that comprise the album as well as a multimedia presentation explaining the photographs and providing context for what viewers are seeing.

- What are your feelings as you look at these photographs?
- What do you see? What do you "hear"?
- Looking at the photographs together, what "story" do they tell?

NOTE 2.9

Additional information on perpetrators including Adolf Eichmann can be found in Lesson 9: Perpetrators, Bystanders, and Collaborators.

9. Explain to students that when Adolf Eichmann (an SS officer who played a major role in the extermination of European Jews) was on trial in Jerusalem in 1961, he claimed that he was merely performing his duty as an obedient soldier. He viewed himself as not personally responsible for his actions, but rather part of a system. Ask students to think about issues of social and personal responsibility by discussing the following questions:

- What does it mean to be "held responsible"?
- What does it mean to "accept responsibility"?
- How is "accepting responsibility" different from being "held responsible"?
- What are some ways that you witness people acting responsibly? What are the benefits to society when people act responsibly?
- What are some ways that you witness people evading responsibility? What is the potential harm to society when people evade responsibility?
- Explain who you believe is responsible for making sure that something like the Holocaust never happens.

10. Have students review the K-W-L charts that they developed at the beginning of Part 1 of this lesson and share additional information that they have added to the "L" column. Have students review the "W" column and identify any questions from their original list that remain outstanding for them or additional questions that have been raised for them as a result of participating in this lesson. Instruct students to choose one of their remaining questions and research the answer and post both the question and answer on the class wiki, website, or blog, or submit to you as a culminating activity.

Reflect and Respond

Either in class or as homework, have students reflect and respond to one or more of the topics below or have them develop a topic that has meaning for them based on the material covered in the lesson.

- In her testimony, Itka Zygmuntowicz recites the poem she wrote in Auschwitz—a poem about freedom. Many children (and adults) used art as a way to spiritually survive the experience of the ghettos, and in some instances, the extermination camps. Write about the importance of the arts in your life and how music, painting, writing poetry, or something similar has helped you during a particularly difficult time.

- Much of this lesson focused on social and personal responsibility. As a result of our class discussions and readings, are there any situations in your life for which you feel you should take more responsibility? If so, how do you plan on taking responsibility/action?

- Throughout this lesson you have considered two important questions regarding the Holocaust: How was the Holocaust humanly possible? and Why did the Holocaust happen? Respond to either or both of those questions in light of the material you have studied.

- In "Hunger Camp at Jaslo," Polish poet Wislawa Szymborska writes: "History counts its skeletons in round numbers. A thousand and one remains a thousand, as though the one had never existed…" How do you interpret these lines in light of learning about the "Final Solution"? What is the poet cautioning us to remember as we learn about the Holocaust? Why is it important to give faces to the victims of genocide and not just think of them in terms of numbers?

Making Connections

The additional activities and projects listed below can be integrated directly into the lesson or can be used to extend the lesson once it has been completed. The topics lend themselves to students' continued study of the Holocaust as well as opportunities for students to make meaningful connections to other people and events, including relevant contemporary issues. These activities may include instructional strategies and techniques and/or address academic standards in addition to those that were identified for the lesson.

1. Visit IWitness (iwitness.usc.edu) for activities specific to Lesson 5: The "Final Solution."

2. Distribute the student handout, *The First Ones,* available on the website in the **Additional Resources** section of the **Lesson Components.** Read the short biography of Yitzhak Katzenelson together. You may then choose to have students read the poem silently, in groups, or as a whole class. Once they have read the poem, discuss it together, using some or all of the discussion questions below.

    - Why do you think the Nazis would go after the children first?
    - How could children be "dangerous" to the Germans?
    - Katzenelson describes the two-year-old girl he sees as looking like a "grandma of a hundred years." Why might such a little child seem like an old person?
    - Why do you think he says that his people "drew consolation" from the children? How might their children be a consolation to Jews?
    - How does Katzenelson end the poem? Is he hopeful or hopeless? How do you know?

3. Provide students with a copy of the *Pyramid of Hate* available on the website (Lesson 3: Nazi Germany under **Download Lesson Resources**). After reviewing the material together, tell students that you want them to consider whether "genocide" should be added to the top of the pyramid or if there are other changes to the graphic that they feel are warranted after learning about the "Final Solution." Instruct students to prepare a revised "pyramid of hate" or prepare a completely different graphic representation that they feel more accurately depicts the escalation of hate. The revised graphic should be accompanied by a short explanatory text that explains the reasoning behind adding genocide to the top of the pyramid or changing the graphic entirely. Students should also be given the option of keeping the graphic exactly as it currently appears, but they must explain why they feel there shouldn't be any changes.

4. Professional and amateur artists of all genres recorded what they saw and experienced during the Holocaust. Some inmate art was sanctioned by camp or ghetto authorities for propaganda purposes or to satisfy Nazi officials who demanded inmates produce personal works of art for their satisfaction. Clandestine art was created at great risk to the artist's life. Thousands of these clandestine pieces, created by children and adults, were discovered in ghettos and

camps after liberation. Artists who survived the Holocaust often created works following liberation to document what they had experienced or to share their interpretations of what the Holocaust meant not only to them personally, but to humanity.

Have students research art that was created either during or following the Holocaust and identify one piece that is particularly significant or moving to them. In a written, oral, or multimedia report, instruct students to share information about the artist and the piece of art they chose, provide background on the circumstances under which the piece of art was created, the medium used, etc. and explain why they chose this particular work of art. Artists that students might want to consider researching include Felix Nussbaum, Fernand Van Horen, Yehuda Bacon, Esther Lurie, Alexander Bogen, Hirsch Szylis, Samuel Bak, Bedrich Fritta, and Petr Ginz.

5. Divide students into small groups and have them research one of the topics below or identify their own topic and prepare a presentation in a format of their choice to share with the class or post on the class website or wiki. Encourage students to include primary source materials in their lessons. In addition to the **Supplemental Assets** available on the website in the **Additional Resources** section of the **Lesson Components,** encourage students to use the United States Holocaust Memorial Museum website (**ushmm.org**) and IWitness (**iwitness.usc.edu**).

Topic #1: Resistance in the Camps

Topic #2: Culture, Religion, and Education in the Camps

Topic #3: Community and Teamwork in the Camps

Topic #4: Children in the Camps

Topic #5: Survival in the Camps

Topic #6: Information about a specific extermination camp

[**NOTE:** Encourage students to learn about all six of the extermination camps—Auschwitz-Birkenau, Belzec, Chelmno, Majdanek, Sobibor, and Treblinka.]

6. Many works of fiction have been written that center on a person's experiences during the Holocaust. These texts often evoke strong emotion, heighten awareness, and provide opportunities for the reader to ask him/herself complex questions—all positive outcomes. Even though such books are clearly identified as fiction, many may still reflect historical inaccuracies in terms of time, place, and events that can lead to an erroneous understanding or representation of what took place during the time period.

Have students work together to develop a rubric for assessing the historical accuracy of works of fiction about the Holocaust. They should identify what specific dimensions (chronology of events, language, depictions of people and places, etc.) upon which a work should be judged and a scale for scoring how successful the author is in achieving each of the characteristics they have identified. After the rubric that has been developed, have students read or re-read—either individually or in groups—one of the books listed below or another similar title and apply the rubric they have developed. If they are unsure if something is accurate, they will need to conduct the necessary research to make an informed decision. After completing the assignment, have students compare their findings/completed rubrics and draw conclusions regarding the possible benefits and challenges of using fiction to learn about the Holocaust.

Possible texts:

- *Number the Stars* by Lois Lowry
- *The Book Thief* by Markus Zusak
- *Milkweed* by Jerry Spinelli
- *The Boy in the Striped Pajamas* by John Boyne
- *Devil's Arithmetic* by Jane Yolen
- *Friedrich* by Hans Peter Richter

EXCERPT FROM *NIGHT*

Elie Wiesel

The beloved objects that we had carried with us from place to place were left behind in the wagon and, with them, finally, our illusions.

Every few yards, there stood an SS man, his machine gun trained on us. Hand in hand we followed the throng.

An SS came toward us wielding a club. He commanded:

"Men to the left! Women to the right!"

Eight words spoken quietly, indifferently, without emotion. Eight simple, short words. Yet that was the moment when I left my mother. There was no time to think, and I already felt my father's hand press against mine: we were alone. In a fraction of a second I could see my mother, my sisters, move to the right. Tzipora was holding Mother's hand. I saw them walking farther and farther away; Mother was stroking my sister's blond hair, as if to protect her. And I walked on with my father, with the men. I didn't know that this was the moment in time and the place where I was leaving my mother and Tzipora forever. I kept walking, my father holding my hand.

Behind me, an old man fell to the ground. Nearby, an SS man replaced his revolver in its holster.

My hand tightened its grip on my father. All I could think of was not to lose him. Not to remain alone.

The SS officers gave the order.

"Form ranks of fives!"

There was a tumult. It was imperative to stay together.

"Hey, kid, how old are you?"

The man interrogating me was an inmate. I could not see his face, but his voice was weary and warm.

"Fifteen."

"No. You're eighteen."

"But I'm not," I said. "I'm fifteen."

"Fool. Listen to what I say."

Then he asked my father, who answered:

"I'm fifty."

"No." The man now sounded angry. "Not fifty. You're forty. Do you hear? Eighteen and forty."

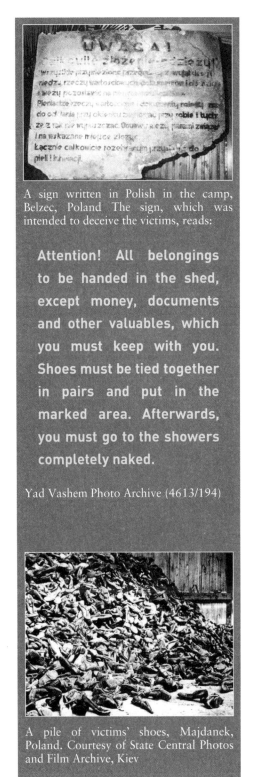

A sign written in Polish in the camp, Belzec, Poland The sign, which was intended to deceive the victims, reads:

Attention! All belongings to be handed in the shed, except money, documents and other valuables, which you must keep with you. Shoes must be tied together in pairs and put in the marked area. Afterwards, you must go to the showers completely naked.

Yad Vashem Photo Archive (4613/194)

A pile of victims' shoes, Majdanek, Poland. Courtesy of State Central Photos and Film Archive, Kiev

He disappeared into the darkness. Another inmate appeared, unleashing a stream of invectives:

"Sons of bitches, why have you come here? Tell me, why?"

Someone dared to reply:

"What do you think? That we came here of our own free will? That we asked to come here?"

The other seemed ready to kill him.

"Shut up, you moron, or I'll tear you to pieces! You should have hanged yourselves rather than come here. Didn't you know what was in store for you here at Auschwitz? You didn't know? In 1944?"

True. We didn't know. Nobody had told us. He couldn't believe his ears. His tone became harsher:

"Over there. Do you see that chimney over there? Do you see it? And the flames, do you see them?" (Yes, we saw the flames.) "Over there, that's where they will take you. Over there will be your grave. You still don't understand? You sons of bitches. Don't you understand anything? You will be burned! Burned to a cinder! Turned into ashes!"

His anger changed into fury. We stood stunned, petrified. Could this be just a nightmare? An unimaginable nightmare?

I heard whispers around me:

"We must do something. We can't let them kill us like that, like cattle in the slaughterhouse. We must revolt."

There were, among us, a few tough young men. They actually had knives and were urging us to attack the armed guards. One of them was muttering:

"Let the world learn of the existence of Auschwitz. Let everybody hear about it while they still have a chance to escape…."

But the older men begged their sons not to be foolish:

"We mustn't give up hope, even now as the sword hangs over our heads. So taught our sages…."

The wind of revolt died down. We continued to walk until we came to a crossroads. Standing in the middle of it was, though I didn't know it then, Dr. Mengele, the notorious Dr. Mengele. He looked like the typical SS officer: a cruel, though not unintelligent, face, complete with monocle. He was holding a conductor's baton and was surrounded by officers. The baton moving constantly, sometimes to the right, sometimes to the left.

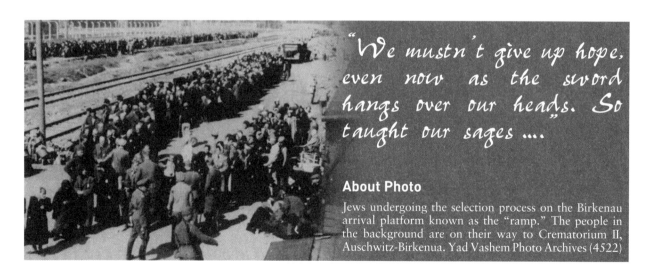

"We mustn't give up hope, even now as the sword hangs over our heads. So taught our sages …."

About Photo

Jews undergoing the selection process on the Birkenau arrival platform known as the "ramp." The people in the background are on their way to Crematorium II, Auschwitz-Birkenua. Yad Vashem Photo Archives (4522)

In no time, I stood before him.

"Your age?" he asked, perhaps trying to sound paternal.

"I'm eighteen." My voice was trembling.

"In good health?"

"Yes."

"Your profession?"

Tell him that I was a student?

"Farmer," I heard myself saying.

This conversation lasted no more than a few seconds. It seemed like an eternity.

The baton pointed to the left. I took half a step forward. I first wanted to see where they would send my father. Were he to have gone to the right, I would have run after him.

The baton, once more, moved to the left. A weight lifted from my heart.

We did not know, as yet, which was the better side, right or left, which road led to prison and which to the crematoria. Still, I was happy, I was near my father. Our procession continued slowly to move forward.

Another inmate came over to us:

"Satisfied?"

"Yes," someone answered.

"Poor devils, you are heading for the crematorium."

He seemed to be telling the truth. Not far from us, flames, huge flames, were rising from a ditch. Something was being burned there. A truck drew close and unloaded its hold: small children. Babies! Yes, I did see this, with my own eyes ... children thrown into the flames. (Is it any wonder that ever since then, sleep tends to elude me?)

So that was where we were going. A little farther on, there was another, larger pit for adults.

I pinched myself: Was I still alive? Was I awake? How was it possible that men, women, and children were being burned and that the world kept silent? No. All this could not be real. A nightmare perhaps.... Soon I should wake with a start, my heart pounding, and find that I was back in the room of my childhood, with my books...

My father's voice tore me from my daydreams:

"What a shame, a shame that you did not go with your mother... I saw many children your age go with their mothers...."

His voice was terribly sad. I understood that he did not wish to see what they would do to me. He did not wish to see his only son go up in flames.

My forehead was covered with cold sweat. Still, I told him that I could not believe that human beings were being burned in our times; the world would never tolerate such crimes....

"The world? The world is not interested in us. Today, everything is possible, even the crematoria...." His voice broke.

"Father," I said. "If that is true, then I don't want to wait. I'll run into the electrified barbed wire. That would be easier than slow a slow death in the flames."

He did not answer. He was weeping. His body was shaking. Everybody around us was weeping. Someone began to recite Kaddish, the prayer for the dead. I don't know whether, during the history of the Jewish people, men have ever before recited Kaddish for themselves.

"*Yisgadal veyiskadash, shmey raba*…. May His name be celebrated and sanctified…." whispered my father.

For the first time, I felt anger rising within me. Why should I sanctify His name? The Almighty, the eternal and terrible Master of the Universe, chose to be silent. What was there to thank Him for?

We continued our march. We were coming closer and closer to the pit, from which an infernal heat was rising. Twenty more steps. If I was going to kill myself, this was the time. Our column had only some fifteen steps to go. I bit my lips so that my father would not hear my teeth chattering. Ten more steps. Eight. Seven. We were walking slowly, as one follows a hearse, our own funeral procession. Only four more steps. Three. There it was now, very close to us, the pit and its flames. I gathered all that remained of my strength in order to break rank and throw myself onto the barbed wire. Deep down, I was saying good-bye to my father, to the whole universe, and against my will, I found myself whispering the words: "*Yisgadal, veyiskadash, shmey raba*…. My heart was about to burst. There. I was face-to-face with the Angel of Death….

No. Two steps from the pit, we were ordered to turn to left and herded into barracks.

I squeezed my father's hand. He said:

"Do you remember Mrs. Schächter, in the train?"

Never shall I forget that night, the first night in camp, that turned my life into one long night seven times sealed.

Never shall I forget that smoke.

Never shall I forget the small faces of the children whose bodies I saw transformed into smoke under a silent sky.

Never shall I forget those flames that consumed my faith forever.

Never shall I forget the nocturnal silence that deprived me for all eternity of the desire to live.

Never shall I forget those moments that murdered my God and my soul and turned my dreams to ashes.

Never shall I forget those things, even were I condemned to live as long as God Himself.

Never.

Excerpt from Elie Wiesel, *Night*, trans. Marion Wiesel (New York: Hill and Wang, 1960). Translation copyright © 2006 by Marion Wiesel. Reprinted by permission of Hill and Wang, a division of Farrar, Straus and Giroux, LLC.

POEMS FROM A CAMP SURVIVOR

Dan Pagis

"Written in Pencil in the Sealed Railway-Car"

here, in this carload
i am eve
with abel my son
if you see my other son
cain son of man
tell him that i

"Testimony"

No no: they definitely were
human beings: uniforms, boots.
How to explain? They were created
in the image.

I was a shade.
A different creator made me.

And he in his mercy left nothing of me that would die.
And I fled to him, rose weightless, blue,
forgiving – I would even say: apologizing –
smoke to omnipotent smoke
without image or likeness.

Poems reprinted with permission from "Testimony" and "Written in Pencil in the Sealed Railway Car" in *The Selected Poetry of Dan Pagis,* translated/edited by Stephen Mitchell (Berkeley, CA: The University of California Press, 1996). © 1996 by the Regents of the University of California.

About the Poet

Dan Pagis was born in 1930, in Bukovina, Romania. He spent three of his adolescent years in a Nazi concentration camp in Ukraine before arriving in Palestine, in 1946. He became one of the most vibrant voices in modern Israeli poetry and is considered a major world poet of his generation. Dan Pagis died in Jerusalem in 1986.

Photo courtesy of Yad Vashem

About Illustration

Zinovii Tolkatchev (1903–1977), **Appell**, 1944. Gouache, charcoal and crayon on paper. Gift of Zigmund A. Rolat, New York, in memory of his parents Henryk and Mania who perished in the Holocaust. Collection of the Yad Vashem Art Museum, Jerusalem. © Yad Vashem. All Rights Reserved.

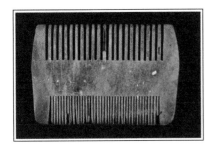

In his memoir *Memory Fields* (Knopf, 1992) Shlomo Breznitz writes:

> "When mother died, with the exception of a few photographs, I did not care to keep any of her material possessions. However, there is one small item that Judith [Shlomo's sister] and I cherish above everything else. It is the dirty and broken comb that she brought back from Auschwitz. She traded it for a full day's ration of bread in order to have a chance to comb her closely cropped head."

"This prayer book was purchased in Auschwitz in 1944. I received it from a Russian inmate in exchange for a portion of my daily ration of bread. It accompanied me throughout my entire journey of suffering in the concentration and death camps in Germany. I donate today this unique prayer book to Yad Vashem in Jerusalem as a memorial for future generations and in memory of my parents David and Malka Kopolovich z"l, my wife's parents Shlomo and Zehava Weiss z"l, my brothers and sisters and all of my relatives who were murdered in the Holocaust."

— Zvi Kopolovich, Holon
18th of Cheshvan, 5750, November 16, 1989

Annie Fisk Levinger was born in Austria; later her family moved to Czechoslovakia. In September 1944, she was deported with her family to Theresienstadt. While in Theresienstadt, Annie married Pawel Bisk, who was deported to Auschwitz three days later. Annie was deported to Auschwitz shortly thereafter. The entire time he was imprisoned in the camp he kept a photograph of his beloved wife. At first, he kept the photograph in his mouth, and then hid it in his sock. Both Annie and Pawel survived the war.

Photos © Yad Vashem

EXCERPT FROM *MAN'S SEARCH FOR MEANING*

Viktor E. Frankl

In front of me a man stumbled and those following him fell on top of him. The guard rushed over and used his whip on them all. Thus my thoughts were interrupted for a few minutes. But soon my soul found its way back from the prisoner's existence to another world, and I resumed talk with my loved one: I asked her questions, and she answered; she questioned me in return, and I answered.

"Stop!" We had arrived at our work site. Everybody rushed into the dark hut in the hope of getting a fairly decent tool. Each prisoner got a spade or a pickaxe.

"Can't you hurry up, you pigs?" Soon we had resumed the previous day's positions in the ditch. The frozen ground cracked under the point of the pickaxes, and sparks flew. The men were silent, their brains numb.

My mind still clung to the image of my wife. A thought crossed my mind: I didn't even know if she were still alive. I knew only one thing—which I have learned well by now: Love goes very far beyond the physical person of the beloved. It finds its deepest meaning in his spiritual being, his inner self. Whether or not he is actually present, whether or not he is still alive at all, ceases somehow to be of importance.

I did not know whether my wife was alive, and I had no means of finding out (during all my prison life there was no outgoing or incoming mail); but at that moment it ceased to matter. There was no need for me to know; nothing could touch the strength of my love, my thoughts, and the image of my beloved. Had I known then that my wife was dead, I think that I would still have given myself, undisturbed by that knowledge, to the contemplation of her image, and that my mental conversation with her would have been just as vivid and just as satisfying.

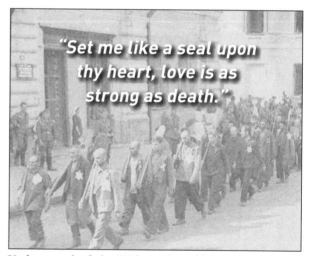

"Set me like a seal upon thy heart, love is as strong as death."

Under guard of the Wehrmacht soldiers, Jews wearing Jewish stars with shovels ("spades") marching through the city on the way to forced labor, Russia, Mogilev, 1941.

About the Author

Viktor E. Frankl, born in Vienna, Austria 1905, was a practicing psychotherapist, university professor, and author. His most widely read work, *Man's Search for Meaning* (Beacon Press, 1959), is an account of his experiences in various concentration camps, including Theresienstadt, Auschwitz, and Dachau. In the book, Frankl explores the transcendent experience amid extreme suffering as well as the nature of moral freedom. His wife, Tilly, to whom he refers in the passage, died in Bergen-Belsen. Viktor Frankl died in Vienna in 1997.

INTERVIEW WITH FRANZ STANGL

About Franz Stangl

Born in Austria in 1908, Franz Stangl joined the Austrian police in 1931 and became a criminal investigations officer in the political division. In 1940, Stangl joined the Euthanasia Program at its Hartheim castle institute—one of six centers where people with mental and physical disabilities and other "asocial" Germans were killed.

Franz Stangl, Yad Vashem
Photo Archive (5318/89)

In March 1942, Stangl became commandant of the Sobibor extermination camp in Poland. Later that year he became commandant of Treblinka where he was responsible for the deaths of 870,000 Jews. After the prisoner revolt in Treblinka in September 1943, Stangl and his staff were transferred to Trieste, Italy to organize anti-partisan actions. He also spent time at the San Sabba concentration camp.

After the war Stangl returned to Austria, where he was arrested by the Americans for being an SS member (they did not know that he had participated in the extermination of Jews). However, Stangl was found out when the Americans began investigating the Euthanasia Program. About to be charged in May 1948, Stangl escaped to Rome, Syria, and eventually Brazil where he and his family lived under their own names until discovered in 1967. Stangl was tried in Germany and sentenced to life in prison, where he died in 1971.

Interview

While in prison Stangl was interviewed by Gitta Sereny, a British journalist. The interviews were published in a book entitled *Into That Darkness*. The following is an excerpt from one of their discussions in prison.

Q: Would it be true to say that you finally felt they weren't really human beings?

A: When I was on a trip once, years later in Brazil… my train stopped next to a slaughterhouse. The cattle in the pens, hearing the noise of the train, trotted up to the fence and stared at the train. They were very close to my window, one crowding the other, looking at me through the fence. I thought then, "look at this; this reminds me of Poland; that's just how the people looked, trustingly, just before they were put in tins."

Q: You said "tins." What do you mean?

A: …I couldn't eat tinned meat after that. Those big eyes… which looked at me… not knowing that in no time at all they'd all be dead…

Q: So you didn't feel they were human beings?

A: Cargo. They were cargo.

Q: When do you think you began to think of them as cargo?

A: I think it started the day I first saw Totenlager [the sub-camp where the gas chambers stood] in Treblinka. I remember Wirth [first commander of the camp] standing there, next to the pits full of blue-black corpses. It had nothing to do with humanity; it couldn't have; it was a mass—a mass of rotting flesh. Wirth said, "What shall we do with this garbage?" I think unconsciously that started me thinking of them as cargo.

Q: There were so many children, did they ever make you think of your children, of how you would feel in the position of those parents?

A: No… I can't say I ever thought that way… you see, I rarely saw them as individuals. It was always a huge mass. I sometimes stood on the wall and saw them in the tube [the passage leading to the gas chamber area]. But—how can I explain it—they were naked, packed together, running, being driven with whips like…

Q: Could you not have changed that?… In your position, could you not have stopped the nakedness, the whips, the horror of the cattle pens?

A: No, no, no. This was the system. Wirth had invented it. It worked. And because it worked, it was irreversible.

Interview reprinted from *Into That Darkness* by Gitta Sereny. © 1974 by Gitta Sereny. Used by permission of Vintage Books, a division of Random House, Inc.

Introduction

Although the Nazis came to power in 1933, it wasn't until the second half of 1941 that Nazi policy began to focus on the annihilation of the Jewish people. This evolution in policy coincided with Germany's invasion of the Soviet Union on June 22, 1941. Nazi leaders saw the invasion of the Soviet Union not only as a bid to gain territory that they felt was vital for Germany, but as an ideological struggle. The brutality of the invasion coalesced with racial antisemitism to further radicalize anti-Jewish polices since Jews were seen as the racial and ideological archenemy—especially the stereotype that Jews were the creators and primary agents of Bolshevism.

Historians note that on July 31, 1941, Hermann Goering, Hitler's second in command, sent an official order to Reinhard Heydrich, the head of the security branch of the SS, to authorize a "Final Solution of the Jewish Question." The exact meaning behind this order is still debated among many Holocaust scholars. Current research shows that mass systematic killing of Jewish men in the newly conquered territory of the Soviet Union began in June, and by August included women and children as well. There is no surviving order by Hitler to expand the murderous activities to encompass all Jews under Nazi control, but most scholars believe such an order was given in the autumn of 1941, or at the latest early in 1942. Even if the exact sequence of events regarding the order is unknown, the fact remains that mass murder continued swiftly, and soon spread to Poland and other European countries. By the end of 1941, many hundreds of thousands of Jews had been murdered; eventually approximately six million Jews would be murdered by the Nazis and their collaborators.

The latest research reveals that although the tone of Nazi anti-Jewish policies came from the highest centers of power in Germany (Adolf Hitler and his senior officials), Nazi officials of lower ranks often had much leeway in the actual implementation and even initiated various aspects of policy. This idea of those at lower levels taking initiative has been called by the British historian Ian Kershaw "working toward the Fuehrer" (Hitler). Throughout the Nazi period there is a dynamic between the "center" and the "periphery" regarding anti-Jewish activities—while the responsibility for anti-Jewish activities rested primarily with the top leaders, there were many other people of different levels in Nazi German society who made a choice to serve the regime.

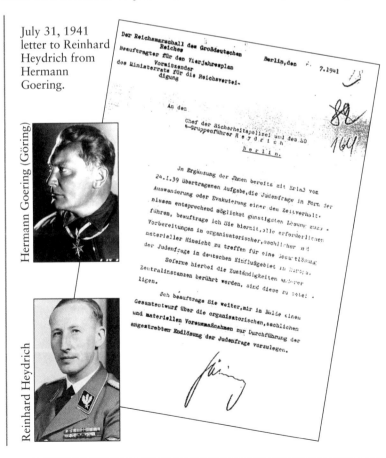

July 31, 1941 letter to Reinhard Heydrich from Hermann Goering.

Hermann Goering (Göring)

Reinhard Heydrich

Einsatzgruppen

When "Operation Barbarossa" (German code name for Germany's invasion of the Soviet Union) began, the Einsatzgruppen, special SS killing units, followed the German army, the Wehrmacht. Their job was to search for opponents of the Reich, including Communists and all Jews—and execute them. There were four units of Einsatzgruppen; the largest unit was composed of 1,000 men. These groups alone did not carry out the destruction of Soviet Jewry—wherever they went, ordinary German soldiers, German police units, and local collaborators were active participants. By spring 1943, the Einsatzgruppen and their collaborators had murdered 1.5 million Jews and hundreds of thousands of others, including Soviet prisoners of war and Sinti-Roma.

The Einsatzgruppen killed their victims—men, women, and children—by gathering them along the edges of ravines, mines, ditches, or pits dug specifically for this purpose. First, they would force Jews to hand over their possessions and remove their clothing. Then they would shoot them and throw the bodies into ditches that often had been dug beforehand by Jews themselves. In this way many Jewish communities were destroyed entirely.

Among the bloodiest massacres was that which occurred at Babi Yar, just outside of Kiev, Ukraine in late September 1941. There, close to 34,000 Jewish men, women, and children were murdered over the course of two days.

About Photos

Left: Einsatzgruppen about to shoot Jews on the outskirts of Kovno, 1941–1942.

Right: A German policeman searching through clothes of murdered Jews, Babi Yar, Ukraine, October 1941. Courtesy of Hessisches Hauptstaatsarchiv

The Extermination Camps

The mobile killing squads proved to be problematic for the Nazi leaders. They required large numbers of executioners, the men suffered from psychological repercussions, and it was difficult to conceal the killing from the surrounding populace. A new method was therefore devised, aimed at solving a number of these issues. First, instead of the killer coming to the victims, the victims would now be brought to "killing centers." The new system of murder by gassing served to reduce the direct contact between the killers and their victims, making the murderers' task easier.

A new phase in the reign of terror was reached when the "Final Solution" was formulated, and extermination camps were constructed with the expressed purpose of killing Jews. Unlike other enemies of the Third Reich, all Jews in Nazi-occupied territory were destined for extermination. In the words of Elie Wiesel, himself a former camp inmate, "While not all victims were Jews, all Jews were victims."

Six camps were considered to be extermination camps. From across Europe, Jews were deported, most commonly like animals in cattle trains, to be slaughtered en masse at these sites. All of the camps—Chelmno, Belzec, Sobibor, Treblinka, Auschwitz-Birkenau, and Majdanek—were in occupied Poland which had the largest prewar Jewish community in Europe. For the most part, the Nazis tried to hide their activities from the local population.

With the exception of Auschwitz-Birkenau and Majdanek—which were also places of detention and labor—the camps had only one purpose: the Jews brought to the extermination camps were to be killed. Jews would arrive at the camp, usually after having spent several days in transit with little or no food or water, and within a few hours after reaching the camp, they would all be dead.

In Auschwitz-Birkenau and Majdanek some transports would go through a selection; however, the vast majority of the arrivals were sent directly to the gas chambers; few were selected for labor. The entire procedure was planned for the greatest possible efficiency. In order to prevent panic, which could impede the killing, the victims were deceived into believing that they were going to have showers. Their personal possessions were taken from them, and they undressed. After their deaths their possessions and even hair and gold fillings were used by the authorities for different purposes. The perpetrators created a system that functioned like an "assembly-line" procedure that has come to be known as industrialized mass murder.

There are few survivors of the four sites that were exclusively extermination camps, since most of the people who reached them were sent immediately to the gas chambers. In these camps, very few prisoners' lives were spared in order to work in the crematoria and in other camp functions. More prisoners survived Majdanek and Auschwitz since, as slave laborers, they were not killed immediately. As a rule, the Nazi exploited slave laborers to the point of death, whereby they were either selected again, this time to be gassed, or died from exhaustion and related complications. Those who survived did so despite the Nazis' murderous intentions. Those who did survive the extermination camps tell of the unimaginable horrors they experienced there every day.

About Photos

Left: Transfer from the deportation trains to cattle cars at the Kolo Station, Lodz, Poland. Yad Vashem Photo Archive (1602/270)

Right: A Magirus van found after the war, suspected as a gas van used for murder in Chelmno camp, Kolo, Poland. Yad Vashem Photo Archive (1264/2)

The Perpetrators

Hundreds of thousands of people were involved, either directly or indirectly, in implementing the "Final Solution," the policy of systematically mass murdering Jews. Some actually engaged in murdering Jews. Others played a role in the bureaucratic process of ordering Jews from their homes to the sites of murder and arranging murder operations. Others became guards or transported Jews to the places where they would be killed. A great many people benefited from the worldly possessions left behind by the murdered Jews, and in this way they too became complicit in the murder process.

The core organizers and planners of the annihilation of European Jewry came from the ranks of the Nazi Party and the SS, who in general fervently believed in Nazi ideology. The driving force of the murders was the SS, among whom were commanders of killing units and Nazi camps; however, it is important to emphasize that the SS members were not the only ones who were actively involved in carrying out the "Final Solution." There were many groups involved from Germany, their allies in the war, and from the lands they occupied. In addition to the SS men, soldiers from the Wehrmacht, and the German police forces took part in these activities. Officials from the civil apparatus that the Germans maintained in the occupied lands also participated in implementing the "Final Solution."

For a wide range of reasons, people from the nations that fell under Nazi domination or were allied with the Nazis also took part in the "Final Solution," either directly or indirectly. Some were motivated primarily by their acceptance of Nazi ideology; others were of German heritage and willingly took up the offer by the Nazi authorities to become their partners; others collaborated with the Nazis in the hope that it would further their own national political agenda; others joined the Nazis in order to ameliorate their own or their family's suffering under the brutal occupation; and still others joined the Nazis in order to escape almost certain death as prisoners of war on the Eastern Front. Regardless of how the door to collaboration swung open, many non-Germans became full and frequently enthusiastic participants in the mass systematic murder of European Jews.

Because of the broad spectrum of people involved in the murder of the Jews in one way or another, responsibility for the murder rests on society as a whole during this period.

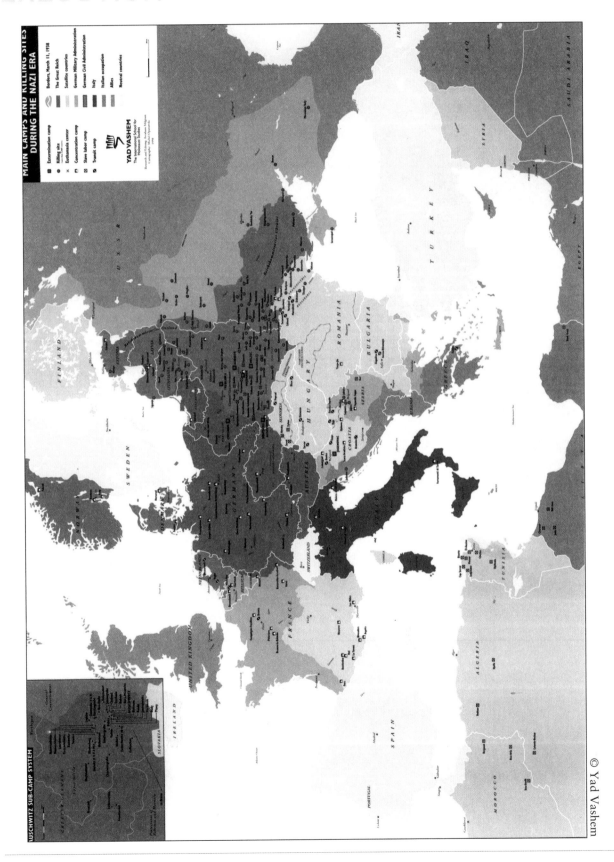

Yad Vashem Photo Archive (10AO8)

Yad Vashem Photo Archive (4613/41)

About Photo

Jewish Partisans in a Forest near the Town, Bialystok, Poland (3774/43)

Yad Vashem Photo Archive

"Resistance does not have to be with a gun and a bullet...."

– Roman Kent, Jewish Survivor

Preparing to Use This Lesson

Below is information to keep in mind when using this lesson. In some cases, the points elaborate on general suggestions listed in the "Teaching about the Holocaust" section in the Introduction to this resource, and are specific to the content of the lesson. This material is intended to help teachers consider the complexities of teaching the Holocaust and to deliver accurate and sensitive instruction.

- The term "resistance" when related to Jews in ghettos and camps during the Holocaust takes on a different meaning than the way students may understand the term. Jews faced an increasingly lethal situation in the ghettos, and once the Nazis adopted the "Final Solution" every single Jew living under Nazi tyranny was sentenced to death.

- Throughout this lesson, help students understand that resistance required great courage and at times physical strength. Those who chose to resist had to grapple with many dilemmas including the possible price of disobeying Nazi orders, the possible effect of their resistance on their families and communities, and the punishment they might have to endure for resisting. These issues are not always obvious and should be brought to students' attention. [See also Preparing to Use This Lesson, Lesson 4: The Ghettos.]

- Emphasize that the fighters of the Warsaw ghetto were Jews who were imprisoned in the ghetto and suffered from the same misfortune as other Jews there. Because their actions were so remarkable it may seem that they were "different" from other Jews in the ghetto. Realizing that what they did was done from within the misery of the ghetto, their deeds seem even more remarkable.

JEWISH RESISTANCE

About This Lesson

 120–180 minutes

❖ INTRODUCTION This lesson provides an opportunity for students to explore Jewish resistance efforts during the Holocaust—focusing on the period from the establishment of the ghettos through the implementation of the "Final Solution." An opportunity is provided for students to learn about the risks of resisting Nazi domination and the means, scope, and intensity of resistance efforts. These ranged from cultural and spiritual resistance in the ghettos to armed resistance of partisans and ghetto and camp prisoners. At their core, these forms of resistance are expressions of the capacity to preserve what is best in humanity in the face of the worst humanity has to offer. This lesson also provides an opportunity for students to consider the role of personal and cultural identity in their lives.

This two-part lesson has material appropriate for history, social studies, Holocaust studies, and English/language arts classes. Instructional strategies used in the lesson include large-group discussion, vocabulary building, brainstorming, small-group work, interpreting visual history testimony, analyzing primary source documents, reading for information, critical thinking, comparing and contrasting information, crafting a written argument, and journaling.

❖ OBJECTIVES After completing this lesson, students will be able to:

- Define resistance within the context of the Holocaust.

- Explain how resistance and rebellion were discouraged in occupied territories.

- Identify various forms of resistance that took place in the ghettos and camps.

- Conclude that designating an action as "resistance" is based on a variety of factors, i.e., what might be considered resistance in one situation may not be considered resistance in another situation.

- Interpret primary source materials—including clips of visual history testimony—that represent a range of resistance efforts against the Nazi regime in Europe.

- Explain the connection between the "Final Solution" and armed resistance.

- Construct an argument, based on evidence from primary and secondary sources, to support the claim that Jews resisted the Nazi regime in a variety of ways.

- Analyze the role of culture, customs, and traditions in individual or group narratives.

RESOURCES & TESTIMONIES

All of the resources used in this lesson can be found in this guide at the end of this lesson and at echoesandreflections.org.

Visual history testimonies are available on the website or on the DVD that accompanies this resource guide.

Teachers are urged to review the lesson procedures to identify other materials and technology needed to implement the lesson.

L6

❖ KEY WORDS & PHRASES

Aktion	ghetto	Sobibor
armed resistance	Holocaust	Sonderkommando
Aryan	*Kadoshim*	spiritual resistance
Auschwitz-Birkenau	liquidated	Treblinka
cantor	*Lodz Ghetto Chronicle*	tyranny
collaborator	Majdanek	underground
Communist	Molotov Cocktail	Warsaw ghetto
concentration camp	Nazi	Warsaw Ghetto Uprising
crematoria	partisans	Yom Kippur
cultural resistance	Passover	Zionist
Einsatzgruppen	Purim	Z.O.B.
extermination camp	Resistance	

❖ ACADEMIC STANDARDS The materials in this lesson address the following national education standards:

Common Core State Standards

- Reading Standards for Informational Text 6–12

- Writing Standards 6–12

- Speaking and Listening Standards 6–12

- Reading Standards for Literacy in History/Social Studies 6–12

- Writing Standards for Literacy in History/Social Studies 6–12

A complete analysis of how this lesson addresses Common Core State Standards by grade level and specific skills is available on the Echoes and Reflections website.

National Curriculum Standards for Social Studies

❶ Culture

❷ Time, Continuity, and Change

❸ People, Places, and Environments

❹ Individual Development and Identity

❺ Individuals, Groups, and Institutions

❻ Power, Authority, and Governance

❿ Civic Ideals and Practices

Procedures

Part 1: Spiritual and Cultural Resistance

1. Begin this lesson by writing the word "resistance" on the board. Have students brainstorm the meaning of the word and suggest situations when an individual or group of people might decide that resistance is appropriate or necessary. Record the students' responses on the board or on chart paper.

2. Introduce students to Roman Kent and show the first clip from Part 1 of Visual History Testimony: *Jewish Resistance*. After students have watched the testimony clip, discuss the

L6

following questions:

- What are the specific examples of resistance Roman Kent shares in his testimony?

- In his testimony, Roman says, "sometimes the easiest resistance is with a gun and a bullet." What do you think he means by this statement? Do you agree with him? Explain your thinking.

- Roman wants people to understand that contrary to what some may think, Jews *did* resist the Nazis during the Holocaust in a variety of ways. Why do you think he feels it is important for people to understand this?

3. Ask students to think about the term "resistance" in the context of the Holocaust. Have them consider and respond to the question, "What were Jews resisting during the Holocaust?"

4. Explain to students that there were many examples of Jewish resistance during the Holocaust even though the risks of opposing the Nazi regime were grave. Using the board or chart paper, record students' thoughts on possible reasons why most people could not resist (e.g., hunger, sickness, isolation, lack of weapons, care for children, parents, or other family members).

5. In addition to the term "resistance," have students think about the term "survival." Take a few minutes to discuss how these terms are similar and how they are different. Ask for volunteers to look the words up in dictionaries and compare the dictionary definitions.

6. On the board or on chart paper, write the heading, "Jewish Resistance during the Holocaust" and below write the subheadings "Cultural/Spiritual Resistance" and "Active/Armed Resistance." While providing students with the definitions below, have a volunteer(s) write key ideas for each form of resistance under the appropriate heading.

Cultural/Spiritual Resistance

Cultural/spiritual resistance during the Holocaust was acts of opposition that originated or found their expression in culture, traditions, and the human spirit to undermine Nazi power and inspire hope among the persecuted Jews. For most Jews, acts of cultural and spiritual resistance were the only possible means to oppose Nazi tyranny. Examples of cultural resistance included creating schools in the ghettos; maintaining religious customs; writing poems and songs or performing concerts or plays; drawing, painting, or secretly photographing observed events; and keeping records of ghetto or camp life and hiding them in the hope that they would be discovered after the war. Acts of cultural/spiritual resistance could be intentional and conscious, or only understood to have been resistance in retrospect.

Active/Armed Resistance

Active/armed resistance during the Holocaust was acts of opposition, defiance, or the sabotage of Nazi plans using weapons or including typical battles and attacks. Examples of armed resistance are the

TESTIMONY VIEWING

About the Interviewee

Roman Kent was born on April 18, 1929, in Lodz, Poland. He was incarcerated in the Lodz ghetto and was later imprisoned in the Flossenbürg, Auschwitz, and Gross-Rosen concentration camps. Roman was also imprisoned in the Auschwitz-Birkenau extermination camp. His interview was conducted in the United States. When the war began, Roman was ten years old.

———

For additional information about Roman Kent, see his Biographical Profile available on the website.

NOTE 1.3

While an immediate response to this question might be "the Nazis," students should also understand that Jews were resisting things like isolation, dehumanization, starvation, and the "Final Solution"—death.

NOTE 1.4

Refer to Lesson 4: The Ghettos and Lesson 5: The "Final Solution" for additional information on life in the ghettos and camps.

NOTE 1.6

It should be understood that in a sense, cultural/spiritual resistance was active since it too involved action. Sometimes Jews simply refused to cooperate or follow a command, and this could be seen as classic passive resistance.

L6

Helen Fagin was born on February 1, 1922, in Radomsko, Poland. She was forced to live in the Lodz, Warsaw, and Radomsko ghettos. Helen escaped during a deportation and then went into hiding in Poland. Her interview was conducted in the United States. When the war began, Helen was seventeen years old.

Ruth Brand was born in 1928 (exact date unknown), in Cuhea, Romania. She was forced to live in the Dragomiresti ghetto and later imprisoned in the Bergen-Belsen concentration camp. Ruth was also imprisoned in the Auschwitz-Birkenau extermination camp. Her interview was conducted in Israel. When the war began, Ruth was eleven years old.

For additional information about Helen Fagin and Ruth Brand, see their Biographical Profiles available on the website.

bombing of a bunker, camp, office, or train, or an uprising or revolt using weapons and arms. Unarmed active resistance could include many things, such as preparing bunkers, forging and using false papers, smuggling food and other items, etc.

7. Explain that spiritual resistance can often be seen as an attempt to maintain one's previous way of life and his or her unique identity. The terrible reality in which Jews lived was expressed by the teacher, Chaim Kaplan who lived in the Warsaw ghetto: "Everything is forbidden to us, but we do everything." Have students consider the meaning of this statement.

8. After introducing students to Helen Fagin and Ruth Brand, show the next two clips from Part 1 of Visual History Testimony: *Jewish Resistance* and discuss the following questions:

   • How would you characterize the activities Helen Fagin initiated in the ghetto?

   • What purpose does the *Gone with the Wind* story serve for the students in Helen's "clandestine school"?

   • What reason does Ruth Brand give for fasting on Yom Kippur, despite the danger of doing so?

   • How were Ruth and the other girls punished for this act of resistance?

   • What does the word "brave" mean to you? Based on your definition, would you describe Helen and Ruth as brave?

9. Distribute the *Cultural and Spiritual Resistance* handout. Have students read the excerpts that were compiled from a variety of documents and then divide the class into small groups. Instruct each group to use the excerpts and clips of visual history testimony that they watched to discuss the following questions:

   • Which of the excerpts on the handout would you identify as examples of resistance and why?

   • How does the information in the excerpts illustrate the need Jews felt to maintain the traditions that had been in place prior to the war? Provide specific examples from the text.

   • What role do traditions, customs, and culture play in people's lives?

   • Why do you think it was so important for Jews to remain connected to the traditions, customs, and culture that were part of their lives even when this connection placed them in immediate jeopardy?

   • Jews in the ghettos tried to maintain their customs from before the war, but at the same time were confronted with a totally different reality. How are these two themes reflected in the excerpts and testimony clips?

   • What were the dilemmas in maintaining traditions and customs during the Holocaust?

10. End this part of the lesson with a whole-group discussion whereby students respond to the following question: How, if at all, has your understanding of resistance, especially as it pertains to the Holocaust, changed over the course of this lesson?

Part 2: Partisans and Armed Resistance

1. Begin this part of the lesson by having students review the definitions of spiritual and armed resistance and provide examples of each.

2. Introduce students to Mira Shelub and Sol Liber and then show Part 2 of Visual History Testimony: *Jewish Resistance*.

TESTIMONY VIEWING

About the Interviewees

Mira Shelub was born on January 13, 1922, in Zdzieciol, Poland. She was forced to live in both the Zdzieciol and Dworzec ghettos and later escaped to the Lipiczany Forest, where, she, along with her sister, joined the partisans until they were liberated, in 1944. Her interview was conducted in the United States. When the war began, Mira was seventeen years old.

Sol Liber was born on December 3, 1923, in Grojec, Poland. He was forced to live in the Warsaw ghetto and was later imprisoned in the Skarzysko-Kamienna, Majdanek, Buchenwald, Treblinka, and Tschenstochau concentration camps. His interview was conducted in the United States. When the war began, Sol was fifteen years old.

_____

For additional information about Mira Shelub and Sol Liber, see their Biographical Profiles available on the website.

Discuss the testimonies using the questions below.

- Were you surprised to learn that there were female partisans? Why or why not?

- What do you learn about the partisans from Mira Shelub's testimony?

- What does Mira say was the goal of the partisans?

- What do you learn about armed resistance in the Warsaw ghetto from Sol Liber's testimony?

- Both Mira and Sol give insight into how resistance during the Holocaust didn't mean "winning," but each and every act remained significant. How were the acts of resistance that Mira and Sol describe "significant"?

3. Prepare students for the material on partisans by asking the questions below:

- What visual image do you have when you hear the word "forest"?

- Is a forest a protected or an exposed place?

NOTE 2.3

Having maps and photographs of the forests of Eastern Europe available for students to see will enhance their understanding of the partisans' struggle. It is important that students understand that the European forests that the partisans faced are probably very unlike forests that they know. These large, dense woodlands and swamps cover thousands of square miles, and because of the harsh and extreme climate in the winter, there are no edible plants.

- What are some possible dangers and difficulties that someone would face if he or she were to survive for any length of time in a forest?

4. Distribute the *Partisans* handout and instruct students to read the material and identify textual evidence to support their responses to the questions below.

   - What dilemmas did a Jewish person face when thinking about whether he or she should flee to the forest?

   - What were the main differences between a Jewish partisan and a non-Jewish partisan?

   - According to information provided in the text, why was it so difficult for people to flee to the forest? Why was it impossible for most Jews to flee to the forest?

   - Why did partisans feel it necessary to keep their location secret—even from local farmers and peasants?

NOTE 2.5

Make sure that students understand that most of the Jewish population—parents of children, the children themselves, the elderly, the sick, and the millions who were murdered before conditions became ripe for revolt—could not take part in the armed uprising.

5. Distribute or show students the pronouncement that was written and read by Abba Kovner at a meeting in Vilna on January 1, 1942. To provide context, explain that Abba Kovner was a young Lithuanian Jew who was a leader of a youth movement that hoped to take part in building a Jewish state in Israel. A young activist in the ghetto, he eventually became the leader of an armed underground. After a wave of murder during the second half of 1941, in which 2/3 of the Jews of Vilna were killed, Kovner was convinced that the Germans had a plan to murder all Jews everywhere. He had no real solid proof, but a strong feeling based on the events that had occurred in Vilna. Thus, the underground members decided to enter the ghetto and when it was about to be liquidated, they hoped to lead an armed uprising. After reading the pronouncement together, have a discussion based on the following questions:

   - To whom is Abba Kovner directing his message? What specific words in the text support your answer? Explain why you think this was his audience.

   - What are Abba Kovner's arguments in favor of resistance?

   - Analyze the following statement from the text: "It is better to die as free fighters than to live at the mercy of murderers." What was Abba Kovner's central argument?

   - Why do you think that most Jews who participated in the revolts were youth?

6. Explain to students that, in addition to the underground partisan resistance that occurred in the villages and countryside of Nazi-occupied territories, there were forms of active resistance including armed revolts that were organized in the ghettos, concentration camps, and even extermination camps during the Holocaust. Stress that it was very difficult for Jews to conduct armed resistance, and have students brainstorm possible conditions or other factors that made armed resistance so difficult. To help put this in context, tell students that the German army in World War II was a very powerful army, and it took nearly six years from the start of the

war and an effort unparalleled in history to defeat it.

7. Distribute the *Armed Resistance in the Ghettos and Camps* handout. Have students read the information aloud or in small groups. Discuss the reading with emphasis on the following questions:

   • What motivated Jews to fight the Nazis?

   • How were their motives similar or different from other examples of resistance that you know about?

   • What does it mean to "offer resistance for its own sake"?

8. After a general discussion of resistance in the camps and ghettos, distribute the *Personal Testimonies* handout. After the class has read the handout (either in groups, individually, aloud, or for homework), have them respond to the following questions, citing specific information and examples from the text to support their answers whenever possible.

   • What difficulties and dilemmas did the fighters face in obtaining weapons?

   • What expressions does Mordechai Anielewicz use to describe the revolt?

   • To whom does Mordechai Anielewicz address his message? Why do you think this is his audience?

   • Why do you think it was important to Mordechai Anielewicz that news of the Warsaw Ghetto Uprising be broadcast over the underground radio?

   • What descriptive word or term would you use to describe this revolt?

   • Why was it important for Zalman Gradowski to leave written testimonies behind?

   • How would you title the Zalman Gradowski passage?

   • What, in your opinion, makes someone a hero? Based on your definition of "hero," is the man who wrote these lines a hero?

   • Antek Zuckerman said about the Warsaw Ghetto Uprising: "If there's a school to study the human spirit, there it [the Uprising] should be a major subject." From the statement, what importance does Zuckerman assign to the Uprising? Cite other examples studied in this lesson that could also be used to support the statement.

9. Assign students the writing prompt below as a culminating activity for this lesson.

   Prompt: Sometimes people who have not studied the Holocaust will ask, "Why didn't Jews fight back?" In his testimony, Roman Kent addresses this very question when he says, "I've heard so many times [it] being said that Jews didn't do anything, that they went like sheep to the ovens, but it's not true…"

   Based on materials studied in this lesson, prepare a written argument to support the claim that Jews did resist the Nazi regime in a variety of ways. The argument should introduce the topic,

NOTE 2.9

In addition to reviewing the written materials covered in this lesson, encourage students to go to the website and review the clips of testimony that they had watched earlier.

establish the significance of the claim, and provide relevant and sufficient evidence from primary and secondary sources to support your argument.

Reflect and Respond

Either in class or as homework, have students reflect and respond to one or more of the topics below or have them develop a topic that has meaning for them based on the material covered in the lesson.

- Reflect on the meaning of unarmed and armed resistance based on the testimonies you heard. Why is one form of resistance more appropriate than another in certain situations? Think of an example of a situation that might warrant each type of resistance.

- In the Krakow ghetto, the underground declared that they were fighting "for three lines in history." Reflect on what you understand this statement to mean and how studying about resistance efforts during the Holocaust influence your understanding of the words and the sentiment they express.

- Think about the role culture, traditions, and customs play in your life. Write about one or more traditions that are particularly important to you, explaining why they are important and how they have shaped—or continue to shape—your identity.

Making Connections

The additional activities and projects listed below can be integrated directly into the lesson or can be used to extend the lesson once it has been completed. The topics lend themselves to students' continued study of the Holocaust as well as opportunities for students to make meaningful connections to other people and events, including relevant contemporary issues. These activities may include instructional strategies and techniques and/or address academic standards in addition to those that were identified for the lesson.

1. Visit IWitness (iwitness.usc.edu) for activities specific to Lesson 6: Jewish Resistance.

2. Using a variety of print and digital sources, have students research other examples of underground movements or partisan resistance during World War II: Italian, Slovakian, Polish, French, Yugoslavian, and others, and prepare a written, oral, or multimedia presentation on their findings. Encourage students to identify how the partisan movement they researched was both different from and similar to the Jewish partisans' movement.

3. Using the information discussed in this and preceding lessons, break students into small groups and have them construct their own "underground newspaper" from one of the camps or ghettos. Articles, announcements, and advertisements should reflect what they have learned about the culture and environment in the ghettos or camps.

4. Have students access *Excerpts from On Both Sides of the Wall* available in the Additional Resources section of the Lesson Components. Have students read the introduction to Vladka Meed and the two excerpts from her autobiography. After reading the text, instruct students, either individually or as part of a small group, to prepare up to five questions they would ask Meed about her experiences as part of the underground if they could have interviewed her (Vladka Meed passed away on November 21, 2012, at the age of 90). Students should then research the answers to their questions using a variety of sources including Vladka Meed's testimony (available on IWitness and YouTube), her Biographical Profile, and her autobiography. Their final piece of writing should be written in interview format, clearly

indicating what questions were posed and how Vladka Meed might have responded.

5. Throughout history, music has been used as a form of resistance and as a catalyst for societal change. During the Holocaust, music was secretly composed and performed in the ghettos as a way to uphold traditions, escape the harsh existence that Jews faced, and to document ghetto life. One such composition, created by Hirsh Glick, became the official song of the partisans. It was translated into several languages and was well known in both the ghettos and concentration camps. Show or distribute a copy of *Never Say* (available in the Additional Resources section of the Lesson Components) and have students identify specific words, phases, or lines that reveal Glick's intended audience as well as the message/s he was attempting to convey in the song. Refer to Yad Vashem's *Heartstrings* exhibition (available on the website in the Additional Resources section of the Lesson Components) so students can hear the song. Ask students if the rhythm is what they had expected or if they had anticipated the song to sound different, and if so, in what way.

Extend this activity by having students research the role of music in resistance efforts, protest, and/or in raising awareness of social issues in the United States, and prepare a multimedia presentation to share their findings. Encourage students to visit "History Now: The Music and History of Our Times" at the Gilder Lehrman Institute of American History website for primary source materials and soundtracks that will support their research (gilderlehrman.org/history-now).

6. Have students gather relevant information from multiple print and digital sources about resistance efforts by enslaved African Americans in the 17th and 18th centuries or interned Japanese Americans during World War II and prepare a multimedia presentation. Their research should include information about both active/armed resistance and cultural/spiritual resistance. Examples of primary source materials (e.g., a newspaper written in an internment camp, photographs, interviews) should be included in the presentation. Have presentations posted on the class website so students will be able to learn about resistance efforts by the group that they did not study and to see a variety of primary sources.

7. Have students pretend they are a film critic for a local media outlet and their assignment is to review one of the following films: *Uprising* (2001), *Escape from Sobibor* (1987), or *Defiance* (2008). After watching the film, have students write a review of the film and recommend whether people should see it or not. The review should comment on such things as acting, cinematography, etc., but the focus of the review should be on whether the film is historically accurate based on what students have learned in this lesson and through additional research on the topic addressed in the film.

CULTURAL AND SPIRITUAL RESISTANCE

Excerpts of Voices from the Ghetto

"In the ghetto, there are, of course, many people who are shaking their heads and refusing to participate in this deception, because in their opinion, the life of the Jews in the ghetto does not permit the shallowness of social life. However, this means repressing the tortured people's fundamental expression of the will to live and shutting off the only avenue of affirming the importance of that life. To sit in a theater again, far from the gloomy atmosphere of the prison, to chat in the lobby of the Cultural Center during the intermission again, to flirt, to show off a new dress or an attractive hairdo—this is a human need that cannot be repressed. This was the way it was for the people who lived in this superior cultural center, as Litzmannstadt [Lodz ghetto] had been in the years preceding the war. And to whomever reads this in the future, the writer wants to say that from his perspective, the suffering of the ghetto was not in the least alleviated by these shows, even if they did provide a few hours of pleasure."[1]

* * *

January 17, 1944

Announcement! Re: Obligatory Registration of Musical Instruments

"For once, a measure not aimed at the stomach of the ghetto dweller, but no less severe on that account. [The ghetto is thirsty for culture...] Now this last vestige of that happiness is to vanish. One can readily imagine what it means for a professional musician, a virtuoso, even a dilettante, to be forced to give up his beloved violin [...] The street will notice nothing; harsh life will go on; and to the torments of hunger and cold will be added the unappeased craving for music."[2]

The ghetto orchestra, Kovno, Lithuania. In front standing from left is Michael Hofmekler, the conductor, and sitting next to him is Boris Stupel who survived Dachau and immigrated to Australia. In the background playing the violin is Yankale who was 13 years-old and standing to his right is Shmaya (Alexander) Stupel (Boris's brother) who perished in Dachau. Yad Vashem Photo Archive (75GO9)

* * *

June 9, 1942

"A hunger for the printed word is now making itself felt more strongly in the ghetto. To ascertain how hungry people are for books, it is enough to take a look at the kilometer-long line at Sonenberg's lending library (even there!) [...] Each reader walks up to the table, requests a couple of titles, finds out if a given book is available (it usually is not), receives a couple of books to choose from, and has to make up his mind in a hurry. There is no time for long deliberation, as there once had been."[3]

* * *

March 4, 1941

"The soup kitchen for the intelligentsia is a regular meeting place of the who's who [...] Only here do they at least have an illusion of things they had become accustomed to in the old days: a certain degree of courtesy [by the staff] in their conduct and attitude toward those who are now destitute and stripped of their status [...] [...] From time to time, the kitchen management organized reading and poetry evenings and concerts. The aim was to give the ghetto inhabitants cultural entertainment and provide financial support for the artists. [...] The moments spent in kitchen number 2 – [...] those are also moments of an exchange of opinions, something like a club in which those people, the who's who meet over lunch."[4]

* * *

Jews in prayer shawls praying in a synagogue in the ghetto, Warsaw, Poland. Yad Vashem Photo Archive (1605/858)

"The *kloyz* [small synagogue] is almost full. The cantor prays melodiously; you would never know from him and the worshippers that the world is on the brinks of an abyss. They are wearing prayer shawls and tefillin. If you closed your eyes for a moment and did not look at these people, at their skinny faces... but just listened to the hum of their prayers, you would be sure you had fallen into a house of God in a time of peace and tranquility. There are young people, too, among the worshippers, and not just a few. They, too, are participating in creating an atmosphere in which the physical is forgotten and the soul is dedicated to sublime, lofty service totally removed from the oppression of the body and making the suffering of the moment pale in significance... I was suddenly suffused with warmth that I hadn't felt since before the war. Someone, something, lifted me, carried me, and placed me in a congregation of Jews from the Middle Ages who were fighting and dying for their religion…. In the world—murder, violence, robbery and fraud; the street, cold; in the heart, anguish and pain; but above them all there hovers a different force, supreme and eternal—the power of past and future generations."[5] —Reuven Feldshaw

* * *

"The living spirit behind the school was Yitzhak Katzenelson [Warsaw ghetto]. He was our most respected and popular teacher. His specialty was *Bible,* and he taught his students to love their people and their heritage, and to strive for national independence. His enthusiasm was contagious and at its height he would start singing and his students and the family in whose apartment they were studying would soon join in. It was usually very difficult to find classrooms in apartments, but there was never a problem in securing one for Katzenelson's lessons."[6]

* * *

"Under conditions of this sort we celebrated Purim, 5701. The Book of Esther was not read in the darkened synagogues, because all public worship is prohibited; but we were happy about the defeat of the Persian Haman. We celebrated Purim in the Zionist soup kitchen at 13 Zamenhof Street, which is the center of all Hebrew-Zionist social activity. Here we always find the atmosphere and the warmth of Zionism. Every so often programs are put on with lectures, songs, instrumental music and recitations. When we come here we forget our troubles and all the terrible events taking place outside. Here you can hear debates and sermons, arguments and quarrels as in the good days. And when your throat is dry you can wet it with a glass of black coffee without sugar. [...]

This year we read the Scroll in the Sephardic pronunciation; then we sang the holiday songs accompanied by a piano, and between one number and the other we even had a bite-three pieces of bread spread with butter, a taste of the traditional poppy-seed tarts, and a glass of sweetened coffee.

Credit for this heroic achievement goes to Dr. I. Schiper, M. Kirszenbaum, Bloch, and Kaminar.

We came sad and left sad, but we had some pleasant moments in between—God remember these men with favor!"[7]

End Notes

[1]Arie Ben-Menachem, *The Lodz Ghetto Chronicles*, Vol. 3, trans. from Hebrew by Marion Duman (Jerusalem: Yad Vashem, 1988), 305.

[2]Lucjan Dobroszycki, *The Chronicle of the Lodz Ghetto, 1941–1944* (New Haven, CT: Yale University Press, 1984), 434.

[3]Ibid., at 201–202.

[4]Ibid., at 28–30.

[5]Reprinted with permission from Yad Vashem Archive O.3/959.

[6]Zivia Luberkin, *In the Days of Destruction and Revolt* (Israel: The Ghetto Fighters' House, 1981), 69.

[7]Chaim A. Kaplan, *The Warsaw Ghetto Diary of Chaim A. Kaplan* (New York: Collier Books, 1973), 256.

PARTISANS

Partisans during World War II were armed units in areas dominated by Nazi Germany and her allies that fought against them behind the front lines. As the war progressed, many countries fell under Nazi domination, either as occupied territory or run by regimes that were allied to Nazi Germany. Frequently civilians and soldiers continued to oppose this situation, and decided to continue the armed struggle against the Nazis and their collaborators.

The partisans generally formed and fought in places that offered them some sort of cover, such as forests, swamps, or mountains. They engaged in a variety of activities, most commonly ambushes and sabotage. Often they sought to disrupt the transport of soldiers and war material, and this meant that frequent targets were rail lines, bridges, and vehicles. Especially in the occupied territory of the former Soviet Union, partisan activity grew, became organized, and took place in coordination with military and government authorities.

When the murder of the Jews struck, many Jews fled to the countryside. They literally fled for their lives. Before fleeing, however, they had to face dilemmas about leaving behind family members who were unable to join them, and the realization that their actions could lead to repercussions in the places from which they had escaped. It is only when Jews were able to obtain weapons that they could engage in partisan activities.

Jewish partisan activity began before other more organized partisan warfare emerged. As a result, already existing Jewish units sometimes were brought under the control of the other partisan units that had firmer military backing, and many Jews as individuals joined those units as well. Owing to anti-Jewish attitudes, in many instances Jews were not wanted in these units, and even when they were allowed to join them,

they often faced discrimination that could be very harsh.

A hallmark of the Jewish partisans was that unlike other partisans who focused strictly on fighting, Jewish partisans also sought to rescue Jews from certain death at the hands of the Nazi regime. The result was that so-called "family camps" came into being. The largest was under the Bielski brothers in Belarus with some 1,200

About Photos

Top: A group of partisans from the "family camp" of Tuvia Bielski in the Naliboki Forest, Poland, May 1944. Ghetto Fighters House Archives (32425)

Bottom: Partisans Kiril Tros (left) and Masha Bruskina (center, holding sign) marched through Minsk, Russia by German troops on October 26, 1941 prior to their public executions. The sign reads in German and Russian "We are partisans and have shot at German soldiers." Bundesarchiv, Bild 146-1972-026-43/CC-BY-SA

Jews, many of whom were non-fighters—older people and children. A similar family camp in the same area—the Zoran unit—had about 800 Jews in it. The non-fighters often performed services for other partisan units, such as sewing clothing, nursing, and repairing weapons. It can be said of the family camps that they fought just enough to justify their existence as partisans, but focused primarily on keeping alive as many Jews as possible. Nonetheless some Jewish units, such as the one in which Abba Kovner was a leader, focused on fighting.

Life in the forests, swamps, and mountains for the Jewish partisans was far from easy and posed many dilemmas. Many were not used to the rough living conditions and their shelter was usually far from adequate. The provision of food, which often was confiscated from local peasants, created tension that endangered them and rarely provided sufficient sustenance. When partisans were wounded or contracted sickness they only had the most primitive medical care, since medical equipment and medicines were not available. Many Jewish partisans fell victim to the "Jew hunts" conducted by the Nazis, who sought to discover Jews in hiding, and to other partisans who fought the Nazis but hated Jews. Like all partisans, Jewish partisans units frequently had to move their base of operations, sometimes in great haste, primarily because the Nazis considered the partisans a very serious problem and invested great effort in discovering and destroying them. In light of all of these hardships, and despite the heroic acts of many of the fighters, relatively few Jews survived the ordeal.

Abba Kovner (back row, center) with members of the United Partisan Organization, a Jewish resistance organization based in the Vilna ghetto that organized armed resistance against the Nazis.

A group of Jewish partisans from the Kovno ghetto in the Rudniki Forest. Yad Vashem Photo Archive (7003/168)

Jewish women and children partisans in the forest near Pinsk, Poland. Yad Vashem Photo Archive (1262/1)

Jewish partisans in forest, Vilna, Poland. Yad Vashem Photo Archive (8409/59)

PRONOUNCEMENT BY ABBA KOVNER

"Jewish youngster, do not trust those that deceive you. Of the eighty thousand Jews in 'The Jerusalem of Lithuania' [Vilna], only twenty thousand have survived. In front of our very eyes, they tore our parents, our brothers, our sisters from us.

Where are the hundreds of men who were abducted for labor by the Lithuanian 'kidnappers'?

Where are the naked women and the children who were taken away from us on the terrible night of the provocation?

Where are the Jews who were taken away on Yom Kippur [taken on that day]?

Where are our brethren from the second ghetto?

Whoever was taken out of the ghetto gates never returned again.

All the roads of the Gestapo lead to Ponary [the woods in the outskirts of Vilna where Jews were shot by the Einsatzgruppen]

And Ponary is death!…

Hitler is plotting to annihilate all the Jews of Europe. It befell the Jews of Lithuania to be the first in line.

Let us not go like sheep to the slaughter!

It's true, we are weak and defenseless, but the only response to the enemy is resistance!

Brothers! It is better to die as free fighters than to live at the mercy of murderers.

Resist! To our last breath."

ARMED RESISTANCE IN THE GHETTOS AND CAMPS

Resistance in the Ghettos

On January 18, 1943, German forces entered the Warsaw ghetto in order to arrest Jews and deport them. To their astonishment, young Jews offered them armed resistance and actually drove the German forces out of the ghetto before they were able to finish their ruthless task. This armed resistance came on the heels of the great deportation that had occurred in the summer and early autumn of 1942, which had resulted in the dispatch of 300,000 Jews, the vast majority of the ghetto's inhabitants to Nazi camps, almost all to the Treblinka extermination camp. About 60,000 Jews remained in the ghetto, traumatized by the deportations and believing that the Germans had not deported them and would not deport them since they wanted their labor. Two undergrounds led by youth activists, with several hundred members, coalesced between the end of the first wave of deportations and the events of January.

During four days in January, the Germans sought to round up Jews and the armed resistance continued. The ghetto inhabitants went through a swift change, no longer believing that their value as labor would safeguard them. With the news of the first incident of fighting they stopped responding to the Germans' calls that they come to the gathering point, known as the *Umschlagplatz*. They began devising hiding places, and the Germans had to enter many buildings and ruthlessly pull out Jews. Many were killed in their homes when they refused to be taken. On the fourth day, having only managed to seize between five and six thousand Jews, the Germans withdrew from the ghetto. The remaining inhabitants believed that the armed resistance combined with the difficulties in finding Jews in hiding, had led to the end of the *Aktion*. As a result, over the next months the armed undergrounds sought to strengthen themselves and the vast majority of ghetto residents and zealously built more and better bunkers in which to hide.

On the eve of Passover, April 19, 1943, German forces again entered the ghetto aiming to liquidate it. This time they were more prepared for resistance, but so were the two Jewish undergrounds and the ghetto population. Mostly with handguns, but also with a few rifles and many homemade Molotov Cocktails, several hundred young Jewish fighters who had no military training or battle experience confronted

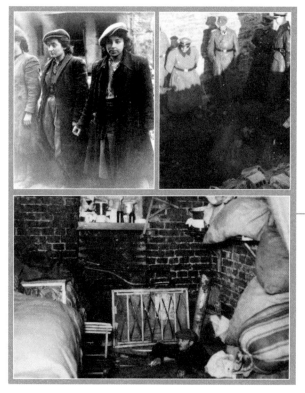

About Photos

Top Left: HeHalutz women captured with weapons during the Warsaw Ghetto Uprising. HeHalutz (The Pioneer) was an association of Jewish youth.

Top Right: Waffen SS soldiers locating Jews in dugouts. National Archives and Records Administration, College Park, 6003996

Bottom: A Jew inside a bunker used for hiding. National Archives and Records Administration

the German military force in pitched battles. In the hand-to-hand combat the Germans were not able to put down the rebellion, since many fighters managed to get away and retreat over the rooftops; nor could the Germans find the non-combatant Jews hiding in the bunkers.

Both sides sustained losses, but the ghetto fighters knew even before they had begun that they could not really defeat the powerful German forces. They fought primarily for the sake of offering resistance, for vengeance, and with the idea that the Germans should pay a heavy price for their lives. They did not believe the fighting could lead to mass rescue, but they did hope that some fighters and ghetto inhabitants might be able to escape from the convulsing ghetto and continue offering resistance as underground members and partisans.

A significant episode in the uprising was the so-called "battle for the flags" that took place in the northern ghetto on Muranowska Street. A group of fighters had managed to hoist two flags at the top of a high building on that street: the blue-and-white flag of the Zionists, and the white-and-red flag of Poland, which had been smuggled into the ghetto through the sewer system. The flags could be seen from outside the ghetto walls, and communiqués concerning them were communicated to the Polish underground and broadcast over Polish radio (certain sections of these communiqués were even picked up by *The New York Times*). The flags flying over the ghetto sparked the imagination and the enthusiasm of the local population—a grave affront to the Germans. The Germans understood this and made Muranowska Street a primary target, bringing in even heavier artillery and increasing manpower in order to take the flags down at any cost.

Yet the fighters were determined to do whatever it took not to give up the flags, which they continued to wave over the ghetto for almost four days. Finally, by Friday, April 23, 1943, after tanks and artillery had pounded the buildings on Muranowska Street to such an extent that the entire street shook, the flags ceased to wave, having been shot to pieces.

When the Germans understood they would be unable to make the Jews report for deportation as planned, they began systematically setting fire to the ghetto, turning it into a vast firetrap. The flames and the heat turned life in the bunkers into hell; the very air felt afire, the goods that had been stored spoiled, and the water was no longer fit to drink. Gradually, the Jews' ability to resist or hide declined. For almost a month the Jews of the Warsaw ghetto fought for their lives. Many of them perished in the fire and smoke; others were murdered in the ghetto streets; those who remained were sent to Treblinka, Majdanek, and other camps.

On May 16, 1943, Jurgen Stroop, the German commander of the forces ordered to put down the uprising, had the Great Synagogue on Tłomackie Street destroyed. After the building had been razed, he declared, "There is no longer a Jewish quarter in Warsaw," meaning

About Photos

During the Warsaw Ghetto Uprising, April–May, 1943, from left to right: Burning of blocks of dwellings during the suppression of the uprising, National Archives and Records Administration; Waffen SS soldier next to destroyed dwellings, National Archives and Records Administration; the ruins of the Great Synagogue on Tłomackie Street destroyed as a sign of the final suppression of the uprising.

About Photos

Left: German storm troopers force Jews of all ages in the Warsaw ghetto out of the bunkers during the Warsaw Ghetto Uprising in April–May, 1943.

Background photo: Waffen SS soldiers leading Jews captured during the suppression of the Warsaw Ghetto Uprising.

National Archives and Records Administration, College Park, 6003996

the Warsaw Ghetto Uprising had been quashed. Even after Stroop's declaration, sporadic resistance continued for a while and a few of the fighters and others did manage to flee by way of the sewer system; some went on to join the Polish underground and continued to battle the Germans.

In addition to the Warsaw Ghetto Uprising, in approximately one hundred other ghettos in Eastern Europe underground fighting organizations were formed. They came into being with goals similar to those of the Warsaw ghetto fighters, understanding they could not defeat the Nazis and to a large extent fighting for its own sake. Nevertheless, some undergrounds put more emphasis on various escape plans that would be implemented in the wake of the fighting. There were cases in which the fighting was spontaneous and others where it was more organized. In most cases, Jewish youth movements were deeply involved. In some places the planned armed resistance was never realized, owing to local conditions. Ultimately each ghetto has its own story. Among all of the ghetto uprisings, the Warsaw Ghetto Uprising was the largest, the longest, and the most influential.

Resistance in the Extermination Camps

The extreme terror of the Nazi camp system made any kind of organized resistance tremendously difficult. Nonetheless prisoners in a number of camps carried out organized acts of resistance. Most notably Jewish prisoners in three extermination camps, Treblinka, Sobibor, and Auschwitz-Birkenau rose up against their persecutors. This happened at a point when it was clear to them that they were destined to be murdered. In Treblinka and Sobibor, the goal was to facilitate escape; in Auschwitz-Birkenau the goal was to disrupt the process of murder.

The first of these uprisings was in Treblinka on August 2, 1943. Six hundred prisoners using mostly knives, clubs, and other "cold" weapons (weapons that do not involve fire or explosions) fell upon their guards and then broke out of the camp. Most of the rebels were killed immediately or very soon after they left the camp. Several dozen managed to escape. In Sobibor, on October 14, 1943, the fate of the fighters was very similar, although somewhat more managed to flee and hide or join the partisans nearby. In Auschwitz-Birkenau, on October 6 and 7, 1944, prisoners who were forced to work in the special unit in the gas chamber complex, the Sonderkommando, managed to blow up one of gas chambers, but they all fell in the ensuing battle. All of these uprisings were born of desperate situations, but nevertheless say much about the spark of humanity and dignity that remained alive among many prisoners even in the unyielding cruelty of the Nazi camps.

PERSONAL TESTIMONIES

"On July 28, 1942, a meeting of 'HeHalutz' was held. It was decided that a Jewish Fighting Organization would be established [...] however, the sum total of the ghetto's weapons at the time was only one pistol!"

From an interview with Marek Edelman, a Warsaw ghetto fighter[2]

Marek Edelman

"Then we collected weapons.

We smuggled it from the Aryan side (we took money by force from all kinds of institutions and private people)..."

Interviewer: How much would you pay for a pistol?

From three thousand to fifteen thousand. The closer to April, the more expensive: the demand in the market increased.

Interviewer: And how much did it cost to get a Jew to the Aryan side?

"Two thousand, five thousand. All kinds of prices. It depended on whether the person looked like a Jew, if he spoke with an accent, and if it was a man or a woman."

Interviewer: That means that for one pistol, it would have been possible to hide one, two or even three people for a month. If you had been offered the choice at that time: one pistol or the life of one person for a month...

"Such a choice was not offered. Perhaps it was even better that it was not offered."

From the last letter of Mordechai Anielewicz, smuggled from the Warsaw ghetto to the underground courier Antek Zuckerman[3]

Mordechai Anielewicz

"It is impossible to put into words what we have been through... I feel that great things are happening and what we dared do is of great, enormous importance... It is impossible to describe the conditions under which the Jews of the ghetto are now living. Only a few will be able to hold out. The remainder will die sooner or later. Their fate is decided. In almost all the hiding places in which thousands are concealing themselves it is not possible to light a candle for lack of air. With the aid of our transmitter we heard the marvelous report on our fighting by the *Shavit* radio station. The fact that we are remembered beyond the ghetto walls encourages us in our struggle. Peace go with you, my friend! Perhaps we may still meet again! The dream of my life has risen to become fact. Self-defense in the ghetto will have been a reality. Jewish armed resistance and revenge are facts. I have been a witness to the magnificent, heroic fighting of Jewish men in battle." —Mordechai Anielewicz, April 23, 1943

From the testimony of Zivia Lubetkin at the Eichmann Trial[4]

Zivia Lubetkin

"It is difficult for me to describe life in the ghetto during that week, and I had been in this ghetto for years. The Jews embraced and kissed each other; although it was clear to every single one that it was not certain whether he would remain alive, or it was almost certain that he would not survive, nevertheless that he had reached the day of our taking revenge, although no vengeance could fit our suffering. At least we were fighting for our lives, and this feeling lightened his suffering and possibly also made it easier for him to die.

I also remember that on the second day—it was the Passover Seder—in one of the bunkers by chance I came across Rabbi Meisel. There had been contacts between us and him, since the days of the Halutz underground in ordinary times as well. The Halutz underground, in its operations, had not always had an easy time on the part of the Jewish population—they did not always accept us. There were those who thought that we were bringing harm to their lives—as I have pointed out, the collective responsibility, the fear of the Germans. But this time, when I entered the bunker, this Jew, Rabbi Meisel, interrupted the Seder, placed his hand on my head and said: *May you be blessed. Now it is good for me to die. Would that we had done this earlier.*"

From the words of Zalman Gradowski, one of the fighters in the Auschwitz-Birkenau revolt[5]

"Dear finder, search every part of the ground. Buried in it are dozens of documents of others, and mine, which shed light on everything that happened here... As for us, we have already lost all hope...

...The future will judge us on the basis of this evidence. May the world understand some small part of the tragic world in which we lived." —Zalman Gradowski, September 6, 1944

NOTE: The revolt in Auschwitz-Birkenau attempted to put an end to the murder by disrupting the operation of the crematoria, and also to create a memory and a testimony to the tragedy of the lives and deaths of the hundreds of thousands of people who were killed in front of their eyes. After writing down and documenting the events, they buried them near the crematoria. This document was written by one of the organizers of the uprising.

From a 1968 interview with Yitzhak "Antek" Zuckerman on the 25th anniversary of the Warsaw Ghetto Uprising[6]

Yitzhak Zuckerman

"I don't think there's any real need to analyze the Uprising in military terms. This was a war of less than a thousand people against a mighty army and no one doubted how it was likely to turn out. This isn't a subject for study in a military school. Not the weapons, not the operations, not the tactics. If there's a school to study the human spirit, there it should be a major subject. The really important things were inherent in the force shown by Jewish youth, after years of degradation, to rise up against their destroyers, and determine what death they would choose: Treblinka or Uprising. I don't know if there's a standard to measure that."

End Notes

[1] Yitzhak Arad, Yisrael Gutman, and Avraham Margaliot, eds., *Documents on the Holocaust, Selected Sources on the Destruction of the Jews of Germany and Austria, Poland and the Soviet Union* (Jerusalem: Yad Vashem, 1981), 293–294.

[2] *Preceding God – An Interview with Marek Edelman of the Warsaw Ghetto Fighters*, trans. from Polish by Hanna Krall (Jerusalem: Adam Publishing House, 1981), 57.

[3] Supra note 1, at 315–316.

[4] *Attorney General* v. *Adolf Eichmann*, 36 I.L.R. 5 (Dist. Jerusalem 1961), aff'd, 36 I.L.R. 277 (S.Ct.1962) (Israel), Trial Transcript. Retrieved from nizkor.org/hweb/people/e/eichmann-adolf/transcripts/Sessions/Session-025-04.html.

[5] Ber Mark, *The Scrolls of Auschwitz*, ed. Isiah Avrech, trans. from Hebrew by Sharon Neemani; adapted from the Yiddish original text (Tel Aviv: Am Oved Publishing House, 1985), 205.

[6] Yitzhak ("Antek") Zuckerman, *A Surplus of Memory: Chronicle of the Warsaw Ghetto Uprising*, trans. from Hebrew by Barbara Harshav (Berkeley: University of California Press, 1993).

About Photo

Max Cohen in His Hiding Place, Haarlem, Holland, October 1942 (6044/9)

Yad Vashem Photo Archive

"Our vision in our church was that we always had to help those people in need...."

– Arie Van Mansum, Rescue and Aid Provider

Preparing to Use This Lesson

Below is information to keep in mind when using this lesson. In some cases, the points elaborate on general suggestions listed in the "Teaching about the Holocaust" section in the **Introduction** to this resource, and are specific to the content of the lesson. This material is intended to help teachers consider the complexities of teaching the Holocaust and to deliver accurate and sensitive instruction.

- It is important for students to understand that people like the ones they will learn about in this lesson were the exception rather than the rule. The Holocaust is a grim reminder of how indifference can become the norm. Reviewing rescue attempts in light of the millions of bystanders makes this lesson even more important to study.

- A rescuer might seem to students as a perfect person with "angelic" characteristics. This can cause students to feel distant from the rescuers' acts. Discuss with students that those individuals identified as "Righteous Among the Nations" (e.g., Oskar Schindler) were "normal" people with human faults even though they performed "righteous acts." In doing so, students can better relate to the rescuers and begin to see that ordinary people can perform extraordinary acts, and such actions can mean the difference between life and death.

- During the Holocaust, six million Jews were murdered, among them 1.5 million children. It is unknown how many people managed to survive through the situations described in this lesson, but it is known that they were only the fortunate few. While students want to relate to successful rescue attempts, they should be reminded that most attempts failed and the victim, and in some cases both the rescuer and the victim, were murdered when they were caught.

- Information about rescuers like the "Righteous Among the Nations" should be taught within the larger context of the Holocaust. Learning about rescuers without focusing on other aspects of the Holocaust might give students the impression that rescuers were the majority, when in fact they were a very small portion of the population.

Lesson 7 RESCUERS AND NON-JEWISH RESISTANCE

About This Lesson

⏱ 180–270 minutes

❖ **INTRODUCTION** This lesson provides students with an opportunity to learn about the types of rescue that occurred in Nazi-occupied Europe and to consider the moral and ethical choices that non-Jews made in order to help Jews survive. The lesson also outlines the obstacles and dangers that hidden children faced during the Holocaust. Throughout the lesson, students have an opportunity to consider the price of apathy and indifference in the face of injustice.

This three-part lesson has material appropriate for history, social studies, ethics, religion, Holocaust studies, and English/language arts classes. Instructional strategies include large-group discussion, brainstorming, analyzing and organizing information, reading for content, critical thinking, interpreting visual history testimony, and journaling.

❖ **OBJECTIVES** After completing this lesson, students will be able to:

- Name the various forms of assistance provided to Jews by non-Jews during the Holocaust.

- Analyze the motivations of non-Jewish rescuers in their efforts to help Jews survive during the Holocaust.

- Evaluate the moral and ethical choices individuals and groups made when deciding whether or not to help Jews.

- Identify the risks involved when non-Jews helped Jews hide or escape.

- Describe the obstacles and dangers that hidden children had to overcome in order to have a chance to survive.

- Discuss both the content and the messages in a clip of visual history testimony.

- Examine the price of apathy and indifference in the face of injustice.

RESOURCES & TESTIMONIES

All of the resources used in this lesson can be found in this guide at the end of this lesson and at echoesandreflections.org.

Visual history testimonies are available on the website or on the DVD that accompanies this resource guide.

Teachers are urged to review the lesson procedures to identify other materials and technology needed to implement the lesson.

L7

❖ **KEY WORDS & PHRASES**

Aktion	concentration camp	*Kristallnacht Pogrom*	"Righteous Among the Nations"
Allies	extermination camp	Nazi	Talmud
antisemitism	"Final Solution"	occupation	Theresienstadt
Aryan	Gestapo	Palestine	underground
Auschwitz-Birkenau	Holocaust	partisans	Vichy
bystander	Judaism	perpetrator	victim
collaboration	*Kindertransport*	resistance	Yad Vashem
Communism	Knesset		

❖ **ACADEMIC STANDARDS** The materials in this lesson address the following national education standards:

Common Core State Standards

- Reading Standards for Informational Text 6–12
- Writing Standards 6–12
- Speaking and Listening Standards 6–12
- Reading Standards for Literacy in History/Social Studies 6–12
- Writing Standards for Literacy in History/Social Studies 6–12

A complete analysis of how this lesson addresses Common Core State Standards by grade level and specific skills is available on the Echoes and Reflections website.

National Curriculum Standards for Social Studies

❷ Time, Continuity, and Change

❹ Individual Development and Identity

❺ Individuals, Groups, and Institutions

❻ Power, Authority, and Governance

❾ Global Connections

❿ Civic Ideals and Practices

Procedures

Part 1: Rescue and Aid Providers

1. Write the word "altruism" on the board. Have students brainstorm the meaning of the term and record their responses. Help students consider the following key elements of altruism if they are not offered during the brainstorming session:
   - directed toward helping another or others
   - involves a high degree of risk or sacrifice to the helper
   - no external reward
   - voluntary action

2. Introduce students to Arie Van Mansum and Leslie Banos and then show Part 1 of Visual History Testimony: *Rescuers and Non-Jewish Resistance*. Follow with a discussion using the questions below.
   - How does Arie Van Mansum say he became involved in helping to hide Jews?
   - To what does Arie attribute his willingness to help Jews during the Holocaust?
   - How does Leslie Banos say he got involved in the resistance movement?
   - What specific things did Leslie and his family do to help people?

TESTIMONY VIEWING

About the Interviewees

Arie Van Mansum was born on March 5, 1920, in Utrecht, Netherlands. He rescued roughly one hundred people, and as a result, eventually spent time in prison, including

continued on page 179

- To what does Leslie attribute his willingness to help Jews during the Holocaust?

- What risks did Arie and Leslie face once they decided to provide aid?

- Do Arie's and Leslie's actions fit the description of "altruism"? Explain your response.

3. On the board or on chart paper, draw a circle and put a "V" in the middle for "victim." Ask students to identify victims of the Holocaust. Draw a larger circle around the first circle and put a "P" for "perpetrator." Have students identify perpetrators during the Holocaust. Draw a third larger circle that intersects the first two and put a "B" for "bystander." Ask students to identify bystanders during the Holocaust. Have students study the diagram and discuss what happens to a bystander when he or she makes the decision to no longer be a bystander but to help the victim (i.e., he or she now also becomes a victim as in the case of Arie Van Mansum).

4. Ask students if deciding to take this risk of becoming a victim yourself is an example of altruism. Allow time for them to share their thinking and also discuss the following questions:

   - What are some possible reasons why people were altruistic during the Holocaust? (e.g., religious beliefs, personal experience, upbringing)

   - Why do you think most people remained indifferent to what was going on around them? (e.g., fear, not seeing others as part of them)

5. Distribute *Those Who Dared to Rescue*. As students read the handout, have them prepare a graphic organizer or make a list of the various forms of rescue by which non-Jews saved the lives of Jews during the Holocaust.

6. Have a large-group discussion reviewing the forms of rescue discussed in the handout. Have students brainstorm the qualities that would motivate people to help others at the risk of their own lives and possibly the lives of their families and friends. Use some or all of the questions below to guide the discussion.

   - Why would someone agree to hide another?

   - What could be the possible motivation for doing so?

   - Think about the terms "help" and "rescue." How, if at all, are these terms different?

   - In the context of the Holocaust, how do you understand the difference between these two terms? Can you think of a specific time when help was needed rather than rescue, and of times when Jews needed to be rescued?

   - What are the possible risks in trying to help someone?

   - What are the possible risks in trying to rescue someone?

   - What are some of the basic human needs that must have been provided by a rescuer to a victim?

About the Interviewees
continued from page 178

imprisonment in the Amersfoort concentration camp. His interview was conducted in Canada. When the war began, Arie was nineteen years old.

Leslie Banos was born on August 16, 1923, in Nyirbator, Hungary. He infiltrated the Nazi administration in Hungary, and along with his aunt and cousin, rescued and aided over sixty people. His interview was conducted in the United States. When the war began, Leslie was sixteen years old.

For additional information about Arie Van Mansum and Leslie Banos, see their Biographical Profiles available on the website.

L7

NOTE 2.7

Encourage students to visit annefrank.org/en/subsites/home/ for an online tour of the Secret Annex and additional information about the people who hid there and the people who helped them for more than two years.

- Would you characterize those individuals who helped Jews as heroes? Why or why not?

- Would you characterize those who rescued Jews as heroes? Why or why not?

7. Distribute *Anne Frank's Legacy,* and read together as a class. Continue the earlier discussion about rescuers, using some or all of the questions below.

- How did you feel reading Miep Gies's speech?

- What reasons did Miep give for helping to hide the Frank family?

- Would you characterize Miep as an altruistic person? Why or why not?

- What does the word "empathy" mean? How is "empathy" different from "sympathy"? [**Optional:** Have students look up the definitions of "empathy" and "sympathy" in a dictionary and share their findings.]

- What life experiences prior to meeting the Frank family prepared Miep to empathize with the Frank family's situation?

- How many people were involved in hiding the Frank family?

- Miep talks about how talking to Anne made her feel she was speaking to a "much older person." Where have you previously seen the idea that children grew up very quickly during the Holocaust? (e.g., Lesson 4: The Ghettos)

- Miep does not see herself as a hero; she says that those in hiding were the heroes. Do you agree with this? Explain your thinking.

- In paragraph three, Miep talks about "blaming the victim" for his or her own troubles. What does it mean to "blame the victim"? What are some contemporary examples of blaming the victim? (e.g., a woman out alone is "asking" to be raped, tourists on vacation "throwing a lot of money around" are "asking" to have their wallets or purses stolen)

- In the description given to us by Miep of the morning ritual, she describes the Jews standing silent. What does victimizing a person do to his or her self image? Why was Miep upset?

- Discuss Miep's statement, "Many children are told to mind their own business only. When those children become adults, they might look the other way if people ask for help." Do you think that parents and other significant adults (e.g., teachers, religious leaders) have a responsibility to teach children to act when they see injustice? What are some ways that adults might model this behavior?

- How does the Holocaust continue to serve as an example of the price of apathy and indifference to individuals and society?

- In addition to apathy, what else might have influenced the behavior and decisions of bystanders during the Holocaust?

Reflect and Respond

Either in class or as homework, have students reflect and respond to one or more of the topics below or have them develop a topic that has meaning for them based on the material covered in the lesson.

- Think about the people you met in Part 1 of this lesson—Leslie Banos, Arie Van Mansum, and Miep Gies. All of them see themselves as "ordinary" people and yet they all did extraordinary things. How might this be explained? Why do you think some people became rescuers during the Holocaust while most remained bystanders? What moral choices were made by rescuers during the Holocaust and what were the ongoing challenges they faced?

- Think about someone whom you would describe as a hero. Write about this person and identify the reasons why you would call him or her a hero. The person can be a public figure, a historical figure, or someone in your personal life.

Part 2: "Righteous Among the Nations"

1. Introduce students to Renee Scott, show Part 2 of Visual History Testimony: *Rescuers and Non-Jewish Resistance*, and discuss the following questions:

   - What does Renee Scott say she did to help rescue Jews?

   - How many false papers does Renee estimate were made each week at the Chamber of Commerce?

   - Why was what Renee did so dangerous?

2. Give students an introduction to the phrase "Righteous Among the Nations." Explain that in 1953, the Knesset (Israeli parliament) passed the Holocaust Martyrs' and Heroes' Remembrance Authority Law, which created Yad Vashem. Yad Vashem received the mandate to identify and recognize non-Jews who had risked their lives during the Holocaust to save Jews in countries that had been under Nazi rule or that had collaborated with the German regime. The historical account of the Holocaust would not be complete without the amazing stories of the "Righteous Among the Nations." Information about Yad Vashem can be found at the beginning of this guide and on the Echoes and Reflections website.

3. Tell students that a committee of judges discusses each and every person who is a candidate for becoming a "Righteous Among the Nations." Ask students to think about what the main criteria for receiving this designation might be and list their answers on the board or chart paper. Distribute *Yad Vashem Criteria for "Righteous Among the Nations"* and review together.

TESTIMONY VIEWING

About the Interviewee
Renee Scott was born on February 13, 1906, in Calais, France. While working for the Chamber of Commerce, she prepared and distributed false passports for Jews. Renee was arrested for her underground activities and transferred from prison to prison until she was eventually imprisoned in Ravensbrück concentration camp where she was selected for forced labor. Her interview was conducted in the United States. When the war began, Renee was thirty-three years old.

For additional information about Renee Scott, see her Biographical Profile available on the website.

L7

4. After reviewing the handout, allow time for students to share their observations about the material. If needed, use guiding questions like those below.

- Do you agree with the "Righteous Among the Nations" criteria? Why or why not?

- Is there something else that you expected to see in the criteria? If so, what?

- Did you think that the overall number of individuals identified as "Righteous Among the Nations" would be higher? Why or why not?

- Are you surprised by any of the information listed on the chart of "Righteous Among the Nations" by country? If so, what surprises you or what question/s does the information raise for you?

5. Distribute *Rescue in Denmark*. Direct the class to turn to the first page of the handout, and choose a volunteer to begin reading out loud. When the reader has finished reading the first paragraph, pause and ask the group:

- How was the situation for Danish Jews different from Jews in other German-occupied countries until 1943?

After reading the second, third, and fourth paragraphs, pause and ask the group:

- What event propelled the underground in Denmark to go into action?

- What made Helsingor (Elsinore) an ideal place for Jews to go if they wanted to escape Nazi-occupied territory?

After reading the fifth and sixth paragraphs, ask the group:

- Why might Ronne and Kior have been interested in helping the Jews?

- What reasons might they have had besides humanitarian ones?

After reading the seventh, eighth, and ninth paragraphs, ask the group:

- How did the underground keep the Jewish children from crying on the boats to Sweden?

- How many trips did the Elsinore Sewing Club take to Sweden?

- In addition to Jews, who else did the Elsinore Sewing Club rescue?

- What risks did the people who were involved with this "club" take when they agreed to help rescue Jews?

- How is the story of the rescue in Denmark unique?

- What kind of cultural and political systems should a nation create in order to be able to participate/organize such a moral action?

6. Close with a general discussion about why students think that some individuals and groups decided not to accept the bystander role during the Holocaust. Encourage them to reflect on ways that they and others that they know do and do not accept the role of bystanders in their school and communities.

Part 3: Hidden Children

1. Begin this part of the lesson by asking students to consider what it meant to hide during the Holocaust. Use the following questions to help guide the discussion:

- What were some of the problems that people in hiding had to face?

- How do you think people in hiding got food? What kind of food did they get?

- What threats did those in hiding face on a daily basis?

- What survival mechanisms did people use?

- How might adults in hiding cope differently than children? What emotions, challenges, or concerns might face an adult in hiding that would not apply to a child?

2. Introduce students to Kristine Keren, Ursula Levy, and Leslie Banos if his testimony was not shown earlier. Show students Part 3 of Visual History Testimony: *Rescuers and Non-Jewish Resistance* and have a discussion using the questions below.

- How long does Kristine Keren say she and her family hid in the sewers?

- What does Kristine say were some of the daily struggles that she and her family faced while hiding?

- Where does Ursula Levy say she and her brother were hidden?

- Why do you think Ursula's mother agreed to have her children baptized by the Catholic Church?

- How does Leslie's testimony provide insight into how difficult it was to hide Jews during the Holocaust?

- What does Leslie say his aunt did in order to feed the people they were hiding?

- After listening to the testimonies of Kristine, Ursula, and Leslie, what role do you think trust played in the experiences of those in hiding?

- How difficult do you think it was for those in hiding to trust anyone?

- What feelings do you have after listening to these testimonies?

3. Have each student complete a "Minute Paper" assessment by responding to the question: What will you remember most from this lesson and why? Instruct students to submit their responses to you before leaving class or, if time permits, have students discuss how they responded to the question with a partner.

Reflect and Respond

Either in class or as homework, have students reflect and respond to one or more of the topics below or have them develop a topic that has meaning for them based on the material covered in the lesson.

- Write a letter to someone that you learned about in this lesson. Tell the person what you are thinking and feeling after learning about his/her experiences.

- Reflect on the meaning of the statement from the Talmud, "He who saves one life, it is as though he has preserved the existence of the entire world."

- Write about a time when you made a conscious decision to help someone in a difficult situation or about a time when someone came forward to help you. Describe the event in detail and tell how you felt during the situation. What were some of the

L7

NOTE 3.2

Encourage students interested in learning more about Kristen Keren's story to read *The Girl in the Green Sweater: A Life in Holocaust's Shadow* written under the name Krystyna Chiger (St. Martin's Press, 2008).

complications or difficulties that you faced? Were there any moral or ethical dilemmas that needed to be addressed? What were your feelings after the situation ended?

Making Connections

The additional activities and projects listed below can be integrated directly into the lesson or can be used to extend the lesson once it has been completed. The topics lend themselves to students' continued study of the Holocaust as well as opportunities for students to make meaningful connections to other people and events, including relevant contemporary issues. These activities may include instructional strategies and techniques and/or address academic standards in addition to those that were identified for the lesson.

1. Visit IWitness (iwitness.usc.edu) for activities specific to Lesson 7: Rescuers and Non-Jewish Resistance.

2. Have half the class read *Anne Frank: The Diary of a Young Girl* (Anchor Books, 1996) and the other half of the class read Miep Gies's *Anne Frank Remembered: The Story of the Woman Who Helped to Hide the Frank Family* (Touchstone, 1988). Have students work in pairs or small groups to develop graphic organizers comparing and contrasting the experiences of Anne Frank and Miep Gies. Encourage students to refer to the **Timeline** available on the website to understand the events that they are reading about within a larger context.

3. Divide the class into pairs of students. Assign each pair one of the names on the *Selected List of "Righteous Among the Nations"* available on the website in the **Additional Resources** section of the **Lesson Components**. Instruct students to research the individual or group and prepare a presentation for the class using one of the formats suggested below or another format of their choice. Among other resources, encourage students to access Yad Vashem's database of the "Righteous Among the Nations." A link to this resource is available in the **Additional Resources** section of the **Lesson Components**.

   • Create an illustrated storyboard of the person's (or group's) rescue actions.

   • Prepare a dialogue between the rescuer and a person who was rescued.

   • Create a collage that represents this person (or group) and his/her/their actions.

   • Write an article that praises the accomplishments of the rescuer.

   Have students present their research projects to the class. At the end of each presentation, ask the class to consider whether the Yad Vashem committee made a good choice in selecting this person or group and give reasons why or why not.

4. Share with students the brief introduction to the *Kindertransport* on the following page. After they have heard or read the introduction, have students work in small groups to generate a list of questions that they still have about this rescue effort. If needed, share a few sample questions with students: How old were the children? How were the children selected? Why did the transports stop in 1940? Where did the children go once they arrived in Great Britain?

   After groups have completed their list of questions, instruct them to organize the questions into sub-topics and then decide who will research the answers to each set of questions. Have students find the answers to the questions using multiple print and digital sources and develop a PowerPoint, written report, or multimedia report to present their findings. Share presentations on the class website or wiki. Students may want to listen to Henry Laurant's (Lesson 2: Antisemitism) testimony available on IWitness and YouTube as he recounts his *Kindertransport* experience or watch *Into the Arms of Strangers: Stories of the Kindertransport* (2000) as part of their research.

Introduction to the *Kindertransport* Following the *Kristallnacht Pogrom* in November 1938, the British government, under increased public pressure and persistent efforts by refuge aid committees, agreed to permit an unspecified number of children to enter Great Britain from Germany and German-annexed territories. The rescue operation brought about 9,000–10,000 children, some 7,500 of them Jewish, from Germany, Austria, Czechoslovakia, and Poland to Great Britain between 1938 and 1940. The informal name for this series of rescue efforts was *Kindertransport* (Children's Transport). Many of the children eventually became citizens of Great Britain, or emigrated to Israel, the United States, Canada, and Australia. Most of these children would never again see their parents, who were murdered during the Holocaust.

5.   Using an online map creator (e.g., ZeeMap, Click2Map, StepMap), have students create their own interactive maps representing the material outlined on the handout *Yad Vashem Criteria for "Righteous Among the Nations."* Maps should indicate those countries where individuals have been awarded this recognition as well as how many people/groups have been identified as "Righteous Among the Nations" per country.

L7

THOSE WHO DARED TO RESCUE

"In those times there was darkness everywhere. In heaven and on earth, all the gates of compassion seemed to have been closed. The killer killed and the Jews died and the outside world adopted an attitude either of complicity or of indifference. Only a few had the courage to care. These few men and women were vulnerable, afraid, helpless–what made them different from their fellow citizens?"[1]

Rescue of Jews by non-Jews was the exception rather than the rule during the Holocaust. Most people never considered helping Jews. The brutal repression of those who helped and fear of such repression, the culture of conformity, the prevailing atmosphere of antisemitism, and in many times and places, the profound suffering engendered by the war, all contributed to an attitude of caring only for "me and mine" and the general abandonment of the Jews to their fate. Nevertheless, it is estimated that out of nine million Jews under Nazi domination, tens of thousands were rescued during the Holocaust by non-Jewish people.

Many rescuers acted out of a sense of altruism, that is, an unselfish desire to help those who were being persecuted. Some performed acts of heroism based upon deeply held religious beliefs or moral codes; others acted in the spur of the moment, offering help to someone they had never seen before as soon as they realized the person was in need. Yet others acted out of loyalty to people with whom they had developed close personal ties. If caught by the Nazis, those who attempted to provide aide to Jews were sent to prisons or concentration camps or immediately executed, depending on the country in which they lived. Rescue put both the immediate family and sometimes even the entire community of the rescuer in peril. Some rescuers survived with their charges until the end of the war, only to be murdered by their neighbors for having had the audacity to help Jews.

To date, over 25,000 non Jews have been recognized by Yad Vashem as "Righteous Among the Nations"—people who chose to rescue Jews with great risk to themselves. Following are a few of their stories.

A very significant rescue group—*Zegota*—was formed in occupied Poland. Zegota took care of thousands of Jews who were trying to survive in hiding, The group sought to find safe hiding places, and helped pay for the upkeep and medical care of the Jews being hidden, despite the death penalty imposed on Poles who aided Jews. In particular, *Zegota* successfully placed thousands of Jewish children in safe houses, orphanages, and convents. One of its main activists was Irena Sendler, a young social worker, who at great personal danger, devised means to enter the ghetto and help the sick and dying Jews. She managed to obtain a permit from the municipality that enabled her to enter the ghetto, allegedly to inspect the sanitary conditions. Once inside, she established contact with activists of the Jewish welfare organization and began to assist them in their work. She helped smuggle Jews out of the ghetto to the "Aryan side "and helped set up hiding places for them. After the Warsaw ghetto was destroyed, Sendler was appointed director of *Zegota*'s Department for the Care of Jewish Children. Sendler, whose underground name was "Jolanta," exploited her contacts with orphanages and institutes for abandoned children to find refuge for Jewish children, telling the institutions that they were Christian. She rescued many hundreds of children and made a great

---

[1]Elie Wiesel, in Carol Rittner and Sandra Meyers, *Courage to Care - Rescuers of Jews during the Holocaust* (New York University Press, 1986), 2.

Famous Diplomats to Rescue Jews

Raoul Wallenberg

Chiune-Sempo Sugihara

Sousa Mendes

effort to keep a record of their true identity.

Some rescuers were diplomats who took the initiative to issue thousands of visas and letters of protection that allowed Jews to immigrate to other countries or enjoy diplomatic protection until immigration became possible. Among the most famous of these were Raoul Wallenberg, Chiune-Sempo Sugihara, and Sousa Mendes from Sweden, Japan, and Portugal respectively.

After Germany invaded France in 1940, American journalist, Varian Fry, was sent by a private American relief organization to help prominent anti-Nazi refugees who were in danger of being arrested by the Gestapo, among them many Jews. Fry's network forged documents, used black-market funds, and created secret escape routes. Artists Marc Chagall and Marcel Duchamp, and political scientist Hannah Arendt were among the famous cultural figures he helped. In September 1941, Fry was expelled from France because his activities angered both the US State Department and the Vichy government.

Oskar Schindler was a businessman and a member of the Nazi Party. He took over a factory formerly owned by Jews outside of Krakow, Poland. At one point he began protecting his Jewish employees from deportation and death by creating a list of workers "essential" to the German war effort and paying the Nazis money for each person on the list. As time passed he took on more employees with the idea of bringing them under his protection. Schindler is an example of an individual who made a dramatic personal change during the course of the war. At the beginning, he was an opportunist who succeeded in making money by exploiting Jews. Once he realized that the Nazis were deporting Jews to murder them, he decided to risk all he had in order to save the Jews he had once exploited.

Moshe Bejsky, one of the Jews saved by Schindler, said after the war: "Schindler was the first German since the beginning of the war that did not fill me with fear... Here is the man who not only managed to save 1,200 people, but who over the years was able to listen and to solve thousands of daily problems that our lives depended on."

Some Jews were saved when they were hidden by non-Jews in and around their homes. Hiding places included attics, cellars, barns, underground bunkers, and even dog houses were used as hiding places for weeks and months. Some Catholic and Protestant clergy hid Jews in churches, orphanages, and convents. In France, the Protestant population of the small village of Le Chambon-sur-Lignon led by Pastor Andre Trocme sheltered several thousand Jews. When the local French authorities demanded that the pastor ceases his activities, his response was clear-cut: "... I do not know what a Jew is. I know only human beings."

Hiding Jews in towns, cities, and on farms required extreme caution. Because of food rationing, feeding extra people was not only difficult, but dangerous since obtaining food beyond the normal

L7

ration was highly suspicious. Getting medical care for ill people also entailed many risks. Anything that looked questionable could lead to neighbors reporting to the authorities and the discovery of hiding places and their inhabitants.

Dr. Giovanni Pesante and his wife Angelica, from Trieste, Italy, hid Hemda, their daughter's Jewish friend, for over a year .When one day Hemda suggested that she leave so as not to jeopardize them, Dr. Pesante said to her," I beg you to stay with us for my sake, not yours. If you leave I will forever be ashamed to be part of the human race."

Jozef Ulma was a farmer who lived with his wife Wiktoria and their six young children in the small town of Markowa, Poland. In the fall of 1942, while the hunt for Jews was going on in the entire area, a Jewish family by the name of Szall came to Markowa to find shelter. When they asked Jozef and Wiktoria to hide them, the couple agreed, and took them in along with two Jewish sisters. Although the Ulma house was at the outskirts of the town, the Jews' presence on the farm was soon discovered. During the night of March 23/24, 1944, German police came to Markowa. They found the Szall family on the Ulma farm and shot them to death. Afterwards they murdered the entire Ulma family: Jozef; Wiktoria, who was seven month pregnant; and their six small children— Stanislawa, Barbara, Wladyslawa, Franciszka, Maria, and Antoni. The eldest of the Ulma children had just begun to attend classes in primary school.

Among the rescuers were those who agreed to adopt Jewish children and raise them as their own. This involved falsifying identification papers to prove that the child had been born into the host family. To protect the children and their host families, the children had to take on the lifestyle and church-going habits of their new families. After the war, some children were lucky to be rejoined to surviving family members, and others were found by representatives of Jewish organizations and returned to Judaism. Some hidden children who were never found, remained in the hands of their rescuers as Christians, and the youngest among them never learned their true identity.

A select group of non-Jews did not engage in rescue directly on the scene, but instead tried desperately to draw attention to Nazi activities to exterminate Jews. Jan Karski, a member of the Polish underground, met with Jewish leaders in the Warsaw ghetto, visited the Izbica ghetto and reported personally to Allied leaders, including President Franklin D. Roosevelt. Although his report did not lead to direct and concerted action, it was important in changing the attitude in the Western world and contributed to various rescue initiatives that came into being toward the end of the war.

The rescuers came from all backgrounds. Scholars have not been able to identify a common thread. They were men and women, young and old, rich and poor, peasants and intellectuals, devout Christians and atheists, Socialists and conservatives. When asked, almost all of them responded that they did not think of themselves as heroes. Many explained themselves saying to the effect: "What I have done is what I should have done."

Yad Vashem has conferred the honor of "Righteous Among the Nations" upon over 25,000 individuals. The process of recognition is ongoing, and each year hundreds of additional stories are verified and the honor granted. Undoubtedly there are many stories that will never be discovered since there are those who tried to rescue Jews but failed and perished along with those they were trying to help. In many of their testimonies and memoirs, Jewish survivors attest to the fact that they received help from more than one individual, even though they may not always remember all them. So for this reason too, we can assume that there are more rescuers than history can recall.

What is known, however, is that among the hundreds of millions of people living under Nazi domination at the time, only a select few took profound risks to rescue Jews. The light of their deeds shines forth through the overwhelming darkness of the war years.

ANNE FRANK'S LEGACY
Miep Gies

Miep Gies helped hide Anne Frank and her family for more than two years (1942–1944) during World War II. It was she who found and saved Anne's diary after the Franks were captured by the Nazis. On March 8, 1972, Yad Vashem recognized Jan Augustus Gies and his wife, Hermine (Miep) Gies-Santrouschitz, as "Righteous Among the Nations." This article is adapted from a speech Miep Gies delivered in June, 1996 in Washington, DC after receiving a lifetime achievement award from the Anti-Defamation League. Miep Gies died in January 2010 at the age of 100.

Ladies and gentlemen, I feel deeply moved and honored by the award you gave me, but I sincerely wonder whether I should be the one to receive it. I like to think that I stand here for Anne and all other victims of the Holocaust. In their name, I thank you very much. People often ask where I found the courage to help the Frank family. Yes, it certainly takes some courage, some discipline and also some sacrifice to do your human duty. But that is true for so many things in life! Therefore, this question surprises me, because I simply cannot think of doing anything else.

So why do people ask this question? Step by step I started to understand that many people wonder why they should assist other people, because when we are young most of us are told that if we behave all right, life will work out fine for us. So, if people have a problem, they must have made a big mistake. Why should we then help them? I, however, helped because I don't believe that people in trouble did something wrong. I knew that from my own life.

I was born in Vienna and grew up during the First World War; a war that was lost by Austria. My mother told me that I had always been a good girl, at home and at school. However, I remember that at the age of nine I did not get enough to eat; I still feel the pain of being hungry. I also remember the shock that I had to leave my home in Vienna and go to Holland in order to recover from tuberculosis. Did I deserve to be that sick? No, I had not done anything wrong. Therefore, although very young, I knew

About Photos

Left: Anne Frank, Amsterdam, Holland. Yad Vashem Photo Archive (b1592/65)

Right: Miep Gies, 1987. Courtesy of Rob Bogaerts/ Nationaal Archief

that you can be in trouble, without this being your own fault. From this I learned that I should help victims and not blame them! I felt the same to be true for the Frank family. So, whatever others would think or say, I *had* to help!

I had also another reason to do so. Many children are told to mind their own business only. When those children become adults, they might look the other way if people ask for help. However, I myself lived in Holland with very social-minded foster parents. They had already five children themselves and had to live on a small salary, but still took me—a very sick child—into their home. Whatever they had, they would always share that with others. It made a deep impression on me. It made me feel, I should do the same in my life. Many children will live and express themselves the same way

L7

their parents and teachers do. For instance, if children hear their parents and teachers speak about *the Asians, the Blacks, the whites, the Jews, the Arabs,* whatever, they most likely will begin to believe that *all* Asians, or *all* Blacks, or *all* whites, or *all* Jews or *all* Arabs act the same. It makes them blame the *whole* group, if one of its members commits a crime. Imagine if this would happen to us, because in our own group of people are criminals too!

Once, in Germany, most children were never told that they should always look at somebody else as an individual. Instead, many Germans used to talk about *the Jews.* Hitler knew that many believe that those who come from another country or have another color of skin cause all problems. Therefore Hitler promised that he would make Germany a country for "Aryans" only and that was exactly what many Germans wanted to hear.

Hitler also did other things that pleased Germans. At the time Anne Frank was born, Germany was in deep trouble and very poor. Hitler knew that people in trouble often like to blame others, even if it is their own mistake. So, Hitler offered *the Jew* as scapegoat, which millions of Germans gladly accepted. And that was the way Hitler got the help he needed to kill six million innocent Jews.

We should explain to children that caring about our own business only can be very wrong. When in Germany, step by step, Jewish life was destroyed, most people, all over the world, looked the other way, because they thought that it was safer to stay out. However, during the Holocaust, not only did six million Jews die, *but ten times that number of non-Jews as well.* Not only Jews lost what they had, but others lost billions and billions too. This proves that if injustice happens to your neighbor, there is no guarantee that it will not come to your home, that it will stop at your doorstep! Therefore, we should *never* be bystanders, because, as we have seen 50 years ago, that can be very dangerous for ourselves as well!

I feel very strongly that we cannot wait for others to make this world a better place. *No, we*

ourselves should make this happen now in our own homes and schools by carefully evaluating the manner in which we speak and by closely examining the ways we form and express our opinions about other people, particularly in the presence of children. We should never forget the victims of the Holocaust. I myself think of the family Frank, the family van Daan and the dentist Dussel. Van Daan and Dussel were the names Anne gave them; their true names were van Pels and Pfeiffer. Also, the helpers got other names from Anne, except for me! Why did she decide to use my own name? The answer I will never receive, but it touches me very much. She probably felt too close to me to alter my name.

Together with Jan, my husband, we were a total of five helpers. We all had our own tasks. In the morning I had to enter the hiding place to pick up the shopping list. When I came in, nobody would speak, just stand in line and wait for me to begin. This was always an awful moment for me, because it showed that these fine people felt so dependent on us, the helpers. They would silently look up to me, except for Anne, who, in a cheerful tone, used to say, "Hello Miep, what is the news?" Her mother disliked this very strongly and I knew that the other people in hiding would afterward blame Otto for what they would call, "proof of a too liberal upbringing!" What struck me most about Anne was her curiosity. She always asked me about everything that went on outside and not only that! She knew that I had just married and therefore she hoped that I would tell her more about being so close with another person. Well, I did not yield to that and that must have disappointed her. However, usually I shared all my information with her.

Anne felt very strongly about her privacy, which I discovered when I once entered the room where she was writing her diary. From her eyes I saw that she was angry; maybe she thought I was spying on her, which was not true, of course. At that moment her mother came in and said, when she noticed this tense situation: "Oh, Miep you should know that our daughter keeps a diary." As if I did not know that: I was the one who always gave her the paper. Anne closed her diary with a bang, lifted up her head, looked at me, and said, "Yes, and about you I am writing, too." Then she left, slamming the door behind her. I hurried back to my office, quite upset.

However, usually Anne was a friendly and a very charming girl. I say *girl,* but talking to her gave me the surprising feeling of speaking to a much older person. No wonder, since the situation made Anne grow very quickly from child to young adult. I did not pay much attention to this, because there were all the other things, like my daily care for 11 people: my husband and I, eight in the attic and also a non-Jewish student, wanted by the Germans, who we were hiding in our home. Otto Frank did not know about this student. He would have forbidden it. "You take too much risk, Miep," he would have said.

The children-in-hiding had a hard time. They missed so much. They could not play outdoors and could not meet with friends. They could hardly move. We did all that was possible to help them, but freedom we could not give them. This was one of the most painful things for me.

Every year on the fourth of August, I close the curtains of my home and do not answer the doorbell and the telephone. It is the day that my Jewish friends were taken away. I have never overcome that shock. I loved and admired them so much. During two years eight people had to live together in a very small place. They had little food and were not allowed to go out. They could not speak to their friends and family. On top of that came the fear, every hour of the day. I have no words to describe these people who were still always friendly and grateful. Yes, I do have a word: *They were heroes, true heroes!*

People sometimes call me a hero. I don't like it, because people should never think that you have to be a very special person to help those who need you! I myself am just a very common person. I simply had no choice, because I could foresee many, many sleepless nights and a life filled with regret, if I refused to help the Franks. And this was not the kind of life I was looking forward to. Yes, I have wept countless times when I have thought of my dear friends, but I am happy that these were not tears of remorse for refusing to help. *Remorse can be worse than losing your life.*

I could not save Anne's life, but I could help her live another two years. In those two years she wrote her diary, in which millions of people find hope and inspiration. I am also grateful that I could save this wonderful diary. When I found it, lying all over the floor in the hiding place, I decided to stow it away, in order to give it back to Anne when she would return. I wanted to see her smile and her say, "Oh, Miep, my diary!" But after a terrible time of waiting and hoping, word came that Anne had died. At that moment I went to Otto Frank, Anne's father, the only one of the family who had survived, and gave him Anne's diary. "This is what Anne has left," I said to him. "These are her words." Can you see how this man looked at me? He had lost his wife and two children, but he *had* Anne's diary. It was a very, very moving moment.

Again, I *could not* save Anne's life. However, I *did* save her diary, and by that I could help her most important dream come true. In her diary she tells us that she wants to live on after her death. Now, her diary makes her *really* live on, in a most powerful way! And that helps me in those many hours of deep grief. It also shows us that even if helping may fail to achieve everything, it is better to try than to do nothing.

This article first appeared in *Dimensions: A Journal of Holocaust Studies* 11(1). © 1997 Anti-Defamation League. All rights reserved.

L7

YAD VASHEM CRITERIA FOR "RIGHTEOUS AMONG THE NATIONS"

Criteria

The criteria for awarding the honor "Righteous Among the Nations," determined by the public committee of Yad Vashem, are as follows:

- An attempt that included the active involvement of the rescuer to save a Jew regardless of whether the attempt(s) ended in success or failure

- Acknowledged mortal risk to the rescuer during the endeavor—during the Nazi regime, the warnings clearly stated that whoever extended a hand to assist Jews placed not only their own life at risk, but also the lives of their loved ones

- Humanitarian motives as the primary incentive—the rescuer must not have received material compensation as a condition of their actions

- There must be testimonial support by the rescued person or archival material concerning the deed

"Righteous Among the Nations"

per country as of January 1, 2016*

Poland	6,620	Moldova	79	China	2
Netherlands**	5,516	Albania	75	Brazil	2
France	3,925	Norway	62	Indonesia	2
Ukraine	2,544	Romania	60	Ireland	1
Belgium	1,707	Switzerland	47	Egypt	1
Lithuania	889	Bosnia	42	Peru	1
Hungary	837	Armenia	24	Chile	1
Italy	671	Denmark**	22	Japan	1
Belarus	618	Great Britain (inc. Scotland)	21	Luxembourg	1
Germany	587			Turkey	1
Slovakia	558	Bulgaria	20	Georgia	1
Greece	328	Sweden	10	Montenegro	1
Russia	197	Macedonia	10	Vietnam	1
Serbia	135	Slovenia	7	El Salvador	1
Latvia	135	Spain	7	Cuba	1
Czech Republic	115	USA	5	Ecuador	1
Croatia	115	Estonia	3	**Total Persons**	**26,119**
Austria	106	Portugal	3		

*These figures are not an indication of the actual number of Jews saved in each country, but reflect material on rescue operations made available to Yad Vashem.

**Includes two persons originally from Indonesia, but residing in the Netherlands.

***The Danish Underground requested that all its members who participated in the rescue of the Jewish community not be listed individually, but as one group.

RESCUE IN DENMARK

The Occupation of Denmark

Christian X
King of Denmark

In Denmark, a country located immediately to the north of Germany, the population was able to lead an unusually normal existence in comparison to other countries in Nazi-dominated Europe, until 1943. The Nazis considered the Danes to be "racially kindred" and followed a policy of trying to convince them to become willing allies of Nazi Germany. Because of this and the fact that the Danish armed forces did not oppose the Nazi occupation in April 1940, the German occupiers permitted Denmark to maintain her own government and allowed an unusual amount of freedom. This freedom enabled Danish society to maintain prewar democratic values including respect for the rights of all citizens. The Germans refrained from pressuring the Danes to act against the Jews, since they thought it would hurt their efforts to win them over to the support of Nazi Germany. Some Danes were won over by the Nazis, even joining SS fighting formations; however, many Danes withstood Nazi efforts.

The Deportation

In spring 1943, with the war more clearly turning against Nazi Germany, anti-Nazi feeling and actions in Denmark became more pronounced. The senior representative of Germany in Denmark, Werner Best, began retreating from the policy of winning over the Danes, and as such in the autumn, he decided it was time to deport the Jews and received permission from Berlin to do so. Just as the deportations were to begin, Best got "cold feet" when he began to think that it might be possible to revive the more lenient policies toward the Danes. Since he could not retract the order for deportations that had been authorized in Berlin, he decided to disrupt the deportations in another way. Essentially he looked for a way to rid Denmark of its Jews without alienating the Danes. So, Best allowed information about the deportations to be leaked ahead of time to the Danish underground.

He let it be known that secret plans had been made for a massive roundup of the 8,000 Jews in the country to take place on the night of October 1–2. Thanks to the loyalty and humanity of a few prominent Danes, the head of the Jewish community was warned about the upcoming Aktion. On September 29, when Denmark's Jews assembled in their synagogue for Rosh Hashanah (Jewish New Year) services, they were given the bad news.

Rescue

Immediately, the Danish underground swung into action. People from all walks of life pulled together and participated in a massive rescue operation. Within a few hours, virtually all of the Jews of Copenhagen, the capital of Denmark and the country's largest Jewish community, were spirited out of their homes, hidden, and then taken in small groups to fishing ports. The Danish fishing fleet was quickly mobilized to ferry them to safety across the water to Sweden. On October 1, when the Germans began their planned roundup, moving from house to house with prepared lists of victims, their knocks went mostly unanswered. All in all, 7,200 Jews were saved.

One incredible story of courage and rescue took place in Elsinore (Helsingor), on the northern coast of Denmark, located only two and one-half miles across the sound from Sweden. Elsinore has always been renowned for its castles and its beautiful vistas, but in 1943, because of a bookbinder, a reporter, a detective, a bookkeeper, and a physician, it became the site where one of Denmark's most effective underground resistance efforts took place.

When the Germans decided to implement the "Final Solution" in Denmark, a newspaper reporter named Borge Ronne was in Elsinore, walking past a friend's house. He noticed ten strangers leap out of two taxicabs and run into a garage that was attached to his friend's house. Ronne immediately rang the doorbell and told his friend what he had seen. "It's all right," was the explanation. "They're Jews who have come to Elsinore to escape the Nazi roundup."

This was the first that Ronne had heard of Jewish persecution, and it got him thinking. A few hours later, he bumped into Erling Kior, an acquaintance of his. Kior was deeply upset by a random shooting by German soldiers that had taken place the night before in his neighborhood. Ronne passed on to Kior the news he had learned about the raids to arrest Jews, and the rescue efforts that had been going on in Elsinore. "How about helping the Jews to get across to neutral Sweden?" asked Ronne. "It would be one way of getting back at the Germans." That meeting was the beginning of the Elsinore group. Ronne and Kior, knowing that they needed additional members, contacted Thormod Larsen, a Danish police officer. They felt that Larsen would be particularly valuable to them because he had access to confidential reports about refugees, underground groups, and Nazi plans in Denmark. For additional assistance, Larsen enlisted the aid of Ova Bruhn. Fishermen were contacted who agreed to cooperate.

Their one concern regarded the transporting of Jewish children. The fishermen knew that if the children cried during their dangerous voyage to Sweden, they would all be in jeopardy. To answer the concerns of the fishermen, Ronne and Kior approached Dr. Jorgen Gersfelt, a physician who practiced in a nearby fishing village. Gersfelt agreed to help them, using sedatives to keep the children quiet during transport.

They called themselves "The Elsinore Sewing Club." Using fishing boats, speedboats, and other means of transportation, the Elsinore Sewing Club made as many as ten trips to Sweden every day. Thanks to these five brave Danes, there was a steady stream of Jews going from Elsinore to Sweden, saving the lives of thousands of Jews. After most of the Jewish refugees were safe in Sweden, the

About Photos

From left to right: Members of the resistance movement in fight with German soldiers, 1945. Courtesy of The National Museum of Denmark; Fishermen aboard the Marie which made about 10 trips to Sweden during the rescue of Danish Jews, 1943. Courtesy of The National Museum of Denmark; Danish Jews being smuggled by ship to Sweden. Courtesy of Yad Vashem.

Elsinore Sewing Club continued its transportation activities, ferrying to safety non-Jewish political resisters and English and American airmen who had been shot down over Denmark while flying bombing missions over Germany. It's important to note that most of the fishermen were paid; however, in no case were people left behind because they were unable to pay.

Despite threats, close calls, and raids by the Gestapo, the Elsinore Sewing Club continued its rescue efforts. By the middle of 1944, Thormod Larsen had been critically shot by the Nazis, Borge Ronne had to flee to Sweden to save his own life, Erling Kior had been captured and was a prisoner in the Porta Westfalica concentration camp, and Dr. Gersfelt was forced into hiding with his wife. Only then did the work of the Elsinore Sewing Club come to an end. In the end, only 500 Danish Jews were deported to the Theresienstadt ghetto, where Danish members of the International Red Cross later visited them. These Jews were never sent to extermination camps, and on April 15, 1945, the Danish Jews were released to the Red Cross and returned to Denmark. About 450 Danish Jews survived Theresienstadt.

L7

About Photo

A Former Inmate near Barracks in the Camp, Bergen-Belsen, 1945 (146 FO 3)

Yad Vashem Photo Archive

"We are free, but how will we live our lives without our families?"

– Anton Mason, Jewish Survivor

Preparing to Use This Lesson

Below is information to keep in mind when using this lesson. In some cases, the points elaborate on general suggestions listed in the "Teaching about the Holocaust" section in the Introduction to this resource, and are specific to the content of the lesson. This material is intended to help teachers consider the complexities of teaching the Holocaust and to deliver accurate and sensitive instruction.

- On May 8, 1945, Nazi Germany's unconditional surrender became official, and Europe was liberated from Nazi rule. The offensives that ultimately defeated the German forces began on the Eastern Front in March 1944 and on the Western Front with D-Day in June 1944; these offensives lasted about one year. As the war was nearing its end, Europe was in complete chaos. Many cities, towns, and villages had been destroyed completely or in part. Multitudes had fled in the face of the fighting, including when possible, those persecuted by the Germans and their partners. Allied troops moving across Europe encountered forced labor camps, concentration camps, extermination camps, and mass graves. While liberation of the Jews was not the primary objective of the Allies, troops did free prisoners, provided food and medical care when possible, and collected evidence for war crimes trials.

- The Allies did not anticipate the enormity of the human challenge that liberation would pose. Essentially the Soviet forces liberated camp inmates and after some initial aid, left them on their own. Over time, the Western Allies set up agencies and a system of displaced persons' camps in which liberated prisoners and the multitudes of displaced people—those who had lost their homes and become refugees—were given shelter and were helped.

- The personal condition of most Holocaust survivors was appalling after all they had endured. Individuals were in need of physical and emotional rehabilitation. It was only after they became stronger that they began to confront the loss of their families and former lives, and began thinking about how to build new lives. This entailed many decisions about where to go and what to do. A primary concern was to find surviving family members. On their own or with the help of organizations like the Red Cross and the United Nations Relief and Rehabilitation Administration (UNRRA), they embarked on their searches. Along with the occupation authorities, these organizations also sought to aid them on a daily basis and to ensure their physical well-being. A common tendency among survivors was that many married and soon thereafter had children. The remnants of European Jewry—hundreds of thousands of broken men and women who had been uprooted from their homes and their former lives—began the long and difficult process of rehabilitating themselves and rebuilding their lives. The period following liberation is often referred to as "Return to Life" or "Returning to Life."

Lesson 8 SURVIVORS AND LIBERATORS

About This Lesson

 180–270 minutes

❖ INTRODUCTION The purpose of this lesson is to provide students with an understanding of the political, legal, social, and emotional status of the Jewish survivors. This lesson also examines the role of the liberators following the defeat of the Nazis at the end of World War II.

This three-part lesson has material appropriate for history, social studies, Holocaust studies, and English classes. Instructional strategies used in this lesson include large-group discussion, small-group work, brainstorming, reading for information, interpreting written and visual history testimony, analyzing literature, critical thinking, and journaling.

❖ OBJECTIVES After completing this lesson, students will be able to:

- Describe the complex emotional ramifications of liberation for Jews at the end of World War II.

- Describe the complex emotional ramifications of liberation for the Allied soldiers who liberated the camps following the defeat of the Nazis.

- Name the serious difficulties and immediate needs that survivors faced after liberation, including efforts to reunite broken families, provide care to children, and reclaim homes and communities.

- Summarize the purpose of displaced persons' camps and what life was like for people living in these camps.

- Analyze the choices made by survivors as they reentered society and began to rebuild their lives.

- Discuss both the content and the messages in written and visual history testimony.

RESOURCES & TESTIMONIES

All of the resources used in this lesson can be found in this guide at the end of this lesson and at echoesandreflections.org.

Visual history testimonies are available on the website or on the DVD that accompanies this resource guide.

Teachers are urged to review the lesson procedures to identify other materials and technology needed to implement the lesson.

L8

❖ KEY WORDS & PHRASES

Allies	death march	liberation
Auschwitz-Birkenau	displaced persons'	Majdanek
Bergen-Belsen	camp (DP camp)	refugee
Buchenwald	extermination camp	"Return to Life"
concentration camp	"Final Solution"	survivor
Dachau	Holocaust	Zyklon B

❖ ACADEMIC STANDARDS The materials in this lesson address the following national education standards:

Common Core State Standards

- Reading Standards for Informational Text 6–12
- Reading Standards for Literature 6-12
- Writing Standards 6–12
- Speaking and Listening Standards 6–12
- Reading Standards for Literacy in History/Social Studies 6–12
- Writing Standards for Literacy in History/Social Studies 6–12

A complete analysis of how this lesson addresses Common Core State Standards by grade level and specific skills is available on the Echoes and Reflections website.

National Curriculum Standards for Social Studies

❶ Culture
❷ Time, Continuity, and Change
❸ People, Places, and Environments
❹ Individual Development and Identity
❺ Individuals, Groups, and Institutions
❾ Global Connections

Procedures

Part 1: "Return to Life"

1. Begin this lesson with a discussion about how students imagine survivors felt after liberation. The following questions can help guide this discussion:

   - How do you imagine survivors felt after learning they were liberated?
   - What do you imagine some of their fears were?
   - The phrase "Return to Life" is often used in connection with the period immediately following liberation. What do you think were the first things the survivors needed in order to "Return to Life"?
   - Do you think the phrase accurately captures the Jewish experience at this time? Explain your thinking.

2. Introduce students to Dennis Urstein, Henry Mikols, and David Abrams and then show Part 1 of Visual History Testimony: *Survivors and Liberators*. Follow with a discussion using some or all of the questions below.

   - How does Dennis Urstein describe conditions in Dachau prior to liberation?

TESTIMONY VIEWING

About the Interviewees

Dennis Urstein was born on February 24, 1924, in Vienna, Austria. He was incarcerated in the Buchenwald, Sachsenhausen, Ohrdruf, Auschwitz I, Mechelen, and Dachau concentration camps. Dennis was also imprisoned in the Auschwitz-Birkenau extermination camp. His interview was conducted in Canada. When the war began, Dennis was fifteen years old.

continued on page 201

L8

- What does Dennis remember about the day of liberation and the days immediately following?

- Dennis mentions that the American soldiers reminded him of a character from his childhood. What is the significance of this memory?

- What conflicting emotions does Dennis explain he felt after learning he was free?

- What does Henry Mikols remember of the liberation of Bergen-Belsen?

- Henry says that he remembers feeling that maybe he was one of "the chosen ones." Do you think this was a common feeling among survivors? How might a feeling like that carry with it a tremendous responsibility in the minds of survivors?

- What other emotions do you think survivors probably experienced after liberation?

- Who does David Abrams say he found upon arriving home?

- Why do you think David wanted to walk up to his house rather than accept the ride that was offered to him? What do you think the walk symbolized for him?

3. Introduce students to Ida Fink and distribute *The Tenth Man*. After reading the short story together, have a discussion using the following questions:

- What is the general tone of this piece? How did you feel reading it?

- What characterizes the image of the returning Jews? What from the text supports your answer?

- What is the theme of this short story and how is it conveyed?

- What is the significance of the lack of face for Chaim the carpenter and other returnees?

- Why don't most of the returnees enter their homes, but remain instead on the threshold?

- What is the significance of the title of the story? [NOTE: In Judaism, prayer with a quorum of ten adults—a *minyan*—is the most highly recommended form of prayer and is required for some prayers.]

- Does the narrator claim that these Jews—individually and as a community—can return to life in this place? Explain how Ida Fink develops the narrator's point of view over the course of the text.

About the Author

Ida Fink was born in 1921, in Zbarazh, Poland. At eighteen, she was studying at the Lvov Conservatory for a career as a pianist, when the Germans invaded Poland in September 1939. Her studies ended, Fink was forced to live in the Zbarazh ghetto, but then fled

continued on page 202

About the Interviewees
continued from page 200

Henry Mikols was born on August 27, 1925, in Poznan, Poland. As a political prisoner, Henry was incarcerated in the Ellrich and Buchenwald concentration camps. From Buchenwald, Henry was sent on a death train to Bremen and then on to Bergen-Belsen, where he was eventually liberated. His interview was conducted in the United States. When the war began, Henry was fourteen years old.

David Abrams was born on December 8, 1928 in Dej, Romania. He was forced to live in the Dej ghetto, and later imprisoned in the Mauthausen, Gunskirchen, Gusen, and Auschwitz concentration camps. His interview was conducted in the United States. When the war began, David was ten years old.

For additional information about Dennis Urstein, Henry Mikols, and David Abrams, see their Biographical Profiles available on the website.

L8

and lived under false papers on the "Aryan side." In 1957, Ida immigrated to Israel. Her short stories, written in Polish, discuss the terrible choices, or lack thereof, that Jews faced during the Nazi period as well as the hardships that survivors faced following the war. Ida Fink died in 2011.

4. Allow time for students to review the range of emotions that Jews felt after liberation. Ask them to consider the following questions:

   • Why was it impossible for Jews to completely embrace the idea of freedom after liberation?

   • What obstacles did survivors still have to overcome—physically, emotionally, and psychologically?

   • What feelings and emotions might those who had been able to escape Nazi-occupied Europe have had to contend with after learning the personal and general extent of the devastation during the Holocaust?

5. Distribute *Holocaust 1944* and *When It Happened*. By way of introduction, tell students that each of these poems was written by a Jewish woman who escaped from Nazi Europe in the late 1930s as a young child. They both spent their childhood in England. In their poems, they examine the questions of guilt and duty with which many survivors struggle.

6. Assign half the class the poem "Holocaust 1944" and the other half "When It Happened." Have students break into pairs, making sure that both partners have been assigned the <u>same</u> poem.

7. Allow time for students to read and discuss their assigned poem with their partners. Have some or all of the following questions posted on the board or on chart paper to help students organize their discussions:

   • Who is the speaker in the poem? To whom is the speaker speaking? What is their relationship to one another?

   • Describe what you think the speaker's experience might have been.

   • Describe what you think the "listener's" (the person to whom the speaker is speaking) experience might have been. What specific words or phrases in the poem support your answer?

   • What emotions is the speaker experiencing? What do you think might be causing these emotions?

   • How did the progression of stanzas include increasing degrees of the speaker's recognition of what was going on? How do these changing degrees of recognition seem to impact the poet's sense of self?

   • What is the theme of the poem? Pick out one line or stanza that you believe contributed significantly to the theme of the poem and explain why you selected this particular line or stanza.

   • What questions are left unanswered for you, as the reader? Why are these questions unanswered?

   • What do you think the poet's motivation was for writing this poem?

8. After the class discusses the poems in pairs, come back together as a whole group. Read both poems as a class and conduct a whole-group discussion, allowing the students to lead

the discussion using their reflections and ideas from the pair-work. Encourage students to listen for different interpretations by other groups that read the same poem that they did.

Part 2: Liberators

1. Share general background on the liberation of the camps to prepare students for this part of the lesson.

   About Liberation As the Allies retook control of lands that had been occupied by the Germans, they came across many Nazi camps. In some instances, the Nazis had tried to destroy all evidence of the camps in order to conceal from the world what had happened there. In other cases, only the buildings remained as the Nazis had sent the prisoners elsewhere, often on death marches.

   However, in many camps, the Allied solders found hundreds or even thousands of emaciated survivors living in horrific conditions, many of whom were dying of malnourishment and disease.

   The liberation of the Nazi concentration and extermination camps began in Eastern Europe when Soviet troops reached Majdanek in July 1944. Soon they found many other camp sites, including Auschwitz-Birkenau, which they liberated on January 27, 1945. This day has been chosen to mark International Holocaust Remembrance Day. The British and American troops who were approaching from the west did not reach the concentration camps of Germany until the spring of 1945. What they found shocked and surprised them. They encountered tens of thousands on the verge of death, as well as piles upon piles of corpses. Although unprepared, the Allied liberators tried to help the survivors; however, many still died in the weeks after liberation.

2. Introduce students to Howard Cwick, Anton Mason, and Paul Parks, show Part 2 of Visual History Testimony: *Survivors and Liberators*, and discuss some or all of the questions below.
   - What does Howard Cwick remember seeing during the liberation of Buchenwald?
   - How does Howard describe the survivors? Why does he believe the survivors were initially afraid of the soldiers?
   - Years after liberation, Howard continues to be moved by his experience. What do his emotions tell you about the impact this experience has had on his life?
   - What food does Anton Mason remember the American soldier giving him? What does Anton say about the value of food in the camp?

NOTE 1.8

Encourage students to visit the online exhibit Life after the Holocaust (ushmm. org/exhibition/life-after-holocaust/exhibition). This exhibit documents the experiences of six Holocaust survivors whose journeys brought them to the United States and reveals the complexities of starting over.

L8

TESTIMONY VIEWING

About the Interviewees

Howard Cwick was born on August 25, 1923, in New York, New York. As a member of the United States Armed Forces, he, along with his fellow soldiers, liberated the Buchenwald concentration camp. His interview was conducted in the United

continued on page 204

NOTE 2.2

To learn more about Elie Wiesel's experiences arriving at Auschwitz-Birkenau, see Lesson 5: The "Final Solution."

About the Interviewees

continued from page 203

States. When the war began, Howard was sixteen years old.

Anton Mason was born on April 19, 1927, in Sighet, Romania. He was forced to live in the Sighet ghetto and was later imprisoned in the Buchenwald, Gleiwitz, Auschwitz, Auschwitz I, and Auschwitz III-Monowitz concentration camps. Anton was also incarcerated in the Auschwitz-Birkenau extermination camp. His interview was conducted in the United States. When the war began, Anton was twelve years old.

Paul Parks was born on May 7, 1923, in Indianapolis, United States. As a member of the United States Armed Forces, he, along with his fellow soldiers, liberated the Dachau concentration camp. His interview was conducted in the United States. When the war began, Paul was sixteen years old.

For additional information about Howard Cwick, Anton Mason, and Paul Parks, see their Biographical Profiles available on the website.

- How does Anton explain so many survivors dying after being fed by the soldiers?

- What does Anton say was the "greatest thing" the soldiers did for the survivors?

- How does Anton say he answered Elie Wiesel when Elie said, "We are free"?

- Anton states that he remembers his "exact words" to Elie; he also states the exact moment of liberation, 3:30 in the afternoon— are you surprised that details such as these are seared in Anton's memory? Why or why not?

- In his testimony, Anton says, "We were happy, we were sad, we were happy that we were free, that we were alive and the Germans had lost. As long as one of us was alive, the Germans lost because they wanted to kill us all, and they couldn't kill us all." What are your feelings listening to Anton explain the feelings Jews had regarding liberation? How does what Anton says fit into what you already know about the "Final Solution"?

- Paul Parks tells about speaking to a young girl in Dachau who many years later sees and remembers him "by his eyes." Do you find it surprising that this woman remembered her liberator after so many years? Why or why not?

- What do you imagine were some of the thoughts and feelings liberators had after their experiences liberating the camps? What kinds of things do you think they thought about in light of what they had witnessed?

- What is the effect of hearing both survivors and liberators talk about liberation? What kind of information do you learn from each?

- What kind of information does the survivor provide that would be impossible to learn any other way?

3. Display *A Liberator's Thoughts*. Tell students that the author of this written testimony is Harry Herder, Jr., who was nineteen at the time he and other US soldiers liberated Buchenwald, in April 1945. Discuss the selection using the following questions:

- What kinds of questions is Harry Herder asking himself following his experience at Buchenwald?

- Why does Harry reflect on his German heritage?

- What choices would Harry have had if in fact he had been a German citizen and in the German army during World War II?

- What role does Harry like to believe his upbringing would have played in his choices?

- What questions does reading this testimony raise for you?

4. To learn more about the survivors and liberators introduced so far in this lesson, assign each student a number from one to six. Instruct students to prepare a list of 3–5 questions that they would like to ask the individual with the corresponding number. After

developing the questions, have students use the Biographical Profiles on the website and/or watch the person's testimony on IWitness (iwitness.usc.edu) or YouTube to find the answers. Have students post their questions and answers on the class website or submit electronically.

1. Dennis Urstein
2. Henry Mikols
3. David Abrams
4. Howard Cwick
5. Anton Mason
6. Paul Parks

Part 3: Displaced Persons' Camps

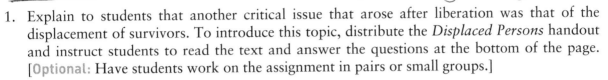
Can't just go home

1. Explain to students that another critical issue that arose after liberation was that of the displacement of survivors. To introduce this topic, distribute the *Displaced Persons* handout and instruct students to read the text and answer the questions at the bottom of the page. [Optional: Have students work on the assignment in pairs or small groups.]

2. Review the *Displaced Persons* handout and the questions together and then introduce students to Malka Baran, David Geslewitz, and Ester Fiszgop before showing Part 3 of Visual History Testimony: *Survivors and Liberators.*

TESTIMONY VIEWING

About the Interviewees

Malka Baran was born on January 30, 1927, in Warsaw, Poland. She was forced to live in the Częstochowa ghetto and later incarcerated in the concentration camp set up on the site of the former ghetto. Her interview was conducted in the United States. When the war began, Malka was twelve years old.

Daniel Geslewitz was born on August 14, 1924, in Lodz, Poland. He was forced to live in the Lodz ghetto and later imprisoned in the Braunschweig, Watenstadt-Hallendorf, Ravensbrück, and Wöbbelin concentration camps. He was also incarcerated in the Auschwitz-Birkenau extermination camp. His interview was conducted in the United States. When the war began, Daniel was fifteen years old.

Ester Fiszgop was born on January 14, 1929, in Brzesc nad Bugiem, Poland. She was forced to live in the Drohiczyn ghetto and later went into hiding in various places, including barns, forests, and attics. Her interview was conducted in the United Sates. When the war began, Ester was ten years old.

For additional information about Malka Baran, Daniel Geslewitz, and Ester Fiszgop, see their Biographical Profiles available on the website.

Use the following questions to continue the discussion about displaced persons' camps:

- What does Malka Baran say she did in the DP camp?
- What does Malka say brought her "back to life"?
- What are some of Daniel Geslewitz's memories of the DP camp?
- How were the examples of life in the DP camp that Daniel describes an indication that the survivors were trying to reestablish themselves and trying to rebuild their lives?
- How does Ester Fiszgop describe her experience in an Italian DP camp?
- In her testimony, Ester says, "I started under the penalty of death—that was my beginning, and then I finished with the penalty of death and I got five years of retirement." What do you think Ester means by this statement?

- Ester says that "no one complained." Why do you think no one complained, despite the horrible conditions?

3. Break the class into six groups. Distribute copies of the photographs from the displaced persons' camps (located at the end of this lesson and on the website) to each group. Have students study the photographs and share their initial observations with others in their group. Prompt students to think about how the photographs represent the choices that survivors made following liberation (e.g., to go on with their lives despite what they had suffered and lost).

4. Assign each group one of the "lenses" below and instruct them to study the photographs again from this particular lens (e.g., If you were a _____ in this camp, what would you notice? How would you explain what you are seeing in the photographs? How might you propose to solve problems that displaced persons might be facing?)

   Lenses:
   - psychologist
   - sociologist
   - doctor
   - policymaker
   - artist
   - educator

5. Have each group select a reporter to share the discussion points made regarding each "lens." Encourage students to listen for differences in perspective depending on the lens that the photographs were viewed.

6. Conclude this lesson with a discussion about the obstacles that survivors faced following liberation and what they did to rebuild their lives. Include the following questions in this summarizing discussion:

   - After all that the survivors went through, what kind of attitudes toward humanity could they have had?

   - What kind of behaviors could they have developed?

   - Would survivors, in your opinion, have been justified had they become criminals and thieves? Explain your thinking.

   - From what you read and heard in the testimonies, what kind of attitude did most survivors adopt? What are the possible reasons for this attitude?

Reflect and Respond

Either in class or as homework, have students reflect and respond to one or more of the topics below or have them develop a topic that has meaning for them based on the material covered in the lesson.

- A frequently cited dictum on Holocaust representation is German philosopher and sociologist Theodor Adorno's statement: "…to write poetry after Auschwitz is barbaric…" How do you interpret this statement? What role do you feel poetry plays in chronicling the individual's experience during or after the Holocaust? What is the value of reading and studying Holocaust poetry? What are the possible limitations?

- Following the Holocaust, many survivors questioned why they had been spared when so many of their family, friends, and neighbors had perished. Similarly, survivors of other catastrophes (e.g., September 11th) also expressed feelings of guilt for having survived. Why do you think people have this reaction? Do you think such feelings influence how the survivors go on to live their lives? If so, how?

Making Connections

The additional activities and projects listed below can be integrated directly into the lesson or can be used to extend the lesson once it has been completed. The topics lend themselves to students' continued study of the Holocaust as well as opportunities for students to make meaningful connections to other people and events, including relevant contemporary issues. These activities may include instructional strategies and techniques and/or address academic standards in addition to those that were identified for the lesson.

1. Visit IWitness (iwitness.usc.edu) for activities specific to Lesson 8: Survivors and Liberators.

2. Like personal diaries, photographs, and oral histories, personal letters can provide us with a more complete understanding of historical events, including valuable insight into the wartime experience. As with other primary documents, letters reflect only the viewpoint of a single individual and may contain mistakes. Their value, however, is that they offer readers a glimpse into the wide range of emotions that people felt as historical events were unfolding. One such letter was written by staff sergeant Horace Evers. As a member of the US Army, Evers was in Munich, Germany hunting down members of the Nazi high command in 1945. Two days after Aldolf Hitler committed suicide, Evers and his unit found themselves in Hitler's private residence. Finding sheets of Hitler's personal stationery with the Nazi swastika embossed over his name, Evers sat down and wrote a letter home to his mother and stepfather about his experience walking through the Dachau concentration camp the day before.

   Show or distribute a copy of *A Liberator's Letter Home, May 2, 1945* (provided in transcript and original letter form) available on the website in the Additional Resources section of the Lesson Components. Discuss the letter using some or all of the questions below.

   • What do you learn about Horace Evers from his letter?

   • What does Evers say his unit was doing in Germany in May 1945?

   • In the letter, Evers describes in vivid detail what he witnessed at the Dachau concentration camp. What were some of the details, and why do you think he included them, especially in a letter to his family?

   • Do you get a sense from the letter that Evers is struggling with what he saw? If so, what line or lines support your answer?

   • What is the irony of Evers writing this letter on Hitler's personal stationery?

   • What is the value of studying personal letters when learning about a historical event? Are personal letters <u>evidence</u> of what happened or should they be studied within the context of other sources? Explain your answer.

   • In addition to letters, what other written communication can be viewed as primary sources (e.g., email)? Do you think when someone is writing a letter, email, text message, etc., they are aware that they are creating a primary source? If they knew the communication would be read many years later, do you think they would write differently? If so, how might what they write be different?

   [NOTE: Encourage students to visit The Center for American War Letters at Chapman University (chapman.edu/research-and-institutions/cawl/index.aspx). The Center currently houses nearly 10,000 previously unpublished letters from the Revolutionary War through emails sent from Iraq and Afghanistan.]

3. As a whole class, read Simon Wiesenthal's *The Sunflower: On the Possibilities and Limits of Forgiveness* (Schocken Books, 1997). In the book, a dying Nazi solider brings Wiesenthal, a concentration camp prisoner, to his deathbed and asks forgiveness for crimes against the Jews.

Wiesenthal says nothing and leaves the soldier's bedside, but later questions his own response. Following the class reading, have students read a sampling of the fifty-three responses to Wiesenthal's question to readers: "What would I have done?" Encourage them to read at least one response that supports forgiveness (e.g., The Dalai Lama, José Hobday), one that does not (e.g., Primo Levi, Herbert Marcuse), and one that is nuanced and provides additional points to consider (e.g., Nechama Tec, Dith Pan), and then craft their own written argument on the topic. The piece of writing should introduce the situation/question, summarize opposing responses, and then state and support their own position with logical reasoning that demonstrates an understanding of the topic.

4. Contact the VFW's Veterans in the Classroom community outreach initiative (vfw.org/Community/VFW-in-the-Classroom). Through this program, a local VFW member is able to help make history "come alive," sharing personal experiences, appropriate memorabilia, uniforms, photographs, and other relevant material. US forces liberated the Buchenwald concentration camp, as well as Dachau, Mauthausen, Flossenburg, and Dora-Mittelbau; check with your local VFW to see if a liberator is available to speak to students. Many Holocaust museums and resource centers also have a Speakers' Bureau of local liberators available to visit the classroom. As a class, generate a list of relevant questions to ask the liberator in advance of his or her visit.

5. The United Nations High Commissioner for Refugees (UNHCR) provides protection, shelter, emergency food, water, medical care and other life-saving assistance to millions of people worldwide, who have been forced to flee their homes due to war and persecution. When possible, UNHCR helps refugees and other displaced people return to their homes voluntarily, safely, and with dignity. Have students research the UHHCR and share their findings in a presentation format of their choice (oral, written, multimedia). The following questions can help guide their research:

   • When and why was the UNHCR created?

   • On what continents has UNHCR worked over the years?

   • What does UNHCR do to assist refugees and internally displaced persons?

   • What challenges does the UNHCR face as it works?

   • In what countries is the UNHCR currently operating and why?

   • Identify one country where the UNHCR is currently operating. Explain the situation and how UNHCR is assisting.

L8

THE TENTH MAN

Ida Fink

The first to come back was Chaim the carpenter. He turned up one evening from the direction of the river and the woods; no one knew where he had been or with whom. Those who saw him walking along the riverbank didn't recognize him at first. How could they? He used to be tall and broad-shouldered; now he was shrunken and withered, his clothes were ragged, and, most important, he had no face. It was completely overgrown with a matted black thicket of hair. It's hard to say how they recognized him. They watched him from above, from the cliff above the river, watched him plod along until, nearing the first houses of the lower town, he stopped and began to sing. First they thought he had gone mad, but then one of the smarter ones guessed that it was not a song, but a Jewish prayer with a plaintive melody, like the songs that could be heard on Friday evenings in the old days, coming from the hundred-year-old synagogue, which the Germans had burned down. The synagogue was in the lower town; the whole lower town had always been Jewish—before the Germans came and during the occupation—and no one knew what it would be like, now that the Jews were gone. Chaim the carpenter was the first to come back.

A dark cloud from the burnt-out fire still lingered over the town, the stench still hung in the air, and gray clouds floated over the marketplace the Germans had burned. In the evening, when the news had spread, a crowd gathered in front of Chaim's house. Some came to welcome him, others to watch, still others to see if it was true that someone had survived. The carpenter was sitting on the front steps in front of his house; the door of the house was nailed shut. He didn't respond to questions or greetings. Later, people said that his eyes had glittered emptily in the forest of his face, as if he were blind. He sat and stared straight ahead. A woman placed a bowl of potatoes in front of him, and in the morning she took it away untouched.

Four days later the next one came back. He was tenant on a neighboring farm and had survived in the forest with the help of the farm manager. The manager brought the tenant back by wagon, in broad daylight. The old man was propped up, half reclining, on the bundles of straw. His face, unlike the carpenter's, was as white as a communion wafer, which struck everyone as strange for a man who had lived so long in the open. When the tenant got down from the wagon he swayed and fell face down on the ground, which people ascribed more to emotion than to weakness. In fact, it was possible to think he was kissing the threshold of his house, thanking God for saving him. The manager helped him up, and supporting him on his arm, led him into the entrance hall.

A week passed and no one came back. The town waited anxiously; people came up with all sorts of conjectures and calculations. The stench of burnt objects faded into the wind and the days became clear. Spring blossomed suddenly as befitted the first spring of freedom. The trees put forth buds. The storks returned.

Ten days later three more men came back; a dry goods merchant and two grain dealers. The arrival of the merchant upset the conjectures and calculations, since everyone knew that he had been taken away to the place from which there was no return. He looked just as he had before the war; he might even have put on some weight. When questioned, he smiled and explained patiently that he had jumped out of a transport to Belzec and hidden in a village. Who had hidden him, and in what village, he didn't want to say. He had the same smile on his face that he used to have before the war when he stood behind his counter and sold cretonnes and percales. That smile never left his face, and it astonished everyone, because no one from this man's family had survived.

For three days the grain dealers slept like logs. They lay on the floor near their door, which was left slightly ajar, as if sleep had felled them the moment they walked in. Their high-topped boots were caked with dried mud, their faces were swollen. The neighbors heard them screaming in their sleep at night.

The grain dealers were still asleep when the first woman returned. No one recognized her. Only when she reached the teacher's house and burst out sobbing did they understand that she was his. Even then, they didn't recognize her, so convincing was her beggar woman's disguise. She had begged in front of Catholic and Orthodox churches, had wandered from church fair to church fair and market to market, reading people's palms. Those were her hiding places. From beneath her plaid kerchief peered the drawn face of a peasant woman.

They asked in amazement: "Is it you?"

"It's me," she answered in her low voice. Only her voice was unchanged.

So there were six of them. The days passed, the gardens grew thick and green.

They're being careful, people said, they're waiting for the front to move—it had been still for so long that an offensive seemed likely. But even when the offensive began and the front made a sudden jump to the west, only a few more came back.

A wagon brought the doctor back. He had lain for nine months in a hole underneath the cowshed of one of his patients, a peasant woman. He was still unable to walk. The accountant and his son and the barber and his wife returned from a bunker in the forest. The barber, who had once been known for his mane of red hair, was bald as a bowling ball.

Every day at dusk, the dry goods merchant left his house and walked towards the railway station. When asked where he was going, he explained, "My wife is coming back today." The trains were still not running.

The farmer, a pious man, spent more and more time by his window; he would stand there for hours on end. He was looking for a tenth man, so that the prayers for the murdered might be said as soon as possible in the ruins of the synagogue.

The days kept passing, fragrant and bright. The trains began to run. The people in the town no longer conjectured and calculated. The farmer's face, white as a communion wafer, shone less often in his window.

Only the dry goods merchant—he never stopped haunting the railway station. He would stand there patiently, smiling. After a while, no one noticed him anymore.

"The Tenth Man" reprinted from Ida Fink, *A Scrap of Time and Other Stories*, trans. Madeline Levine and Francine Prose (Evanston: Northwestern University Press, 1995), 103–106.

About the Author

Ida Fink was born in 1921, in Zbarazh, Poland. At eighteen, she was a music student at the Lvov Conservatory when the Germans invaded Poland in September 1939. Fink was forced to live in the Zbarazh ghetto, but then fled and lived under false papers on the "Aryan side." Her short stories, written in Polish, discuss the terrible choices, or lack thereof, that Jews faced during the Nazi period as well as the hardships that survivors faced following the war. Ida Fink died in 2011.

Photo courtesy of Yad Vashem (5027/650)

HOLOCAUST 1944

Anne Ranasinghe

To my mother

I do not know
In what strange far off earth
They buried you;
Nor what harsh northern winds
Blow through the stubble,
The dry, hard stubble
Above your grave.

And did you think of me
That frost-blue December morning,
Snow-heavy and bitter,
As you walked naked and shivering
Under the leaden sky,
In that last moment
When you knew it was the end,
The end of nothing
And the beginning of nothing,
Did you think of me?

Oh I remember you, my dearest,
Your pale hands spread
In the ancient blessing
Your eyes bright and shining
Above the candles
Intoning the blessing
Blessed be the Lord....

And therein lies the agony,
The agony and the horror
That after all there was no martyrdom
But only futility -
The futility of dying
The end of nothing
And the beginning of nothing.
I weep red tears of blood.
Your blood.

[The lines "Pale hands 0. Lord" is a reference to the Jewish prayer over the Sabbath candles, traditionally performed by the mother in the home.]

From *Holocaust Poetry*, ed. Hilda Schiff (New York: St. Martin's Press, 1995), 142–143.

About the Poet

Anne Ranasinghe, born on October 2, 1925, as Anneliese Katz in Essen, Germany, is an internationally renowned poet from Sri Lanka. Escaping from Nazi Germany to England, she married a Sri Lankan professor and became a citizen of Sri Lanka in 1956. Although primarily a poet, she has also published short stories, essays, and translations. Her works have been broadcast on radio and published in seventeen countries and translated into nine languages.

L8

WHEN IT HAPPENED

Hilda Schiff

I was playing, I suppose,
when it happened.
No sound reached me.
The skies did not darken,
or if they did, one flicked
away the impression:
a cloud no doubt, a shadow perhaps
from those interminable aeroplanes
crossing and recrossing
our sunbleached beaches, Carbis Bay
or the Battery Rocks, where
all summer long we had dived
and cavorted in and out of
the tossing waters, while
the attention of the adults,
perpetually talking,
seemed focused,
unaccountably,
elsewhere.

No sound reached me
when it happened
over there on that
complicated frontier
near Geneva. (Was the sun
shining there too?)
I did not hear you cry out,
nor feel your heart thump wildly
in shock and terror. 'Go back,'
they shouted, those black-clad figures.

'Go back. You are not permitted to cross.'
Did the colour drain from your face?
Did your legs weaken?
'You are under arrest,' they barked.
'Go back and wait.' Back to the
crowd waiting for the train, the train. . .East?
Did you know what it meant?
Did you believe the rumours?
Were you silent? Stunned? Angry?

Did you signal to them then,
When it happened?
To the welcoming committee
one might say, on the other
side of the border.
To your husband and his friends
just a few yards away,
there, beyond the barbed wire,
beyond the notices saying,
'Illegal refugees will be shot.'
They called across, they said,
'Run, jump, take the risk,'
the frontier is such a thin line,
the distance so short between you and us,
between life and death,
(they said afterwards).
How was it you lacked
the courage (they said
afterwards, drinking tea).

No sound whatsoever disturbed me
when it happened.
I slept well. School
was the same as usual.
As usual I went swimming,
or raced down the hill
on my scooter or on foot
laughing with friends.
Often at night
in the dark of my bed,
I would hear the trains being
shunted down at the station,
their anguished whistling
stirring my imagination
drawing me towards oblivion.
At last, no more embarrassing letters
arrived in a foreign language
witnessing my alienation
from the cricketing scene.

Distracted and displaced
when it happened
I did not hear you ask
which cattle truck to mount,

nor, parched in the darkened
wagon, notice you beg for
a sip of water. On the third day,
perceiving the sound of Polish voices,
I did not catch you whisper to your neighbour,
'It is the East. We have arrived.'
Nor, naked and packed tight
with a hundred others
did I hear you choking
on the contents of those well-known
canisters marked 'Zyklon B Gas'
(It took twelve minutes, they say.)
I was not listening
when it happened.

Now I hear nothing else.

[*Carbis Bay and Battery Rocks are beaches in England. Cricket is a very popular sport in England, almost representative of British culture, similar to baseball in the United States.*]

From *Holocaust Poetry*, ed. Hilda Schiff (New York: St. Martin's Press, 1995), 135–137.

About the Poet

Hilda Schiff compiled and introduced the book, *Holocaust Poetry*, which is one of the main works on Holocaust poetry. A poet herself, and also a short story writer and editor, Hilda Schiff was born in central Europe and came to England as a small child. She was educated at the Universities of London and Oxford, where she went on to teach and engage in research.

L8

A LIBERATOR'S THOUGHTS
Harry J. Herder, Jr.

I thought of my German heritage, my Grandfather Hugo who had come to the United States from Germany while he was still a teenager, my mother's grandparents who had come over from Germany long before that...

I wondered...suppose my ancestors had not come to the United States; suppose they had stayed in Germany, and, through some fluke, the two people who had become my mother and father had met, and I had been born a German citizen. What would I be like? Would I be like the people who had instituted and guarded a place like Buchenwald? Could I have been that? Would I have been in the German army? The answer to the last question is obvious—certainly I would have been in the German army. But what kind of work would I have done? I hoped that I would not have been like most of the Germans I had seen. I could have accepted a likeness to some members of the German army whom we had fought, but there were many I would have been uncomfortable with. Much of what I had seen ran counter to everything my mother had brought me up believing.

Excerpted from "Liberation of Buchenwald" by Harry J. Herder, Jr. Full text available at remember.org/liberators. html#Lib.

DISPLACED PERSONS

At the close of the war in German territory there were millions of refugees and people who had been removed from their homelands and brought to Germany by the Nazi German regime. These people became known as "displaced persons," or "DPs." Some six million people returned to their native countries in the aftermath of the fighting; however, between 1.5 and 2 million refused to do so. Some were afraid they would be called traitors in their homelands, since in some capacity they had served the Nazis. Others—especially the Jews—felt they had no reason to go home, since their families and communities had been obliterated.

The Jewish refugee situation was completely different from that of non-Jewish refugees. They were a tiny remnant that had survived a great destruction in that one-third of the world Jewish population had been murdered during the Holocaust. Some Jewish survivors, especially from Western European counties, returned to their homelands with the general flow of refugees, expecting to be treated with consideration, but usually being greeted with callousness. Others, especially from Central and Eastern European countries, decided not to return to their former homes, knowing that there was really nothing to go back to and that going back would force them to confront the burden of their memories with no one left to share them. Some realized that returning to their homes could lead to confrontation with hostile elements of the local population, who were happy that the Jews had "disappeared."

Special DP camps were set up to provide shelter and food for the displaced persons. In general, DP camps were organized and run by the United States, British, and French armies and an agency of the United Nations, the United Nations Refugee Relief Agency (UNRRA). Initially conditions in these camps were deplorable, with Jews sometimes being forced to live alongside those who had recently persecuted them. On a visit to a camp in 1945, Earl Harrison, President Harry Truman's Special Envoy to the UNRRA, wrote to the President, "We appear to be treating the Jews as the Nazis treated them, except that we don't exterminate them." Reports by influential individuals eventually resulted in improved conditions and the establishment of Jewish camps in the American-administered zone of Germany. The DP camps operated until as late as 1953, when the last camp was closed down.

250,000 Jews
in DP camps by 1946

In Germany: 185,000

In Austria: 45,000

In Italy: 20,000

L8

Questions

- What percent of the total number of displaced persons returned to their homes after World War II?
- Why did most Jews not want to return to their former countries?
- What can you conclude about conditions in the DP camps based on the reading?
- What do you think were the different motivations of the Allies to deal with the issue of the DPs?
- Do you think there should have been Jewish DPs camps? Why or why not?

BABIES IN A DISPLACED PERSONS' CAMP (LANDSBERG, GERMANY)

Yad Vashem Photo Archive (1486/605)

A KINDERGARTEN IN A DISPLACED PERSONS' CAMP (SALZBURG, AUSTRIA)

Yad Vashem Photo Archive (3380/452)

A KINDERGARTEN IN A DISPLACED PERSONS' CAMP (BERGEN-BELSEN)

Yad Vashem Photo Archive (1201)

A BOY EATING IN A DISPLACED PERSONS' CAMP (GERMANY)

Yad Vashem Photo Archive (177GO2)

About Photo

German Civilians Forced to
Walk by a Row of Corpses,
Ludwigslust, Germany, 1945
(1822/2)

Yad Vashem Photo Archive

"How can they [Holocaust Deniers] still continue and poison so many minds with their vicious propaganda?"

– Brigitte Altman, Jewish Survivor

Preparing to Use This Lesson

Below is information to keep in mind when using this lesson. In some cases, the points elaborate on general suggestions listed in the "Teaching about the Holocaust" section in the Introduction to this resource, and are specific to the content of the lesson. This material is intended to help teachers consider the complexities of teaching the Holocaust and to deliver accurate and sensitive instruction.

- Examining the topic of responsibility and guilt for the Holocaust is an important, yet difficult, task. Allowing opportunities to examine the roles of both individuals and nations regarding the issue of trying to prevent what happened to Jews and other groups asks students to examine the complex boundaries of responsibility and the cost to a society that does not act. Adolescents are often interested and eager to discuss issues of fairness and consequences as they struggle to understand the world outside of themselves. The study of the Holocaust raises many topics that may lead students to question, analyze, and redefine their own beliefs and values.

- When the Western Allies began to learn about Nazi atrocities, they declared, in December 1942, that at the end of the war leading Nazis would be tried for their part in the unprecedented devastation caused by the war that they had begun and the crimes they had committed. Those among the highest Nazis leaders who were still alive and could be brought to justice were charged with Conspiracy to Wage Aggressive War, Crimes against Peace, War Crimes, and Crimes against Humanity, and were tried at the International Military Tribunal at Nuremberg. In the wake of this trial, others were carried out in many places in Europe; however, in the end, only a small fraction of Nazi criminals were ever brought to justice.

- While questions abound regarding whether the free world should have done more sooner to help the victims of the Holocaust, these questions in no way take away from the fact that Americans (and all Allies) in great numbers gave their lives to liberate Europe. The memory of the more than one million United States servicemen and women who were killed and wounded in World War II must be honored.

Lesson 9 PERPETRATORS, COLLABORATORS, AND BYSTANDERS

About This Lesson

 270–360 minutes plus time for research

❖ **INTRODUCTION** This lesson provides an opportunity for students to examine the complex issues of responsibility and guilt within the context of the Nazi occupation of Europe. Students will also learn about the war crimes trials following World War II and consider the responsibility of the free world to provide a safe haven for refugees attempting to escape Europe. This lesson also provides students with an introduction to Holocaust denial as a contemporary form of antisemitism.

This four-part lesson has material appropriate for history, social studies, Holocaust and genocide studies, art, ethics, and English/language arts classes. Instructional strategies and techniques used in the lesson include large-group discussion, small-group work, brainstorming, reading for information, comparing and contrasting information, interpreting visual history testimony, analyzing primary source documents, critical thinking, interpreting art, and journaling.

❖ **OBJECTIVES** After completing this lesson, students will be able to:

- Define collaborator and collaboration within the context of World War II and the Holocaust.

- Describe the role of those who collaborated with the Nazis during World War II.

- Explain the role of the railroad system in the implementation of the "Final Solution."

- Differentiate between the concepts of "guilt" and "responsibility" when discussing the actions or inactions of individuals or groups during the Holocaust.

- Explain the purpose and outcomes of the Nuremberg Trials as well as other war crimes trials that took place after the war.

- Analyze the role and responsibility of the individual perpetrator within the Nazi system by learning about people like Rudolf Hoess and Adolf Eichmann.

- Summarize the goals and outcomes of the Evian Conference and Bermuda Conference.

- Evaluate the culpability of the free world in what ultimately happened to the Jews of Europe.

- Interpret a variety of primary sources including visual history testimony, artwork, and government documents.

- Define Holocaust denial.

RESOURCES & TESTIMONIES

All of the resources used in this lesson can be found in this guide at the end of this lesson and at echoesandreflections.org.

Visual history testimonies are available on the website or on the DVD that accompanies this resource guide.

Teachers are urged to review the lesson procedures to identify other materials and technology needed to implement the lesson.

L9

- Identify the role of the individual to ensure a safe and free society.

❖ **KEY WORDS & PHRASES**

Allies	Fascism	partisans
antisemitism	"Final Solution"	perpetrator
Auschwitz-Birkenau	genocide	propaganda
Bermuda Conference	ghetto	refugee
bystander	Great Depression	Reich
collaboration	hate group	revisionism
concentration camp	Holocaust	"Righteous Among the Nations"
crimes against humanity	Holocaust denial	Sobibor
Eichmann Trial	nationalism	SS
Einsatzgruppen	Nazi	survivor
European Jewry	Nazi ideology	Vichy
Evian Conference	Nuremberg Trials	Wannsee Conference
extermination camp	Palestine	war crimes trial

❖ **ACADEMIC STANDARDS** The materials in this lesson address the following national education standards:

Common Core State Standards

- Reading Standards for Informational Text 6–12
- Writing Standards 6–12
- Speaking and Listening Standards 6–12
- Reading Standards for Literacy in History/Social Studies 6–12
- Writing Standards for Literacy in History/Social Studies 6–12

A complete analysis of how this lesson addresses Common Core State Standards by grade level and specific skills is available on the Echoes and Reflections website.

National Curriculum Standards for Social Studies

❶ Culture

❷ Time, Continuity, and Change

❸ People, Places, and Environments

❹ Individual Development and Identity

❺ Individuals, Groups, and Institutions

❻ Power, Authority, and Governance

❾ Global Connections

❿ Civic Ideals and Practices

L9

Procedures

Part 1: Perpetrators and Collaborators

1. Write the following words on the board or on chart paper: "guilt" and "responsibility." Allow time for students to brainstorm the meaning of each term. Leave the brainstorming activity visible, and encourage students to add to the definitions as they proceed with the lesson.

2. Introduce students to Jan Karski and Dennis Urstein and show Part 1 of Visual History Testimony: *Perpetrators, Collaborators, and Bystanders*. Follow with a discussion using the questions below.

   • In his testimony, Jan Karski talks about his meeting with President Franklin D. Roosevelt. How does he say Roosevelt responded to his questions about what he should tell the Polish people?

   • Does Jan Karski feel the President's response was adequate? How do you know?

   • What does Dennis Urstein say about what was learned from the Holocaust?

   • In his testimony, Dennis quotes Freud. To whom is he referring? Why do you think he quotes Freud?

   • Who does Dennis believe was guilty for the Holocaust and why?

   • Dennis uses the question "What are we doing about it?" as a call to action. What is he asking people to do?

3. Provide students with the following background information on the role of the railroad system in the implementation of the "Final Solution."

   About the Role of the Railroad System The railroad played a crucial role in the implementation of the "Final Solution." The organization and coordination of transports was a complicated matter, especially in a wartime setting. With the growing shortage of supplies and the priority given to military transports, the allocation of trains for the deportation of Jews was not always easily achieved. It took the close cooperation of all agencies—the SS, the civilian officials of the German Railway, the Ministry of Transportation and, in some cases, the Foreign Office to overcome the difficulties and allow the transports to run so that hundreds of thousands of Jews could be deported to their deaths.

   The transports were accompanied by a detail of guards who were usually recruited from the police. Their task began with the boarding of the train and ended when they handed the transport over to the person in charge at the destination. Hauptmann Salitter was an officer in charge of escorting a

continued on page 226

TESTIMONY VIEWING

About the Interviewees

Jan Karski was born in 1914 (exact date unknown), in Lodz, then a part of the Russian empire. After the fall of Poland in 1939, he joined an underground organization and was chosen to become a courier for the Polish government-in-exile. He was smuggled into the Warsaw ghetto and the Izbica camp to observe conditions. He was sent to the United Kingdom and United States to report on the situation of the Jews in Poland. His interview was conducted in the United States. When the war began, Jan was twenty-five years old.

Dennis Urstein was born on February 24, 1924, in Vienna, Austria. He was incarcerated in the Buchenwald, Sachsenhausen, Ohrdruf, Auschwitz I, Mechelen, and Dachau concentration camps. Dennis was also imprisoned in the Auschwitz-Birkenau extermination camp. His interview was conducted in Canada. When the war began, Dennis was fifteen years old.

For additional information about Jan Karski and Dennis Urstein, see their Biographical Profiles available on the website.

L9

transport of 1,007 Jews that left Dusseldorf for Riga on December 11, 1941. Jews were assembled at the slaughterhouse yard in Dusseldorf. From there they were taken to the railway station where they boarded the train that took them to Riga. Salitter produced a detailed report of the entire trip with recommendations for his superiors.

4. Divide the class into small groups and distribute *Salitter's Report*. Before they begin reading the document, share with students that men who took jobs like Salitter's were not forced to do so and that the job was considered prestigious. As students study the document, have them pay close attention to both the tone and language used in the report.

5. While reading the report, instruct each group to select a recorder to keep a list of all the people appearing in the document who participated in this deportation. When students have finished reading the document, have them add other people who are not mentioned in the document but who also must have taken part in this deportation (e.g., someone had to write the lists of people who would be sent to their deaths, the neighbors, the people in Riga, the people who would murder them later, the officers who gave the orders).

6. In a whole-group discussion, have students answer the questions below, citing textual evidence for their responses whenever possible.

   • What are the main issues that Salitter refers to in the report?

   • In his report on the argument he had with the stationmaster, Salitter complains that the latter clearly does not know the meaning of the term "Jew" and its implications. What does this seem to indicate about Salitter's attitude toward the task he is performing?

   • What appears to be Salitter's reason for recommending that the Jews be provided with water?

   • Why might Salitter have attempted to put children with their mothers?

   • Is there any evidence of Salitter's attitude toward his role or toward Jews in the report? If so, explain his attitude toward each.

   • Based on the report, how would you characterize Salitter's role in the murder process?

   • Who of the perpetrators mentioned in the report is not German? What was their role?

   • What were their possible motives for collaborating with the Germans?

7. Using the notes from the students' small-group work, prepare a composite list of all the people appearing in the document who participated in the deportation and ultimate fate of Jews in the transport. Have groups also offer additional names of those not mentioned in the document. Next to each person's name on the list, have students determine, on a scale of 1 to 4, each person's level of responsibility in what happened to the Jews. Have students support their choices and discuss areas of disagreement.

   1 = Not responsible

   2 = Minimally responsible

   3 = Somewhat responsible

   4 = Guilty

8. To ensure that students understand the meaning of the words "collaboration" and "collaborator" within the context of World War II and the Holocaust, distribute the *Collaborators* handout and read together. Follow with a discussion using some or all of the

questions below.

- Why would people cooperate with the Germans in the military takeover and administration of their countries? (e.g., fear, agreement with the Nazi ideology, opportunity to advance themselves)

- Why did some people cooperate with the Nazis in the annihilation of the Jews?

- Why did the Germans use locals to help carry out the "Final Solution"?

- At what point does not intervening to stop a human catastrophe make a person (or nation) not just a bystander, but a collaborator?

- Were the collaborators responsible for what happened to the Jews? Explain your answer.

Part 2: War Crimes Trials

1. Distribute the *War Crimes Trials* handout. Have students review the text and answer the questions that follow. [Optional: This can be assigned for homework beforehand or students can read and discuss the questions in small groups.]

2. Introduce students to Edith Coliver and Regina Zielinski; show Part 2 of Visual History Testimony: *Perpetrators, Collaborators, and Bystanders,* and follow with a discussion using the questions below.

   - What does Edith Coliver say were her father's messages to her after he learned that she would go to the Nuremberg Trials as a translator?

   - What information do you learn about Hermann Goering and Rudolf Hoess from listening to Edith's testimony?

   - How does Edith support her statement "the legacy of Nuremberg is still with us"?

   - When does Regina Zielinski say she was contacted to testify in a war crimes trial? What conclusions can you draw based on that information?

   - What kinds of questions does Regina say she was asked at the trial? What strategies were used to try to trick her while she was testifying?

   - Why was it so difficult for Regina to testify?

   - What is the difference between giving testimony to USC Shoah Foundation and testifying in court?

   - Why was it important to bring witnesses to testify in the war crime trials?

   - Do you think the trials were important? If so, why?

3. Distribute the *Rudolf Hoess* handout and read together as a whole

TESTIMONY VIEWING

About the Interviewees
Edith Coliver was born on July 26, 1922, in Baden, Germany. She did not experience life in the ghettos or concentration camps. In 1938, she, along with her family, fled to the United States. Her interview was conducted in the United States. When the war began, Edith was seventeen years old.

Regina Zielinski was born on September 2, 1925, in Siedliszcze, Poland. She was forced to live in the Siedliszcze ghetto and was also imprisoned in the Sobibor extermination camp. Her interview was conducted in Australia. When the war began, Regina was fourteen years old.

———
For additional information about Edith Coliver and Regina Zielinski, see their Biographical Profiles available on the website.

L9

group. Follow with a discussion, using some or all of the questions below. Instruct students to cite textual evidence to support their answers.

- In the handout there are two different sources. What are they? How are the two sources different? Might those differences influence what Hoess says in each? If so, how?

- What was Hoess's role in the "Final Solution"?

- How did Hoess describe the process of gassing at Auschwitz? Based on his choice of words, how would you characterize his tone as he described this process? What does this suggest about his attitude toward his crimes?

- What was Hoess's explanation for why he went through with the murders, despite admitting to feeling sympathy for the victims?

- Does Hoess express any moral reservations about the murder of the Jews? Why does he say that he thinks they were wrong? What does that say about his beliefs?

- In your opinion, what was the objective of the postwar criminal trials? After reading Hoess's testimony, do you think these aims were achieved? Explain your response.

4. Continue by distributing the *Adolf Eichmann* handout and read together. Ask students to consider some or all of the following questions:

- What was Eichmann's role in the "Final Solution"?

- How were Eichmann's and Hoess's roles different?

- How does Eichmann explain his actions during the war?

- Eichmann, Hoess, and Salitter defend their actions as soldiers who were only following orders. Do you see this as justification for their actions? Why or why not? What were their choices?

- After reading Eichmann's answers, do you think he regretted his actions? Why or why not?

- Hoess commanded the largest extermination camp—Auschwitz-Birkenau—and was on the site of murder on a daily basis. Eichmann was responsible primarily for the logistics of deportation to camps like Auschwitz-Birkenau. He generally worked out of an office far from those camps, although in his posting in Budapest in 1944, he directed the deportations to that camp. Do you think one of these men was guiltier than the other? Explain your response.

- What role might ideology have played in the motivations and actions of these men?

- Does Dan Pagis's poem "Testimony" available on the website (Lesson 5: The "Final Solution" under Download Lesson Resources) contradict or support what you have learned about Eichmann, Hoess, and Salitter?

- What does "crimes against humanity" mean? [Optional: Have students look up "crimes against humanity" in the Glossary on the website.]

- Do you think the perpetrators who carried out the Holocaust can ever be sufficiently punished? Explain your thinking.

Reflect and Respond

Either in class or as homework, have students reflect and respond to the topic below or have them develop a topic that has meaning for them based on the material covered in the lesson.

In her testimony, Edith Coliver states: "We were hoping that this [the Nuremberg Trials] would pave the way for the vanquished to try the victors. It didn't happen." Many Holocaust survivors have said that justice after the Holocaust was never achieved. What do you think made survivors feel this way? What does the concept of "justice" mean to you? Do you think it is possible that justice could ever be served with an event the magnitude of the Holocaust?

Part 3: Bystanders

1. Provide students with background on the MS *St Louis* using the information below.

> **About the MS *St. Louis*** The MS *St. Louis,* a German ship, left Hamburg, Germany for Cuba on May 13, 1939, with 937 passengers, most of them Jewish refugees. These passengers possessed landing certificates for Cuba, arranged for them by Manuel Benitez Gonzalez, the Cuban Director General of Immigration. Officially, the certificates were free, but Gonzalez took money for them. Jealousy of Gonzalez's gain, local dislike of Jewish immigration, and the government's fascist tendencies led them to cancel the validity of the certificates on May 5, 1939, before the departure of the ship. When the ship reached Havana on May 27, its passengers were denied entry. The American Jewish Joint Distribution Committee (JDC) tried to negotiate on their behalf, but the Cuban president insisted that the ship leave its harbor. The ship left Havana on June 2, steering in circles while negotiations continued. An agreement was reached whereby the JDC would pay $453,000 in exchange for entry into Cuba. The JDC could not meet its deadline, however, and the ship returned to Europe where the refugees were taken in by Belgium, France, Great Britain, and the Netherlands. Many of these refugees later came under the net of German occupation and were murdered by the Nazis.

2. Introduce students to Sol Messinger and Liesl Loeb and show Part 3 of Visual History Testimony: *Perpetrators, Collaborators, and Bystanders.* Conduct a whole-group discussion using the following questions:

   • What did you learn about the ill-fated journey of the MS *St. Louis* by watching Sol Messinger's testimony?

   • How far is Cuba from the United States? How do you think passengers felt being so close to the United States and freedom, but not being allowed to come ashore?

   • What was the significance of "mañana"—the first Spanish word that Sol learned? What did "mañana" mean to the passengers on the MS *St. Louis*?

   • How does Liesl Loeb describe the emigration process for Jews living in Germany?

   • The quota number Liesl's parents had was in the 14,000s. She says that by the time her mother's sister was able to get to the consulate and get a number, they were in the 70,000s. What do these figures tell you about the desire of the Jewish population

TESTIMONY VIEWING

About the Interviewees

Sol Messinger was born on June 16, 1932, in Berlin, Germany. He was imprisoned in the Agde internment camp in France, and later fled to the United States with his family. His interview was conducted in the United States. When the war began, Sol was seven years old.

Liesl Loeb was born on June 17, 1928, in Rheydt, Germany. She did not experience life in the ghettos or concentration camps. In May 1939, she fled to the United Kingdom and later to the United States. Her interview was conducted in the United States. When the war began, Liesl was eleven years old.

For additional information about Sol Messinger and Liesl Loeb, see their Biographical Profiles available on the website.

L9

to leave Germany at the time?

- How does what these two individuals have shared compare/contrast to treatment of immigrants and/or refugees coming to the United States today?

3. As an introduction to the topic of the responsibility that other countries had in intervening in what was taking place in Europe, have students read the statements below (which should be prepared in advance on the board or chart paper) and decide with which position they identify most.

- Nations should be responsible for the safety of other nations and ethnic groups who are in danger at any cost.

- Nations should be responsible for the safety of other nations and ethnic groups who are in danger if it suits their interests.

- Nations should be responsible for the safety of other nations and ethnic groups who are in danger only if it doesn't cost too much tax money.

- Nations should be responsible for the safety of other nations and ethnic groups who are in danger if it doesn't involve risking human lives.

- Nations should not be responsible for the safety of other nations and ethnic groups who are in danger.

4. Divide students into small groups and have them discuss their responses. Emphasize that the goal is not to persuade classmates to change their minds about which statement they chose, but rather to share ideas and thinking on the topic.

5. Explain to students that they will examine the issue of ways that the free world reacted to the fate of Jews by studying what came to be referred to as "the Jewish refugee problem."

6. Distribute and read the *Evian Conference* and *Bermuda Conference* handouts. Follow with a discussion using the questions below.

- Compare the two conferences; what were their official goals?

- What was the outcome of these conferences?

- Do you believe that antisemitism was a factor in the outcome of these conferences? On what have you based your response?

- What role, if any, should the United States play in helping to provide a safe haven to refugees from countries where gross human rights violations, genocide, or potential genocide is taking place?

7. Introduce students to Felix Nussbaum and show *The Refugee*. Have students study the painting and then share their interpretations of it by discussing the following questions:

- What do you believe the artist was attempting to say to the world through this work?

- What do you think the globe in the painting represents?

- What might the bundle next to the man represent?

- How does the man in the picture perceive the world?

- Comment on Nussbaum's choice of color, line, and shape. What is the overall effect of his choices?

- Do you think this piece of art accurately reflects how Jewish refugees felt during the late 1930s? Identify specific examples from one or more of the texts or visual history testimonies to support your response.

- Do you think this painting could have meaning for present-day refugees? Explain your thinking.

L9

8. Next, show students *Portrait of an Unidentified Man*. Have students study the painting and then share their interpretations of it by discussing the following questions:

- What do you think the title of this painting means?

- How does Nussbaum portray gloom and despair in this painting?

- Compare this painting to *The Refugee*. What similarities do you see in the artist's choice of light and color?

- Does viewing the two paintings together tell a story? If so, what is the story?

- Do you think that earlier works by Nussbaum (pre-1939) were similar in style to these paintings? Why or why not?

9. To help students consider whether Nussbaum's style was different in his earlier works, show them *Shore at Rapallo,* and have them discuss the difference in the artist's style between 1934 and 1939. Explain that Nussbaum painted this picture of Rapallo in 1934, while visiting Italy with his companion and future wife, Felka Platek. Nussbaum spent time at the seaside resort with his parents, who were thinking of settling in Switzerland. This was the last summer that Nussbaum would spend with his parents, who returned to Germany and were eventually deported to Auschwitz and murdered.

10. Introduce students to Samuel Bak, and show the painting *Thou Shalt Not Kill.* Have students study the painting and then share their interpretations of it by discussing the following questions:

- What do you believe Samuel Bak was attempting to say to the world through this work?

- Why do you think he chose this symbol to express his idea?

- Who do you think the artist addresses in this painting?

- Comment on Bak's choice of color, line, and shape. What is the overall effect of his choices?

11. Provide students with background information on the debate regarding the role of the United States and other Allies with respect to the Holocaust.

> **About the Allied Nations and the Holocaust** A hotly debated topic since the end of World War II has been the role of the Allied nations with respect to the Holocaust. For Americans, specifically, the controversy centers around the failure of the United States government to admit European Jewish refugees in sufficient numbers into the United States before, during, and after the war, and the decision of the US military not to bomb Auschwitz-Birkenau and the railroad lines leading to the camp. Among the central issues are: "What did Americans and their government know about the systematic murder of European Jews, and when did they know it?" and "When

continued on page 232

About the Artists

Felix Nussbaum was born in Osnabrueck, Germany, and studied in Hamburg, Berlin, and Rome. He and his companion, Felka Platek, settled in Belgium in 1935. In 1940, he was arrested and sent to the camps of Saint Cyprien and Gurs in southern France. Nussbaum managed to escape, and lived in hiding in Brussels, Belgium until he was caught in 1944 and sent to Auschwitz, where he was murdered.

Samuel Bak was born in 1933, in Vilna, Lithuania. He began to draw at an early age. His drawings were first displayed in the Vilna ghetto in 1943. Bak and his mother escaped the destruction of the Vilna ghetto by seeking refuge in a Benedictine convent. After liberation, Bak studied painting in Munich. In 1948, he and his mother immigrated to Israel. He studied art at the Bezalel Academy of Arts and Design in Jerusalem and at the École des Beaux-Arts in Paris.

L9

the US government had substantial evidence of the Holocaust, why did it not act more effectively and quickly to rescue Jews?

The intensity and violence of the war veiled the assault on European Jewry, especially once the "Final Solution" was underway. Nonetheless, information about the anti-Jewish persecution and the systematic mass murder emerged in real time. During the earlier phases of persecution, reports were published in the press and were made by diplomats to their home offices, including to the State Department in Washington, DC. For the US, the flow of information let up significantly after the American entry into the war in December 1941. During the period of the murder, the unprecedented nature of that information made it very difficult to comprehend. Furthermore, the Western Allies were far from the scene of the murder until late spring 1944. Given this situation, it is difficult to know how much more could have been done to save the victims; however, there is evidence that shows that many governments stood by even after they came to understand that Jews were being systematically mass murdered.

12. In small groups or as a whole class, read each of the excerpts listed on the *Primary Source Readings* handout. After determining the central idea of each excerpt, have students develop a list of essential questions based on the documents to stimulate additional thought and inquiry on the topic of how United States' officials responded to events as they were unfolding in Europe from 1933 to 1944.

Reflect and Respond

Either in class or as homework, have students reflect and respond to one or more of the topics below or have them develop a topic that has meaning for them based on the material covered in the lesson.

- Write about your feelings toward your country and its role in the Holocaust. As you respond, consider what you see as the role of the United States in current world conflicts.

- Reflect on the meaning of British historian Sir Ian Kershaw's assertion that "the road to Auschwitz was built by hate, but paved with indifference." What do you think Kenshaw means by this statement? What have you learned about bystanders that would support his sentiment?

- When human catastrophes occur, especially a catastrophe the magnitude of the Holocaust how is responsibility determined? Are there "levels" of responsibility or is everyone—perpetrator, collaborator, and bystander—ultimately equally responsible and, therefore, equally guilty for the crimes committed? What is the difference between responsibility and guilt?

- What is the role of the individual within a society to ensure that all of its citizens are free and safe? Is the responsibility of an individual in a democratic society even greater than that of an individual living in an autocratic society? Why or why not? Should the individual play the same or a similar role regarding the freedom and safety of people outside his or her community or country?

Part 4: Holocaust Denial

1. Have students consider the meaning of the word "denial" and "revisionism" and then discuss the meaning of "Holocaust denial." [Optional: Have students look up "Holocaust denial" and "revisionism" in the Glossary on the website.]

2. Introduce students to Brigitte Altman and show Part 4 of Visual History Testimony: *Perpetrators, Collaborators, and Bystanders.* Discuss the following questions:

   • What does Brigitte Altman say is the goal of Holocaust revisionists?

   • How does Brigitte respond to those who say the Holocaust never happened?

3. The issue of Holocaust denial is a difficult and complex topic. It may be approached by asking the students if they think that it is possible, based upon all of the evidence that they have studied, to question that the Holocaust really occurred. Explain that some antisemitic groups and individuals have stated that the Holocaust did not really happen. These deniers make the following claims:

   • The number of Jews murdered (six million) is a gross exaggeration.

   • There was no Nazi program to exterminate Europe's Jews.

   • Mass killings in gas chambers did not occur.

   • Jews were one of many groups who suffered during World War II and were not singled out for persecution.

4. Individually or in small groups, have students research the topic of Holocaust denial with emphasis on the questions below. Encourage students to consult the Echoes and Reflections website for information on the topic as well as the United States Holocaust Memorial Museum (ushmm.org) and Southern Poverty Law Center (splcenter.org) websites while conducting their research. Have students share their findings in a whole-group discussion.

   • Who are the individuals and groups who have promoted Holocaust denial? Describe their political agendas.

   • What arguments do they use to back up their claims?

   • What arguments can you use to counter their claims?

   • What court cases have centered on the issue of Holocaust denial?

5. Tell students that one way that those who deny the Holocaust have spread their propaganda in the past has been by purchasing scholarly sounding ads in college and community newspapers. Today much of their activity is through the Internet and social media, where there is a tremendous amount of material that promotes the denial and distortion of the Holocaust. Among other central ideas, they frequently call for an "open debate on the Holocaust," and claim that while Nazi antisemitism did exist, this hatred did not result in an organized killing program. They also question the authenticity of the United States Holocaust Memorial Museum in Washington,

TESTIMONY VIEWING

About the Interviewee

Brigitte Altman was born on August 15, 1924, in Klaipeda, Lithuania. She was forced to live in the Kaunas ghetto and later escaped and lived under false identity on a farm near Marijampole, Lithuania. Her interview was conducted in the United States. When the war began, Brigitte was fifteen years old.

———

For additional information about Brigitte Altman, see her Biographical Profile available on the website.

NOTE 4.3

In addition to denial of the Holocaust, there are several related phenomena in public discourse today: trivializing the Holocaust, diminishing the place of the Holocaust in history, and relativizing the Holocaust by drawing superficial parallels between it and other events. In some places around the world, Holocaust denial is a mainstream idea (e.g., the 2006 government-sponsored Holocaust denial conference in Iran), whereas in other countries, denial is very much on the margins. In yet other places, it is the related phenomena that are in or near the mainstream of discussion about the Holocaust.

L9

DC and other major museums and archives around the world.

In Canada and Western Europe, Holocaust deniers have been successfully prosecuted under racial defamation or hate crimes laws. In the United States, however, the First Amendment guarantees the right of free speech, regardless of political content. While the First Amendment guarantees Holocaust deniers the right to produce and distribute their propaganda, it in no way obligates social media, Internet service providers, and other media outlets to provide them with a forum for their views.

6. Explain to students that they will now assume the role of a college newspaper staff. Following an intensive campaign to secure new ads to financially support their print and/or online school paper, they have been approached about publishing a Holocaust denial ad. The group is divided on the issue—half the "newspaper staff" believes that a Holocaust denial ad should be allowed to be published in the school newspaper and the other half believes it should not be permitted. Have students either self-select their side of the argument or randomly assign half the class to the argument in favor of printing the ad and half the class to the argument against printing the ad. Have groups develop their arguments and conduct a debate on the topic.

7. Have a closing discussion that asks students to consider some or all of the following questions:

- Do you think that Holocaust denial is a contemporary form of antisemitism? On what do you base your response?

- If you believe Holocaust denial is a form of antisemitism, why has this expression of hatred been so slow to disappear from society?

- Why is Holocaust denial dangerous?

- Why is it important to be aware of Holocaust denial?

- What is the role of individuals in the face of this phenomenon?

Making Connections

The additional activities and projects listed below can be integrated directly into the lesson or can be used to extend the lesson once it has been completed. The topics lend themselves to students' continued study of the Holocaust as well as opportunities for students to make meaningful connections to other people and events, including relevant contemporary issues. These activities may include instructional strategies and techniques and/or address academic standards in addition to those that were identified for the lesson.

1. Visit IWitness (iwitness.usc.edu) for activities specific to Lesson 9: Perpetrators, Collaborators, and Bystanders.

2. In this lesson, students examine *Salitter's Report,* a report that outlines a transport of 1,007 Jews in December 1941 from Dusseldorf to Riga. Provide students with *Hilde Sherman's*

NOTE 4.7

Consider expanding the discussion to other forms of bigotry (e.g., racism, heterosexism, sexism) and have students share their thinking on why these expressions of hatred are also slow to disappear from society.

L9

Testimony available on the website in the Additional Resources section of the Lesson Components. Have students carefully study the two texts, noting similarities and differences in the description of places, the sequence of events, how people interacted over the course of the transport, etc., and present their findings in a graphic organizer (e.g., Venn diagram).

3. Instruct students to research the facts behind the proposed bombing of Auschwitz and conduct a debate to discuss whether or not Auschwitz should have been bombed by the Allies.

4. Have students research how the Holocaust was covered in media, especially newspapers, in their state, city, or town. After gathering relevant information, instruct students to develop an argument to support or refute the idea that this event was accurately covered and reported to the public. If unable to locate local or state coverage, research how the Holocaust was covered in national media (e.g., *The New York Times*). Have students prepare a written or oral summary of their findings and conclusions. Encourage students to develop and respond to essential questions that this research prompts, e.g., "Had large media outlets like *The New York Times* done more to cover the Holocaust, would it have galvanized other media to do the same?" "Why was the media hesitant to cover what was happening to the Jews of Europe or, if they did cover these events, why were the articles buried inside the paper?" "What is the role of media in alerting and educating the public about events happening in the world?"

5. During the 1994 genocide in Rwanda, up to one million people perished and as many as 250,000 women were raped, leaving the country's population traumatized and its infrastructure decimated. Since then, Rwanda has embarked on an ambitious justice and reconciliation process with the ultimate aim of all Rwandans once again living in peace. In the years following the genocide, more than 120,000 people were detained and accused of bearing criminal responsibility for their participation in the murder of ethnic Tutsis. To deal with such an overwhelming number of perpetrators, a judicial response was pursued on three levels:

   • the International Criminal Tribunal for Rwanda,

   • the national court system, and

   • the Gacaca courts.

   Have students research the structure and goals of each of these responses as well as what the effects have been on reconstructing Rwandan identity and securing justice for the victims and their families. Encourage students to gather relevant information from multiple print and digital sources and present their findings in a PowerPoint or cloud-based presentation (e.g., Prezi), a written report, or decide on another format to present their work.

SALITTER'S REPORT

I. Preparing the Transport

The Jew transport planned for 11 December 1941 included 1,007 Jews... The transport was compiled of Jews of both sexes, of various ages—from babies to 65-year-olds... On the way from the slaughterhouse yard [the designated assembly point] to the platform, a male Jew attempted to commit suicide by throwing himself in front of the streetcar. But he was caught by the streetcar's bumper and only slightly injured. He recovered during the trip, and realized that he could not avoid sharing the fate of the evacuees. An elderly Jewish woman walked away from the platform without anyone noticing—it was raining and it was very dark—entered a neighboring house, took off her clothes and sat on a toilet. However a cleaning woman noticed her and she too was led back to the transport.

II. Boarding the Train

Departure of the transport was planned for 9:30. The Jews were therefore brought to the loading ramp ready to board at 4:00 a.m. However, the *Reichsbahn* [The German Railway] could not have the train ready so early, allegedly due to lack of personnel. Subsequently the loading of the Jews did not begin until 9:00 a.m. The loading of the Jews into cars was carried out in great haste, as the Reichsbahn insisted that the train must depart on time. It is therefore no surprise that some cars were overloaded (60–65 persons) while others had only 35–40 passengers. This caused problems throughout the entire trip to Riga, since individual Jews repeatedly attempted to get into the less crowded cars. As much as time permitted, I allowed them, in some cases, to make changes, as there were also mothers who had been separated from their children. ... The loading of the train ended at 10:15 and...the train left the Dusseldorf-Derendorf station at about 10:30....

III. The Train Moves

I realized that the car reserved for the guards had not been put in the middle, but was at the end of the train, i.e. it was car no. 21... Due to a faulty heating system, the steam pressure did not reach the last cars of the train. Because of the cold, the guard squad's clothing did not dry. (It rained during the entire transport). Thus, I had to deal with guards who could not stand duty because of illness....

The commander of the transport could not see the whole train from his position. Whenever the train stopped, the Jews tried to contact the people at the railway stations, to have their letters mailed or to ask for water. As a result I had to put two guards in one of the cars at the front...

At 11:10 [on 12 December] Konitz was reached. [Salitter wanted to rearrange the train so that the guards' car would be in the center of the train]. This was agreed upon at first, but then the station master declared that...it would not be possible...he told me that the train would have to leave right away. A rearrangement of the train would be impossible... The conduct of the stationmaster seemed strange to me, and I informed him that I would take the matter up with his superiors. He responded that I would be unable to reach his superior. He had his orders. The

L9

train would have to leave, as there were two other trains en route.

He suggested that I remove the Jews from the center car and put them in the guards' second-class car. Then I could move my guards to the empty car. I think someone from the upper echelons should see to it that this railway man is informed that members of the German police are to be treated differently than the Jews. I have the impression that this is a man who still speaks of 'those poor Jews' and for whom the term 'Jew' is totally unknown....

...At Tilsit: There...the car of the guards was put in the front of the train and they finally got some heating. The guards appreciated the warmth very much...as their uniforms were soaked and they could finally dry them.... Normally, the train ride from this point to Riga would take 14 hours, but since there was only one track and our train had only a secondary priority, the trip was often delayed for long periods of time....

IV. Journey's End

...We arrived in Riga at 21:50. The train was kept at the station for one and a half hours.... The train stood there without heat. The temperature outside was minus 12 centigrade.... At 1:45 a.m., we relinquished responsibility for the train over and six Latvian guards were charged with watching it. Because it was past midnight, dark, and the platform was covered with a thick layer of ice, it was decided to transfer the Jews to the Sarnel ghetto only on Sunday morning....

...Riga has a population of about 360,000. Among them were approximately 35,000 Jews. As in other places, the Jews were very prominent in business. After the entry of the German army, their shops were closed and confiscated. The Jews were closed in a ghetto surrounded by barbed wire. At this time, there are only 2,500 male Jews who are being used for labor. The remaining Jews were used elsewhere or shot by the Latvians.... The Latvians, as far as I can tell, are friendly to Germany and many of them speak German.... Their hatred is directed mainly towards the Jews. Therefore, from the moment of their liberation, they have played an important part in the elimination of these parasites. However they seem to find it strange, as I have heard from the railway workers, that Germany brings the Jews to Latvia, instead of eliminating them in their own country.

V. Conclusions

(a) The provisions [for the guards] were good and sufficient.

(b) the pistols and ammunition provided were sufficient....

(c) the two search lights served their purpose well....

(d) the assistance of the [German] Red Cross [to the German guards] is commendable....

(e) In order to supply the Jews with water, it is essential that the Gestapo get in touch with the *Reichsbahn* and coordinate one hour stops every day at a railway station in the Reich. Because of the time table, the *Reichsbahn* was reluctant to comply with the transport commander's wishes. The Jews are usually on the road for 14 hours or more before the transport leaves and have used up all the drinks they had taken with them. When they are not provided with water during the trip, they try, in spite of the prohibition, to leave the train at every possible spot or ask others to get them water.

(f) It is also essential that the *Reichsbahn* prepare the trains at least 3–4 hours ahead of departure, so that the loading of the Jews and their belongings can be conducted in an orderly fashion.

(g) The Gestapo has to make sure that the *Reichsbahn* place the car for the guard detachment at the center of the train…. This is essential for the supervision of the transport….

(h) The men in the guard squad gave me no reason to complain. With the exception of the fact that I had to prompt some of them to act more energetically against Jews who wanted to disobey my orders, they all behaved well and fulfilled their duty well. There were no incidents of disease or any other troubles.

Signed: Salitter, Hauptmann of the Schupo

The Fate of the Jews in Riga

On November 30, 1941 the first transport of Jews from Germany arrived in Riga. In the coming months another 24 transports with a total of over 25,000 Jews arrived. One of these was the transport guarded by Salitter. Thousands of these Jews were murdered upon arrival. The rest were put in concentration camps in the area. The Germans conducted periodic mass executions of Jews by shootings in the nearby Rumbuli Forest.

Security Police

The transports were accompanied by a detail of guards who were usually recruited from the police. Their task began with the boarding of the train and ended when they handed the transport over to the person in charge at the destination. Captain Salitter was an officer in charge of escorting a transport of 1,007 Jews that left Dusseldorf for Riga on December 11, 1941.

About Photos

Left: Jews being led to the deportation train by German Police, Wiesbaden, Germany. Yad Vashem Photo Archive (1046/6)

Background photo: Jews boarding a deportation train, Bielefield, Germany. Yad Vashem Photo Archive (1286/3)

L9

COLLABORATORS

To collaborate (collaboration and collaborator): **refers generally to the act of cooperating with or sharing the duties of another person.**

This term has many positive applications: for example, two or more individuals may collaborate on a book, play, piece of music, building project, etc. However, in the context of World War II, the term "collaborators" applies to those who aided the Nazis. Collaboration took many forms. There were those who actually assisted the Nazis in the military takeover of their countries, those who fought in various military formations on the side of Germany, those who revealed the names and locations of partisan fighters to the Nazis, those who cooperated in the German governing of their countries, and those who helped directly or indirectly in the murder of Jews.

When the Germans occupied Poland they unleashed a regime of terror that was directed against the Polish people. They put an end to the Polish state and institutions, and caused the death of up to three million Poles, many through outright murder. Terror on various scales was employed by the Nazis throughout their occupied territories. Since the largest group of Jews lived in prewar Poland, because Poland was far away geographically from Western Europe, and because Poland was considered by the Nazis to be beyond the sphere of the civilized world, Poland became the dumping and killing ground for most of European Jewry. Primarily owing to the exceedingly harsh Nazi regime in Poland and prevalent antisemitic attitudes, out of the general Polish population relatively few extended aid to Jews; after the war, those who had were honored with the designation "Righteous Among the Nations."

In France

After the German invasion of France in 1940, Marshal Philippe Petain signed a ceasefire with Germany. The Germans occupied northern France; in southern France, an autonomous government that collaborated with Germany was set up with its capital at Vichy. This government and the southern portion of the country came to be known as "Vichy." The Vichy government strove to assert whatever independence it could. One way it did so was by initiating anti-Jewish measures before the Germans could impose their own on them. In practice, this meant that the Vichy government collaborated with the Germans in the persecution of Jews. Jews were forbidden to participate in public activities and were deprived of their civil rights. Throughout all of France, initially non-French Jews, and later French-born Jews were removed to concentration camps by French police and the camps were administered by French officials. Later these Jews were sent to extermination camps.

To a certain extent, official French collaboration decreased over the years of the war, although some segments of the society actively collaborated until the very end. Much of the French population kept silent and was even favorable toward anti-Jewish measures as long as they were directed against Jewish property. However, those attitudes changed somewhat when the Germans began deporting French-born Jews. Some French people found it difficult to accept that Jews, especially French citizens, were being deported and began helping Jews, mainly in 1943–1944. At a certain stage, the Germans realized they couldn't necessarily rely on the French authorities, and they became more involved in hunting down Jews, frequently with the help of French citizens who continued to collaborate with them. Deportations continued until France was liberated in the summer of 1944. But after the first wave of deportations of 1942, in which more than half the total number of Jews were dispatched from France to Nazi camps in the East, the number of deportees declined. This decline resulted from many factors, one of which was the growing reluctance of people in France to support the deportations.

In the Netherlands

The Holocaust in the Netherlands unfolded differently from France. Initially, the Germans offered the Dutch collaboration. They considered the Dutch racially and culturally related to the Germans. There was a significant Dutch Nazi Party, and numerous Dutch officials collaborated with the Nazis. When German authorities realized, however, that many other Dutch were reluctant to cooperate with them, they hardened their approach and, among other things, implemented more severe anti-Jewish steps. Thus, there existed side-by-side a significant movement toward collaboration and a significant movement toward opposing such collaboration. The German occupation of the Netherlands is considered the most ruthless in Western Europe. The percentage of Jews deported to the extermination camps was the highest among Western European countries: 77 percent out of 140,000 were murdered; a considerable number went into hiding: 25,000 Jews were assisted by Dutch citizens, out of which about 8,000 were turned in by Dutch collaborators.

In Italy

Under the dictator Benito Mussolini, Fascist Italy and Nazi Germany drew closer toward the end of the 1930s. In 1938, Italy, on its own initiative, legislated very harsh racial laws, with no specific demands from Hitler to do so. In 1940, it joined the war and arrested Jews who were not Italian citizens and deported them to concentration camps, though the conditions in these camps were a far cry from the deadly German camps. The Italians refused to deport Jews from their territories. But a series of events in 1943 changed that. Mussolini was ousted and Italy reached an armistice with the Allies in September 1943. In turn, the Germans invaded and put Mussolini back into power. It was at this point that Italian authorities stopped blocking deportations and German occupiers and Italian collaborators began hunting down Jews. With the assistance of the Italian Fascist guard, out of the approximately 44,000 Jews living in Italy in September 1943, more than 8,000 were deported, mostly to the Auschwitz-Burkina extermination camp.

Although Italy was an ally of Nazi Germany throughout most of the war, Italian society was divided between those who championed collaboration with the Germans and those who opposed it. Even among those who embraced collaboration with Nazi Germany, some fully identified with Nazi ideology and its goals whereas others were less supportive and even opposed the Nazis' murderous anti-Jewish policies. To a large extent, the unfolding events of the war, the short-lived German occupation of Italy, the fact that the small and ancient Italian Jewish community was well-integrated, and that helping Jews was considered by many as an act of resistance against both the German occupation and Italian Fascist regime, all combined to disrupt the deportations once they began.

As research has progressed over the years, the characterization of the Vatican as a silent collaborator has changed. Today we understand that the role of the Vatican regarding the persecution of the Jews was not black and white. Some Catholic institutions such as churches, monasteries, convents, and even the Vatican hid Jews from the Nazis. Others were less forthcoming. The stance and actions of Pope Piux XII remain a matter of passionate debate. It is unclear to what extent actions taken by the Church to help Jews were authorized by him, and there is much discussion regarding his statements about the persecution, especially since his language was not explicit.

In Other Countries

In most countries, the German occupation fueled ingrained popular antisemitism among some of the population that resulted in enthusiastic cooperation with the Germans in carrying out the "Final Solution." Frequently there were local issues that contributed to this support as well. Significant collaboration with the Nazis occurred in Croatia, Hungary, Romania, the Baltic countries, and Ukraine, among other places. In some of these countries, government officials worked hand in glove with the Nazis to facilitate the murder of Jews. Local residents served as guards in the concentration camps, played a role in rounding up Jews for deportations, and also engaged in murder. In the Soviet Union, the Germans established special mobile killing squads, Einsatzgruppen, to carry out executions of Soviet government officials, Communists, partisans, Sinti-Roma, and above all, Jews. These Nazi killing squads were directly aided by Ukrainian, Lithuanian, Estonian, Latvian, and Romanian citizens. At Babi Yar near Kiev in Ukraine, close to 34,000 Jews were murdered by German Einsatzgruppen with the aid of Ukrainian killing squads in only two days. Many Soviet prisoners of war—who had been treated murderously by the Germans—decided to take up German offers to join them; they were trained as fighters and concentration camp guards.

Though the exact number of people who collaborated with the Germans in the murder of the Jews will never be known, it is clear that without widespread collaboration and silent approval, the Nazis could not have murdered six million Jews from all over Europe.

L9

WAR CRIMES TRIALS

The Nuremberg Trial, 1945/6

At their meetings during World War II, Franklin Roosevelt, President of the United States; Winston Churchill, Prime Minister of Great Britain; and Joseph Stalin, Premier of the Soviet Union, discussed among many other important issues the fate of the Nazis in Germany who were responsible for World War II. Churchill thought after their identities were verified, they should simply "be shot." Roosevelt, however, was determined to put the Nazis on trial as war criminals to make the world aware of their crimes.

The first international war crimes trial ever held began on November 20, 1945, in Nuremberg, Germany and lasted for eleven months. The International Military Tribunal (IMT) was set up by the Allies—the United States, Great Britain, the Soviet Union, and France. Each of the Four Powers provided one judge and one alternate and each provided prosecutors. The Chief Prosecutor was Robert Jackson of the United States who was on leave from his position as a Justice of the Supreme Court. Defendants were selected to represent a cross-section of German diplomatic, economic, political, and military leadership. The indictments were based upon four counts or principles.

"The wrongs which we seek to condemn and punish have been so calculated, so malignant, and so devastating that civilization cannot tolerate their being ignored because it cannot survive their being repeated."

—Robert H. Jackson, Chief Prosecutor,
International Military Tribunal,
November 21, 1945

The Charges

Count One: Conspiracy to Wage Aggressive War
The defendants charged under Count One are accused of agreeing or planning to commit crimes as outlined in Count Two.

Count Two: Waging Aggressive War, or "Crimes against Peace"
This evidence is defined as "the planning, preparation, initiation, and waging of wars of aggression," which were also wars in violation of international treaties, agreements, and assurances.

Count Three: War Crimes
This count deals with acts that violate traditional concepts of the law of war, e.g., the use of slave labor; bombing civilian populations; the Reprisal Order (signed by Field Marshal Wilhelm Keitel, a

defendant; this order required that fifty Soviet soldiers be shot for every German killed by partisans); the Commando Order (issued by Keitel, ordered that downed Allied airmen be shot rather than taken captive). War crimes are defined as "murder, ill treatment, or deportation to slave labor or for any other purpose of civilian population or in occupied territory, murder or ill-treatment of prisoners-of-war or persons on the seas, killing of hostages, plunder of public or private property, wanton destruction of cities, towns, or villages or devastation not justified by military necessity."

Count Four: Crimes against Humanity

This count applied to defendants responsible for the extermination camps, concentration camps, and killing rampages in the East. Initially, crimes against humanity were understood to be crimes committed by a government against its own people, and there was some question as to whether the concept could be applied internationally. These crimes are defined as "murder, extermination, enslavement, deportation, and other inhumane acts committed against any civilian population before or during the war, or persecutions on political, racial, or religious grounds in execution of or in connection with any crimes within the jurisdiction of the International Military Tribunal, whether or not in violation of domestic law of the country where perpetrated."

The Defendants

On November 20, 1945, twenty-one Nazi defendants filed into the dock at the Palace of Justice in Nuremberg, Germany. Another defendant named in the indictments, Martin Bormann, was believed dead, although neither he nor his body was ever found. All pleaded "not guilty." Some claimed that they were simply following orders when they helped oversee the transport of Jews and other targeted groups. Others claimed that the court had no jurisdiction, that is, no authority to conduct the trials.

Karl Doenitz
Supreme Commander of the Navy; in Hitler's last will and testament, he was made Third Reich President and Supreme Commander of the Armed Forces. Sentenced to ten years in prison.

Hans Frank
Governor-General of occupied Poland. Sentenced to hang.

Wilhelm Frick
Minister of the Interior. Sentenced to hang.

Hans Fritzsche
Ministerial Director and the head of the radio division in the Propaganda Ministry. Acquitted.

Walther Funk
President of the Reichsbank. Sentenced to life in prison.

Hermann Goering
Reichsmarschall, Chief of the Air Force. Sentenced to hang. Committed suicide a few hours before the sentence was to be carried out.

Rudolf Hess
Deputy to Hitler. Sentenced to life in prison.

Alfred Jodl
Chief of Army Operations. Sentenced to hang.

Ernst Kaltenbrunner
Chief of Reich Main Security Office whose departments included the Gestapo, Sipo, and SD. Sentenced to hang.

Wilhelm Keitel
Chief of Staff of the High Command of the Armed Forces. Sentenced to hang.

Erich Raeder
Grand Admiral of the Navy. Sentenced to life in prison.

Alfred Rosenberg
Minister of the Occupied Eastern Territories. Sentenced to hang.

Fritz Sauckel
Chief of Slave Labor Recruitment. Sentenced to hang.

Hjalmar Schacht
Minister of Economics. Acquitted.

Arthur Seyss-Inquart
Commissar of the Netherlands. Sentenced to hang.

Albert Speer
Minister of Armaments and War Production. Hitler's chief architect. Sentenced to twenty years in prison.

Julius Streicher
Editor of the antisemitic newspaper *Der Stürmer*, Director of the Central Committee for the Defense against Jewish Atrocity and Boycott Propaganda. Sentenced to hang.

Konstantin von Neurath
Protector of Bohemia and Moravia. Sentenced to fifteen years in prison.

Franz von Papen
German statesman and diplomat. Acquitted.

Joachim von Ribbentrop
Minister of Foreign Affairs. Sentenced to hang.

Baldur von Schirach
Reich Youth Leader. Sentenced to twenty years in prison.

About Photo

The twenty-one Nazi defendants in the dock at the Nuremberg Trials, circa. 1945–1946.

Courtesy of National Archives Collection of World War II Crimes Records, National Archives Identifier: 540127

Additional War Crimes Trials

Between 1946 and 1949, 185 more defendants were tried by US Military Tribunals. The American prosecutors brought charges on crimes such as conducting medical experiments upon concentration camp inmates; forced labor; confiscation of Jewish property; mass murder charges against members of the Einsatzgruppen; cases against the huge German companies, I.G. Farben and Krupp Corporations on the use of slave labor; charges against the SS Race and Settlement Office for carrying out policies of genocide; and senior military officers for abuses against prisoners of war and civilians in occupied countries. Twenty-four of those indicted were sentenced to death, twenty sentenced to life imprisonment, and eighty-seven to shorter jail terms. The others were acquitted or released.

Many European countries held war trials of Nazi perpetrators. In 1945, England conducted the Bergen-Belsen Trials. Bergen-Belsen was a concentration camp located in Germany where, among others, Anne Frank died. Although it was not an extermination camp, the British soldiers who liberated it found sickening conditions in the camp, unburied bodies, disease, and starvation. A total of eleven people, eight men and three women, were condemned to death for mistreatment of prisoners at the Bergen-Belsen concentration camp. Nineteen others were sentenced to life in prison.

Due to the enormous scope of the Nazi crimes committed in Poland, the authorities of liberated Poland considered catching the criminals and punishing them one of their prime missions. In November 1944, the trial against some of the Majdanek extermination and concentration camp staff was held while the war was still raging in Poland. The Poles, together with the Soviets, put on trial, among the rest, the commanders of Auschwitz, Rudolf Hoess and Arthur Liebehenschel, who were sentenced to death and hanged. Most of the other criminals got away since they fled westwards and the Polish had only minor success in getting them extradited.

By the end of the war, the unprecedented magnitude of the Nazi crimes came to be known, as well as the vast number of criminals. The Allies realized that it would be impossible to put all of the criminals on trial.

The process of "denazification," the expurgating of Nazism and its influence in Germany, was originally undertaken by the occupying powers. This process included punishing former Nazis according to their classification as Major Offenders, Offenders, Lesser Offenders, or Followers. But by 1948, it became clear that this also was too complicated and too large a task for them to carry out. The Allies transferred the process to the German authorities, but in the climate of the Cold War, by 1954, it was phased out.

In 1950, the Western Allies removed preventive measures on the West German courts. Now the judicial system of West Germany could investigate and punish all Nazi crimes. This didn't happen immediately, mainly because the Germans were much more interested in rebuilding their country and their economy. The Germans abolished the death sentence, including in trials of Nazi criminals.

Moreover, German politicians understood that persecution of Nazis was not popular among the German voters. Due to the Cold War, the Western Allies themselves were much more interested in making West Germany its ally and agreed to disregard the light or lack of punishment of Nazi criminals. In the early 1950s, the Germans took advantage of this situation and released on amnesty many Nazis, some who had been accused of grave crimes. In 1958, the Central Office of the Judicial Administrations of the Länder for the Investigation of Nazi Crimes was established in Ludwigsburg. This led to more investigations and trials. Eventually over 5,000 cases were investigated and nearly as many were brought to trial.

In West Germany, Poland, and the Soviet Union, trials of concentration camp staff were also held in later years. The camps included Auschwitz, Sobibor, Dachau, Bergen-Belsen, Majdanek, Treblinka, Chelmno, Belzec, Sachsenhausen, and Ravensbrück. Some of these staff members were sentenced to death. In other East European countries there were trials against people who were considered to have been fascists, many of whom had a role in the persecution of local Jews.

In 1960, Israeli agents captured Adolf Eichmann in Argentina. Eichmann, who had been a central figure in organizing the logistics of the "Final Solution," was brought to Israel where he stood trial the following year. He was found guilty and became the only convicted criminal to be executed by the State of Israel.

In the 1970s, a new wave of war crime investigations began with the establishment of the Office of Special Investigation (OSI) in Washington, DC. These new investigations were largely supported by Jewish organizations in the United States and particularly the Simon Wiesenthal Center. The objective of the OSI was to pursue possible war criminals who had obtained US citizenship through false statements. Similar war crimes laws were set up in Canada, Australia, and Great Britain. The British War Crimes Act of 1991 limited its jurisdiction to crimes committed in Germany or in German-occupied territory.

As public consciousness about the Holocaust grew from the middle of the 1980s onward, several important war crimes trials were held in France, both of Germans and Vichy functionaries who had collaborated with the Nazis.

Following the fall of the Communist regimes in Eastern Europe, several governments established historical commissions to explore the events of World War II and its aftermath in their countries. Each of these commissions delved into the role of its citizens in the persecution of the Jews. For many reasons the commissions and their findings were often flawed, but despite the flaws, they symbolize an important step in self-examination and accepting responsibility.

All of these trials notwithstanding, the vast majority of Nazi war criminals were never brought to justice.

Discussion Questions

a. What countries conducted the first Nuremberg Trial in 1945–46? Why do you think it was these particular countries?

b. Why do you think that Winston Churchill suggested summarily executing the Nazi leaders?

c. Why do you think that this trial was held in Germany rather than in one of the Allied countries or in a neutral country?

d. Why do you think that the countries conducting this trial had an equal number of judges and prosecutors?

e. Consider the "not guilty" defense based on the reason of "following orders." Do you think that there is ever a situation when this defense could be valid? Explain your answer.

f. Consider what Robert Jackson said about why it was so important to have war crimes trials. Do you agree with his assessment? Why or why not?

L9

RUDOLF HOESS

Rudolf Hoess, the director of the most infamous extermination camp, was, by his own admission, history's greatest mass murderer, personally supervising the extermination of approximately 1.1 million people in Auschwitz-Birkenau. In 1947, Hoess was hanged for his role in the murder of the victims of Auschwitz.

During trial, 1946

Excerpt from Rudolf Hoess's Testimony at the Nuremberg Trials

The Preseident: Stand up. Will you state your name?

Witness: Rudolf Franz Ferdinand Hoess.

Q: During an interrogation I had with you the other day you told me that about sixty men were designated to receive these transports, and that these sixty persons too had been bound to the same secrecy described before. Do you still maintain that today?

A: Yes, these sixty men were always on hand to take the detainees not capable of work to these provisional and, later on, to the other installations. This group, consisting of about ten leaders and sub-leaders, as well as doctors and medical personnel, had repeatedly been told both in writing and verbally that they were bound to strictest secrecy as to all that went on in the camps.

Q: And after the arrival of the transports did the victims have to dispose of everything they had? Did they have to undress completely; did they have to surrender their valuables? Is that true?

A: Yes.

Q: And then they immediately went to their death?

A: Yes.

Q: I ask you, according to your knowledge, did these people know what was in store for them?

A: The majority of them did not, for steps were taken to keep them in doubt about it so that the suspicion would not arise that they were to go to their death. For instance, all doors and all walls bore inscriptions to the effect that they were going to undergo a delousing operation or take a shower. This was proclaimed in several languages to the detainees by other detainees who had come in with earlier transports and who were being used as auxiliary crews during the whole action.

Q: And then, you told me the other day, that death from gassing occurred within a period of three to fifteen minutes. Is that correct?

A: Yes.

Q: Did you yourself ever sympathize with the victims, thinking of your own family and children?

A: Yes.

Q: How was it possible then for you to carry out these actions?

A: In spite of all the doubts which I had, the only one and decisive argument was the strict order and the reason given for it by the *Reichsfuehrer* Himmler.

Q: To what do you attribute the particularly bad and shameful conditions which were found on invasion by Allied troops, and which to an extent were photographed and filmed?

A: The catastrophic situation at the end of the war was due to the fact that, as a result of the destruction of railways and of the continuous bombing of the industrial works, for example, Auschwitz with its 140,000 detainees... The number of sick became immense. There were next to no medical supplies; plagues raged everywhere. Detainees who were capable of work were used continuously. By order of the *Reichsfuehrer*, even half-sick people had to be used wherever possible in industry. As a result every bit of space in the concentration camps which could possibly be used for lodging was filled with sick and dying detainees.

Q: Did you learn that towards the end of the war concentration camps were evacuated, and, if so, who gave the orders?

A: Let me explain. Originally there was an order from the *Reichsfuehrer*, according to which camps, in the event of an approaching enemy or in the event of air attacks, were to be surrendered to the enemy. Later on, with respect to the case of Buchenwald, which had been reported to the Fuehrer, there was...no, at the beginning of 1945, when various camps came within operational sphere of the enemy, this order was withdrawn. The *Reichsfuehrer* ordered the Higher SS and Police Leaders, who in an emergency case were responsible for the security and safety of the camps, to decide themselves whether an evacuation or a surrender was appropriate.

Auschwitz and Gross-Rosen were evacuated. Buchenwald was also to be evacuated, but then the order from the *Reichsfuehrer* came through to the effect that no more camps were to be evacuated. After Buchenwald had been occupied, it was reported to the Fuehrer that internees had armed themselves and were carrying out plunderings in the town of Weimar. This caused the Fuehrer to give the strictest order to Himmler to the effect that in the future no more camps were to fall into the hands of the enemy, and that no internees capable of marching were to be left behind in any camp.

Excerpt from Rudolf Hoess's Autobiography

"...What are my opinions today concerning the Third Reich?... I remain, as I have always been, a convinced National-Socialist in my attitude to life... The concentration camps before the war had to be depositories in which to segregate opponents of the state... similarly, they were necessary for the preventive war on crime... I also see now that the extermination of the Jews was fundamentally wrong. Precisely because of this mass extermination, Germany has drawn upon herself the hatred of the entire world. It in no way served the cause of antisemitism, but on the contrary brought the Jews far closer to their ultimate objective... I have sufficiently explained how the horrors of the concentration camps could come about. I for my part never sanctioned them. I myself never maltreated a prisoner, far less killed one. Nor have I ever tolerated maltreatment by my subordinates... I knew very well that prisoners in Auschwitz were ill-treated by the SS, by their civilian employers, and not least of all by their fellow-prisoners. I used every means at my disposal to stop this. But I could not."

—*Commandant of Auschwitz: The Autobiography of Rudolf Hoess*
(London: Weidenfeld and Nicolson, 1959), 176

ADOLF EICHMANN

Adolf Eichmann was the head of the Jewish section in the SS security apparatus, through which the Nazis dealt with their political, racial, and ideological enemies. He did not make policy, but he did make many decisions concerning the organization of the murder and showed much initiative and enthusiasm for his mission.

Eichmann was involved in all stages of the persecution of the Jews. Most of the time he was a bureaucrat, but at several junctions he also was active in the field. After the annexation of Austria in 1938, he set up the Central Office for Jewish Emigration, which worked to push Jews out of Austria. He set up a similar office in Prague the following year. During the first years of the war, he worked on various plans to isolate Jews and push them out of German territory.

During trial, 1961

On the orders of his direct superior, Reinhard Heydrich, Eichmann organized the Wannsee Conference to coordinate the murders; the conference took place in Berlin, in January 1942. Once the "Final Solution" was launched, Eichmann's office issued the orders regarding when and where deportations were to happen. Eichmann himself paid several visits to extermination camps to check on their efficiency and progress, and was directly responsible for the Theresienstadt ghetto.

Eichmann personally directed the 1944 deportations from Hungary, which were closely coordinated with and carried out by Hungarian authorities. For a time, Eichmann took part in negotiations with the Jewish leadership, in which he suggested that in exchange for the lives of Hungarian Jewry, Germany would receive desperately needed material goods. These negotiations were never completed.

In May 1960, Israeli secret service agents found Eichmann living in Argentina under a false name. They kidnapped him and brought him to Israel to stand trial under the Nazis and Nazi Collaborators (Punishment) Law of 1950. He was indicted on fifteen counts, including crimes against the Jewish people, crimes against humanity, war crimes, and membership in various criminal organizations, including the SS, the Security Service (SD), and the Gestapo. The charges against Eichmann also included crimes against the Poles, Slovenes, Roma, and Czechs.

Eichmann was found guilty on all counts as a key figure in the "Final Solution." On December 15, 1961, he was sentenced to death and was executed.

Excerpt from Adolf Eichmann's Testimony in an Israeli Court

Judge: Did you never experience a conflict, what one could call a conflict of conscience? Between your duty and your conscience.

Eichmann: One could call it a state of being split.

Q: Being split?

A: A conscious split state, where one could flee from one side to the other.

L9

Q: It was necessary to abandon one's personal conscience?

A: Yes, one could say that. Because one could not control or regulate it oneself.

Q: Except if one accepted the personal consequences.

A: One could have said, I refuse to do this, but I don't know what would have happened then.

Q: If there had been more civil courage, things would have been different, don't you think so?

A: Of course, if this civil courage had been hierarchically organized.

Q: Then it wasn't fate, an inevitable fate.

A: It's a question of human behaviour. That's how it happened, it was wartime, everyone thought: "It was useless to fight against it, it's only a drop in the ocean. What use is it? There's no point in it, it will do neither good nor harm." It was also connected to the times, I think, with the era, with ideological education, rigid discipline, and all that kind of thing.

Q: At that time it was very difficult for individuals to accept the consequences of refusing to obey orders.

A: One was living at a time where crime was legalized by the state, it was the responsibility of those who gave the orders.

Q: According to you, the idealist you claim to have been is defined as someone who executes the orders he receives from above to the best of his ability.

A: For me that meant adherence to the nationalism being preached, and, as a nationalist, to do my duty according to the oath of allegiance. That's how I understood it. Today I realize that all nationalism taken to extremes leads to gross egoism and from there it is only a small step to radicalism.

Q: The general outlines both strategically and tactically, of the extermination of the Jews were planned as a campaign psychologically, like psychological warfare, using tactical deception and so on.

A: I believe that it gradually crystallized during the course of events. And if necessary Himmler gave orders directly. I do not think that originally—how can I put it—a discussion about what actions were to be taken, in which the whole thing was planned down to the last detail.... I believe it somehow resulted automatically....

Q: So you say it evolved organically over the course of time.

A: Yes. That's how I'd describe it.

EVIAN CONFERENCE

After Germany annexed Austria in March 1938, President Franklin D. Roosevelt called for an international conference to promote the emigration of Austrian and German refugees and create an international organization whose purpose would be to deal with the refugee problem. The President invited delegates from thirty-two countries, including the United States, Great Britain, France, Canada, six small European democratic nations, the Latin American nations, Australia, and New Zealand. The conference was convened in Evian, France from July 6–16, 1938. Its declared goal was to deal with the refugee problem, however, Roosevelt made it clear that no country would be forced to change its immigration quotas, but would instead be asked to volunteer changes.

During the conference, it became painfully obvious that no country was willing to volunteer anything significant to help the refugees, whom everyone understood were Jewish refugees. The British delegate claimed that Britain was already fully populated and suffering from unemployment, so it could not take in a larger number of refugees. His only new offer consisted of allowing British territories in East Africa to take in small numbers of refugees. The French delegate declared that France had reached "the extreme point of saturation as regards admission of refugees." Myron C. Taylor, the American delegate, allowed that the United States would make the previously unfilled quota for Germans and Austrians available to these new refugees. Other countries claimed the Depression as their excuse for not accepting refugees. Only the Dominican Republic, a tiny country in the West Indies, volunteered to take in refugees—in exchange for huge amounts of money. The world's democracies had made it extremely clear that they were not willing to help European Jewry.

The only operative step taken at the conference was the establishment of the Intergovernmental Committee on Refugees (ICR). Its goals were to help safe haven candidate countries develop opportunities for refugee settlement, and to try and convince Germany to allow organized emigration. However, ICR member countries did not give the organization either the funding or the authority it needed to make a real difference.

About Photo

U.S. delegate Myron C. Taylor delivers a speech at the Evian Conference on Jewish refugees from Nazi Germany. Evian-les-Bains, France, July 15, 1938.

Photo courtesy National Archives and Records Administration, College Park, MD

BERMUDA CONFERENCE

By the end of 1942, reports revealed that the Nazis intended to exterminate European Jewry. Both in the United States and Britain, Jewish and non-Jewish groups demanded that their governments take a stand against the atrocities. The two governments then planned a conference to address public opinion. They chose inaccessible Bermuda as the conference's venue in order to control the number of reporters and representatives of non-governmental organizations attending. Members of the Joint Distribution Committee and the World Jewish Congress were not permitted to attend. The conference was convened on April 19, 1943. Its declared goal was to deal with the issue of wartime refugees.

The organizers severely limited the issues that could be discussed. They insisted on downplaying the persecution of the Jews and the "Final Solution," and presented the issue of refugees only in its more universal aspects. Furthermore, the Americans refused to consider changing their strict immigration quotas to let in more Jewish refugees, while the British refused to consider Palestine as a safe haven for Jewish refugees. They would not even discuss sending food packages to concentration camp prisoners. The Americans also betrayed their lack of seriousness by not sending a high-ranking delegation with the authority to make decisions.

At the conference itself, the attendees spent much time talking about renewing the Intergovernmental Committee on Refugees (ICR), which had been created at the 1938 Evian Conference for the purpose of negotiating with the Germans about refugees. However, the point was moot because, as negotiating with the Nazis was no longer an option, no one was willing to fund the committee. No other solution suggested was deemed acceptable by the two governments, either. Thus, nothing was accomplished, and the Bermuda Conference did not save one Jew.

About Photo

Delegates to the refugee conference in Bermuda.

Left to right: George Hall, British delegate; Dr. Harold W. Dodds, Chairman of the US group; Richard K. Law, British Undersecretary of State for Foreign Affairs; Rep. Sol Bloom, New York; Osbert Peake, British Undersecretary for the Home Office.

Courtesy of the Library of Congress, Prints & Photographs Division, NYWT&S Collection, LC-USZ62-132703

THE REFUGEE

Felix Nussbaum, 1939

About Painting

Felix Nussbaum (1904-1944), **The Refugee (European Vision)**, 1939. Oil on canvas. Collection of the Yad Vashem Art Museum, Jerusalem. © Yad Vashem. All Rights Reserved.

L9

PORTRAIT OF AN UNIDENTIFIED MAN
Felix Nussbaum, 1941

About Painting

Felix Nussbaum (1904-1944), **Portrait of an Unidentified Man,** Brussels, 1941. Oil on canvas. Gift of the Freund family in memory of Hilda Freund. Collection of the Yad Vashem Art Museum, Jerusalem. © Yad Vashem. All Rights Reserved.

SHORE AT RAPALLO
Felix Nussbaum, 1934

About Painting

Felix Nussbaum (1904–1944), **Shore at Rapallo,** Brussels, 1934. Oil on canvas. Gift of Charles Knoblauch in memory of his family members who perished in the Holocaust. Collection of the Yad Vashem Art Museum, Jerusalem. © Yad Vashem. All Rights Reserved.

THOU SHALT NOT KILL, DIPTYCH

Samuel Bak, 1970

About Paintings

Samuel Bak (1933–), **Thou Shalt Not Kill,** diptych, 1970. Oil on canvas, 122x162 cm. each. Gift of the artist. Collection of the Yad Vashem Art Museum, Jerusalem. © Yad Vashem. All Rights Reserved.

"Diptych" is a work made of of two matching parts.

PRIMARY SOURCE READINGS

Dispatches from US Consulates in Germany (1933)

❖ *April 10–Dispatch from George S. Messersmith*

"...It is the undisguised intention of the National Socialist Party to get absolute control of all forms of German Government and of intellectual, professional, financial, business, and cultural life.... The (1933) forcing of the Jewish judges from the courts... [is] brought about by Party pressure and action.... It is a question as to whether such direct ruthless and complete control of a civilized people has ever been achieved in so short a time by a minority."[1]

❖ *July 8–Dispatch from George A. Gordon*

"...Consistently and relentlessly the Jews are being eliminated from practically all walks of life. Nazi doctors and lawyers are "conducting bitter, relentless boycotts against their Jewish colleagues.... Nazi leaders have repeatedly boasted in the past that one of the first acts of a Nazi regime would be to set up ghettos in Germany...the outward and official manifestations of antisemitism in present day Germany fail to reveal the real brutality and truculence of the Nazi toward the Jews, and that they are determined to make life for Jews in Germany well nigh insufferable."[2]

US Newspaper (1942)

❖ *December 18–The New York Times (front page)*

11 ALLIES CONDEMN NAZI WAR ON JEWS; United Nations Issue Joint Declaration of Protest on 'Cold-Blooded Extermination' 11 ALLIES CONDEMN NAZI WAR ON JEWS

WASHINGTON, Dec. 17 -- A joint declaration by members of the United Nations was issued today condemning Germany's "bestial policy of cold-blooded extermination" of Jews and declaring that "such events can only strengthen the resolve of all freedom-loving peoples to overthrow the barbarous Hitlerite tyranny."

Excerpts from Official Reports and Statements (1944)

❖ *From "Report to the Secretary [of the Treasury, Henry Morgenthau, Jr.] on the Acquiescence of this Government in the Murder of the Jews," initiated by Randolph Paul for the Foreign Funds Control Unit of the Treasury Department (January 13, 1944)*

"[State Department officials] have not only failed to use the Governmental machinery at their disposal to rescue Jews from Hitler, but have even gone so far as to use this Government machinery to prevent the rescue of these Jews.

"They have not only failed to cooperate with private organizations in the efforts of these organizations to work out individual programs of their own, but have taken steps designed to prevent these programs from being put into effect.

"They not only have failed to facilitate the obtaining of information concerning Hitler's plans to exterminate the Jews of Europe but in their official capacity have gone so far as to surreptitiously attempt to stop the obtaining of information concerning the murder of the Jewish population of Europe.

"They have tried to cover up their guilt by: concealment and misrepresentation; the giving of false and misleading explanations for their failures to act and their attempts to prevent action; and the issuance of false and misleading statements concerning the 'action' which they have taken to date. While the State Department has been thus 'exploring' the whole refugee problem, without distinguishing between those who are in imminent danger of death and those who are not, hundreds of thousands of Jews have been allowed to perish."

❖ *From Treasury Secretary Henry Morgenthau Jr.'s Personal Report to the President (January 16, 1944)*

"…The facts I have detailed in this report, Mr. President, came to the Treasury's attention as a part of our routine investigation of the licensing of the financial phases of the proposal of the World Jewish Congress for the evacuation of Jews from France and Rumania [sic]. The facts may thus be said to have come to light through accident. How many others of the same character are buried in State Department files is a matter I would have no way of knowing. Judging from the almost complete failure of the State Department to achieve any results, the strong suspicion must be that they are not few.

"This much is certain, however. The matter of rescuing the Jews from extermination is a trust too great to remain in the hands of men who are indifferent, callous, and perhaps even hostile. The task is filled with difficulties. Only a fervent will to accomplish, backed by persistent and untiring effort can succeed where time is so precious."

❖ *From Presidential Statement (March 24, 1944)*

On March 24, 1944, President Roosevelt issued a strong accusation and warning which was published widely in Allied and neutral nations and airdropped in leaflet form by the millions over Nazi-occupied territories. Finally, the President had become convinced of the facts concerning Hitler's war against the Jews. Now he acted forcefully, but too late to save the millions who had already gone to their deaths.

"In one of the blackest crimes of all history—begun by the Nazis in the days of peace and multiplied by them a hundred times in time of war—the wholesale systematic murder of the Jews of Europe goes on unabated every hour…. That these innocent people, who have already survived a decade of Hitler's fury, should perish on the very eve of triumph over the barbarism which their persecution symbolizes, would be a major tragedy…. It is therefore fitting that we should again proclaim our determination that none who participate in these acts of savagery shall go unpunished…. That warning applies not only to the leaders but also to their functionaries and subordinates in Germany and in the satellite countries. All who knowingly take part in the deportation of Jews to their death in Poland or Norwegians and French to their death in Germany are equally guilty with the executioner. All who share the guilt shall share the punishment."

"Hitler is committing these crimes against humanity in the name of the German people. I ask every German and every man everywhere under Nazi domination to show the world by his action that in his heart he does not share these insane criminal desires. Let him hide these pursued victims, help them to get over their borders, and do what he can to save them from the Nazi hangman. I ask him also to keep watch, and to record the evidence that will one day be used to convict the guilty."

End Notes

[1]*Foreign Relations of the United States Diplomatic Papers 1933*, Vol. II (Washington, DC: United States Government Printing Office, 1949), 226–227.

[2]Ibid., at 354–356.

About Photo

A Jewish Woman Sitting with Her Children before Their Execution, Lubny, Ukraine (2725/21)

Yad Vashem Photo Archive

"Great crimes start with little things...."

– Jan Karski, Rescue and Aid Provider

Preparing to Use This Lesson

Below is information to keep in mind when using this lesson. In some cases, the points elaborate on general suggestions listed in the "Teaching about the Holocaust" section in the **Introduction** to this resource, and are specific to the content of the lesson. This material is intended to help teachers consider the complexities of teaching the Holocaust and to deliver accurate and sensitive instruction.

- The Nazi belief that they needed to murder babies and children was central to their racial ideology. This ideology claimed that Jews were guilty of ruining the world the minute that they were born (or even conceived) and, therefore, they should not be "allowed" to live. The murder of children is characteristic of genocides—it is the most effective way to ensure the destruction of a group.

- The Holocaust is one of history's most extreme human events with both unique and universal aspects, and it is critical that students understand the difference between the two. It is important that students first study the unique historical event of the Holocaust and only then proceed to drawing universal conclusions. Help students understand that the word "compare," which is often used when discussing the Holocaust in relation to other genocides or mass killings, does not mean to "equate" as many mistakenly believe.

- Studying the Holocaust and other genocides can leave students feeling that the events they are learning about happened so long ago and in locations so far from their own communities that there is little or no relevance to their own lives. Identifying opportunities for students to visit local museums, centers, memorials, and/or to spend time with members of their communities who can provide a first-person account of events can help students build knowledge, broaden their experiences, and begin to make meaningful connections to events in their own lives.

THE CHILDREN

About This Lesson

180–270 minutes plus time for research

❖ **INTRODUCTION** The purpose of this lesson is for students to understand the effects of the Holocaust on its most innocent victims—children—since targeting babies and children was an important step in the attempt by the Nazis to erase the Jews and their future. Students will also research post-Holocaust genocides and analyze children's rights violations. In addition, students are provided an opportunity to develop a position on whether an event the magnitude of the Holocaust could happen again and to consider the role and responsibility of the individual in seeing that it does not.

This three-part lesson has material appropriate for history, social studies, Holocaust and genocide studies, English/language arts, and ethics classes. Instructional strategies used in this lesson include large-group discussion, small-group work, comparing and contrasting information, interpreting visual history testimony, analyzing primary source documents, research skills, critical thinking, oral presentation, and journaling.

❖ **OBJECTIVES** After completing this lesson, students will be able to:

- Describe the situation that children faced during the Holocaust.

- Discuss both the content and the messages in a clip of visual history testimony.

- Summarize the causes and effects of post-Holocaust genocides.

- Analyze the violation of children's rights during the Holocaust and during genocides that have taken place since.

- Construct an argument to support whether or not something the magnitude of the Holocaust could happen again.

- Recommend actions that individuals can take to prevent genocide.

❖ **KEY WORDS & PHRASES**

Aktion	Gross-Rosen	prejudice
Auschwitz-Birkenau	Holocaust	Sinti-Roma
bystander	Kovno ghetto	Treblinka
Chelmno	Lodz ghetto	victim
extermination camp	Nazi ideology	Warsaw ghetto
genocide	occupation	Yom Hashoah
ghetto	perpetrator	

RESOURCES & TESTIMONIES

All of the resources used in this lesson can be found in this guide at the end of this lesson and at echoesandreflections.org.

Visual history testimonies are available on the website or on the DVD that accompanies this resource guide.

Teachers are urged to review the lesson procedures to identify other materials and technology needed to implement the lesson.

L10

❖ **ACADEMIC STANDARDS** The materials in this lesson address the following national education standards:

Common Core State Standards

- Reading Standards for Informational Text 6–12
- Writing Standards 6–12
- Speaking and Listening Standards 6–12
- Reading Standards for Literacy in History/Social Studies 6–12
- Writing Standards for Literacy in History/Social Studies 6–12

A complete analysis of how this lesson addresses Common Core State Standards by grade level and specific skills is available on the Echoes and Reflections website.

National Curriculum Standards for Social Studies

❶ Culture

❷ Time, Continuity, and Change

❸ People, Places, and Environments

❹ Individual Development and Identity

❺ Individuals, Groups, and Institutions

❻ Power, Authority, and Governance

❾ Global Connections

❿ Civic Ideals and Practices

Procedures

Part 1: Children of the Holocaust

TESTIMONY VIEWING

About the Interviewees

Vladka Meed was born on December 29, 1921, in Warsaw, Poland. She was forced to lived in the Warsaw ghetto but later escaped and hid under false identity in Poland. She is known for her valiant efforts to help

continued on page 263

NOTE 1.1

Additional information on Vladka Meed can be found in Lesson 6: Jewish Resistance.

1. Introduce students to Vladka Meed and Roman Kent and then show the first two clips from Part 1 of Visual History Testimony: *The Children*. Discuss the testimony using the questions below.

   - What do you learn from Vladka Meed's testimony?

   - What does Vladka's testimony tell us about what life was like for some children in the Warsaw ghetto?

   - What do you learn from listening to Roman Kent describe his experience during the Holocaust?

   - What conclusions can you make about the fate of children based on Roman's testimony?

   - What are some other things that you have learned about the fate of children during the Holocaust? How have you learned this information?

   - What is the connection between Nazi ideology and the fate of Jewish children during the Holocaust?

   - What are your feelings after hearing these testimonies?

2. Provide students with background information on children and the Holocaust.

About Children and the Holocaust

Full statistics for the tragic fate of children and youth who died during the Holocaust will never be known; it is estimated that 1.5 million Jewish children and youth were murdered. In many respects, Jewish children were treated just like adults by the Nazis and their collaborators, suffering from the same difficult and terrible situations that adult Jews faced. Like the adults, many suffered through the deadly conditions in ghettos and camps, the terror of shootings and deportations, and the horrors of the industrialized mass murder. Being smaller and less able to understand what was going on around them, the youngest children often had the hardest time. Older children sometimes were better equipped to try to cope with their situations.

The systematic murder of Jewish babies and children—who could not be rationally blamed for anything—was a direct result of Nazi racial ideology. In the eyes of the Nazis, Jewish babies were born guilty of ruining the world and sentenced to death before they took their first breath.

Most Jewish children under the age of fourteen or fifteen were selected to be put to death immediately upon arrival at extermination camps. Not only in the camps, but in the ghettos, in hiding, and in all of occupied Europe, Jewish children were often the first to die.

Throughout Europe during the war, children were on the forefront of suffering both from Nazi policies and from the war itself. They were among the first victims of Nazi murder during the outset of the war when German children and adults who had been institutionalized with mental and physical disabilities were murdered. Sinti-Roma children whom the Nazis deported also had a terrible fate. Although they were not necessarily killed immediately, the vast majority of these children also met their death at the hands of the Nazis and their collaborators.

For all children and youth who survived the war, the difficulties they experienced frequently left their mark on them both physically and psychologically.

3. Divide the class into small groups of four students each. Distribute a copy of each of the four photographs to the groups and instruct each student in the group to randomly select one of the photographs. Have each student study his or her photograph individually and consider the questions below and develop their own questions about the photograph.

   • What does the picture say to you?

About the Interviewees
continued from page 262

aid those in danger. Her interview was conducted in the United States. When the war began, Vladka was eighteen years old.

Roman Kent was born on April 18, 1929, in Lodz, Poland. He was forced to live in the Lodz ghetto and later incarcerated in the Flossenbürg, Auschwitz, and Gross-Rosen concentration camps. Roman was also imprisoned in the Auschwitz-Birkenau extermination camp. His interview was conducted in the United States. When the war began, Roman was ten years old.

_____

For additional information about Vladka Meed and Roman Kent, see their Biographical Profiles available on the website.

NOTE 1.3

Encourage students to come up with four or five questions.

L10

- If this picture was part of a video, what do you imagine you would hear?

- What questions come to your mind as you look at the picture?

4. After students have had ample time to study the photographs individually, instruct group members to share their thoughts and questions about the photographs with one another. Each group member should assume the role of discussion leader while presenting some of the questions he or she developed about a particular photograph. At the end of this activity, share information about the photographs.

5. Introduce students to Vladka Meed (if she was not introduced earlier), show the third clip from Part 1 of Visual History Testimony: *The Children*, and discuss some or all of the questions below.

- What do you learn about Janusz Korczak from listening to Vladka Meed's testimony?

- What kind of man do you think Janusz Korczak was? How does Vladka's testimony help shape your thoughts about him?

- How would you characterize Janusz Korczak's action of not leaving the children although he had the opportunity?

- Janusz Korczak believed that all children are good and if properly loved and cared for, all children would grow up to be great achievers. Do you agree with this philosophy? Why or why not?

- Do children's rights need special attention? Explain your thinking.

6. Distribute the *Janusz Korczak* handout. As a whole-group, read the biographical information and selections from Korczak's "The Child's Right to Respect." Have a whole-group discussion using the questions below.

- How would you characterize Janusz Korczak's philosophy as it pertains to the rights of children?

- Do you agree with his philosophy of what it means to respect a child? Why or why not?

- What specific passage in "The Child's Right to Respect" is particularly meaningful to you and why?

- Do you feel that children in today's society are respected in a way consistent with Janusz Korczak's philosophy? Explain your response by giving specific examples from personal experience or contemporary events that you've heard or read about in the media.

7. Display *Geneva Declaration of the Rights of the Child* and review together. Ask students when they think this declaration was written and adopted.

8. Have students discuss what each of the five principles means and give examples of ways that the principles were violated during the Holocaust. Have students compare the *Geneva Declaration*

to Janusz Korczak's "The Child's Right to Respect" and consider how the two documents are similar and how they are different. Ask students if they think the Geneva Declaration was drafted before or after the Holocaust and solicit reasons for their response. At the end of the discussion, tell students that the Geneva Declaration was written and adopted in 1924, following World War I.

Reflect and Respond

Either in class or as homework, have students reflect and respond to one or more of the topics below or have them develop a topic that has meaning for them based on the material covered in the lesson.

- Reflect on what you think are the rights that all children are entitled to and why. Why do you think the rights of children are violated so often? What are the short- and long-term dangers to a society that does not protect and care for its children?

- Explain the meaning of the statement, "Some are guilty, all are responsible." Discuss whether you believe this statement to be applicable to what happened to children during the Holocaust?

- Whose moral obligation was it to save children who were victims during the Holocaust? Explain what you think might have been done to prevent the death of 1.5 million Jewish children.

Part 2: Genocides after the Holocaust

1. Review the meaning of the term *genocide* using the definition available on the website (Lesson 1: Studying the Holocaust under **Download Lesson Resources** or in the **Glossary**).

2. Introduce students to Leo Bach and show Part 2 of Visual History Testimony: *The Children*. Follow with a discussion using the questions below.

   - In his testimony (provided in 1992), Leo Bach refers to several genocides or genocidal acts that have taken place since the Holocaust. What areas of the world does he mention? [**Optional:** Have students locate countries named on a world map.]

   - What other genocides do you know about that Leo does not mention?

   - Do you think Leo feels that the world learned anything from the Holocaust? What specifically does Leo say that supports your answer?

3. Distribute the *Genocide Case Study* handout. Explain to students that they will work in small groups to research post-Holocaust genocides. They will then present their findings to the class in an oral or multimedia presentation. Their research must include both primary and secondary source materials. Students are encouraged to include sources such as maps, pictures, videos, diary entries, etc. As many questions as possible on the *Genocide Case Study*

L10

handout should be answered, with special attention to the questions related to children.

4. Distribute the *Declaration of the Rights of the Child, 1959* handout for students to use in answering the question specific to that document or alert them to where the document is available on the website. Review the document together as a whole group.

5. Post-Holocaust genocides or atrocities that may be characterized as genocide or genocidal acts have occurred in the countries/regions listed below. Assign each group one of the topics for its research.

- Bosnia-Herzegovina
- Burma
- Cambodia
- Democratic Republic of the Congo
- Indonesia and East Timor
- Rwanda
- Sudan and South Sudan

6. After providing sufficient time for students to complete their research, assign a schedule for presentations or have groups post their multimedia presentations on the class website. After all students have heard or watched all of the presentations, conduct a whole-group discussion using the following questions:

- Based on the information presented in these reports/presentations, can you come to any conclusions about why genocides occur?
- What, if anything, do the perpetrators appear to have in common?
- What, if anything, do the targeted groups appear to have in common prior to the acts of genocide taking place?
- What is the overall effect of these atrocities on children?
- Are you surprised by how many of the rights of children are ignored when genocide occurs? Why or why not? Whose responsibility is it to see that children's rights are not violated under any circumstances?
- In what ways were people and communities changed as a result of the atrocities you researched? How do people and communities continue to suffer from what happened?
- Do you think that the world community should have played a greater role in preventing these genocides or in intervening once it was known that they were happening? Explain your answer.
- How did the free world respond in these cases of genocide? How was the response different or the same as the response during the Holocaust? [NOTE: To learn about the response of the free world during the Holocaust, see Lesson 9: Perpetrators, Collaborators, and Bystanders.]
- What kinds of actions can individuals around the world take so as not to be bystanders to such atrocities?
- In light of the study of these genocides, what do you think was learned from the Holocaust?

Part 3: Could It Happen Again?

1. Introduce students to Jan Karski, Joseph Berger, and William McKinney and show Part 3 of Visual History Testimony: *The Children*. Follow with a discussion using the questions below as a guide.

   - Jan Karski states that "great crimes start with little things" and then goes on to give examples of things people should not do. What are some of the examples he gives? Which, if any, of his suggestions do you think are particularly difficult for people to put into practice and why?

   - Does Joseph Berger believe that anything was learned from the Holocaust? How does he support his argument?

   - William McKinney states in his testimony that it is time to "eliminate bloodshed." What do you think would be needed in order to achieve this goal?

   - Do you think that individuals play a role in helping to make the world a peaceful place? If so, explain the role of the individual.

   - What are some things that you can do to prevent prejudice and bigotry in your school, community, society, and beyond? What are some things that your teachers, parents, religious and community leaders can do?

2. Referring to the clips of testimony shown earlier, remind students that Joseph Berger believed that the Holocaust could happen again, while Jan Karski felt that it could not. Ask students to consider their thoughts on this topic and then allow time for students to participate in a round-table discussion on the question: "Could an event the magnitude of the Holocaust happen again?" Encourage students to refer to specific information that they have learned throughout their study of the Holocaust as they develop and present their arguments. [Optional: Divide students into two groups based on whether they believe something the magnitude of the Holocaust could happen again or not. Have each group prepare its argument and share with others in the class using the "Fishbowl" strategy.]

Reflect and Respond

Either in class or as homework, have students reflect and respond to one or more of the topics below or have them develop a topic that has meaning for them based on the material covered in the lesson.

- Consider the questions posed by Professor Yehuda Bauer, one of the world's premier historians of the Holocaust, "What did the Nazis leave behind? What are their literary, their artistic, their philosophical, their architectural achievements?" Write about what you believe to be the lasting legacy of the Nazis.

- A study of the Holocaust will often raise more questions in people's minds than it will provide answers. What questions,

TESTIMONY VIEWING

About the Interviewees

Jan Karski was born in 1914 (exact date unknown), in Lodz, then a part of the Russian empire. After the fall of Poland in 1939, he joined an underground organization and was chosen to become a courier for the Polish government-in-exile. He was smuggled into the Warsaw ghetto and the Izbica camp to observe conditions. He was sent to the United Kingdom and United States to report on the situation of the Jews in Poland. His interview was conducted in the United States. When the war began, Jan was twenty-five years old.

continued on page 268

NOTE 3.1

To learn more about the role that individuals can play in the face of injustice, see Lesson 2: Antisemitism and Lesson 7: Rescuers and Non-Jewish Resistance.

About the Interviewees

continued from page 267

Joseph Berger was born on September 20, 1937, in Subotica, Yugoslavia. He was imprisoned in the Bergen-Belsen concentration camp. His interview was conducted in the United States. When the war began, Joseph was one year old.

William McKinney was born on February 1, 1923, in Uniontown, Pennsylvania. As a member of the United States Armed Forces, he, along with his fellow soldiers, liberated the Buchenwald concentration camp. His interview was conducted in the United States. When the war began, William was sixteen years old.

For additional information about Jan Karski, Joseph Berger, and William McKinney, see their Biographical Profiles available on the website.

at this stage, do you have about the Holocaust? About human behavior in general? About the role of perpetrators and bystanders? About the resilience of the human spirit?

- What from your study of the Holocaust will you remember most and why?

Making Connections

The additional activities and projects listed below can be integrated directly into the lesson or can be used to extend the lesson once it has been completed. The topics lend themselves to students' continued study of the Holocaust as well as opportunities for students to make meaningful connections to other people and events, including relevant contemporary issues. These activities may include instructional strategies and techniques and/or address academic standards in addition to those that were identified for the lesson.

1. Visit IWitness (iwitness.usc.edu) for activities specific to Lesson 10: The Children.

2. Child survivors are the last living witnesses to the Holocaust. Contact a local Holocaust museum or resource center to request a child survivor visit the classroom. As a class, generate a list of relevant questions to ask the survivor in advance of his or her visit.

3. Many communities have museums, centers, memorials, or survivors and refugees who can share their personal experiences with human rights violations and genocides in addition to the Holocaust, thereby promoting awareness on a range of topics and often encouraging civic action. Such resources are often representative of a particular community's history and/or immigration experience. For example, the Oregon Nikkei Legacy Center in Portland (oregonnikkei.org) reflects the large Japanese-American population in the Pacific Northwest and their experience with internment during World War II, and because states including Maine and Idaho are home to many refugees from war-torn Sudan, groups like the Holocaust and Human Rights Center of Maine (hhrc.uma.edu) and the Idaho Human Rights Education Center (idaho-humanrights.org) have made it part of their mission to educate the community on the genocide in Darfur by providing resources, exhibits, and speakers. Following a visit to a local museum or center or after meeting with a guest speaker, have students conduct a short research project to answer a self-generated question based on something they have seen or heard that they would like to explore further.

4. As a class, read and discuss current and past reports from *The State of the World's Children* on the UNICEF website unicef.org/sowc.

5. Have students plan an event in their school or community commemorating Holocaust Remembrance Week (Yom Hashoah Week), which is usually observed in the United States in April, a week after the end of the Passover Holiday. Yom Hashoah marks the anniversary of the Warsaw Ghetto Uprising. Invite parents,

family members, community members, and school staff and students to the event. As a class, decide what the day will include and what each student's role will be. Additional information about Yom Hashoah and guidelines for planning commemoration activities are available on the Echoes and Reflections website.

6. To provide an opportunity for students to learn more about individuals who survived genocide and human rights violations, help them create a book club to meet on a regular basis either in person or online. Share selected titles with book club members, but let the students come to consensus on which book to read. Students should also decide when they will meet, how much of the book they will have read prior to meeting, and the role they will play in the discussion (e.g., decide if there will be a "discussion leader" for each title). Teachers are encouraged to help facilitate book club meetings, but resist turning the club into an extension of the academic day.

Below is a list of sample titles only; this list is not intended to be comprehensive. Teachers are encouraged to share titles that are age appropriate.

- *A Long Way Gone: Memoirs of a Boy Soldier* (Ishmael Beah)
- *Farewell to Manzanar* (Jeanne Wakatsuki Houston and James Houston)
- *First They Killed My Father: A Daughter of Cambodia Remembers* (Loung Ung)
- *Hidden Roots* (Joseph Bruchac)
- *Left to Tell: Discovering God amidst the Rwandan Holocaust* (Immaculee Ilibagiza)
- *Not My Turn to Die: Memoirs of a Broken Childhood in Bosnia* (Savo Heleta)
- *Rena's Promise: A Story of Sisters in Auschwitz* (Rena Kornreich Gelissen)
- *Tears of the Desert: A Memoir of Survival in Darfur* (Halima Bashir)
- *The Knock at the Door: A Mother's Survival of the Armenian Genocide* (Margaret Ahnert)
- *Ticket to Exile: A Memoir* (Adam David Miller)

PHOTOGRAPH #1

Yad Vashem Photo Archive (4789)

L10

PHOTOGRAPH #2

Yad Vashem Photo Archive (12FO7)

PHOTOGRAPH #3

Yad Vashem Photo Archive (4062/116)

PHOTOGRAPH #4

Yad Vashem Photo Archive (4062/459)

JANUSZ KORCZAK

Janusz Korczak was born Henryk Goldszmit in 1878. He grew up in Warsaw, Poland. Korczak chose to study medicine as a young man because he wanted to help people. He specialized in pediatrics and was an extremely popular doctor in the community because of his compassion for the poor children who lived in the Warsaw slums. In addition, Korczak wrote children's books, stories, plays, and a few books about education. He even had a radio show in which he gave advice to parents.

Korczak founded the Jewish Orphanage in Warsaw and soon his life was dedicated to the orphanage where he lived and worked twenty-four hours a day. As the Jews of Warsaw were being forced into the ghetto in 1940, Korczak insisted on remaining with his children and moved his orphanage into the ghetto. Korczak continued to run the Jewish orphanage according to the values that had guided him in the past, and he tried to insulate his children from the reality of the Nazi occupation. In the ghetto period, his efforts focused on providing livable conditions for the two hundred children in the orphanage; he even tried to expand his activities to encompass other abandoned children in the ghetto.

Korczak could have hidden outside of the ghetto with the aid of Christian friends, but he refused to leave. In August 1942, as the overwhelming majority of the people who had been imprisoned in the Warsaw ghetto were being deported, Korczak realized that his charges were to be deported immediately. He knew that they were headed for deportation from the ghetto, but, rather than frighten the children, he told them they were going on a picnic. Although Korczak could have been saved, and was begged by his friends and admirers to let them help him, he chose to remain with the children. Korczak perished along with nearly 200 children in the gas chambers of Treblinka, as did his most senior coworker Stefania Wilczynska. It is known that many other staff members of other Jewish orphanages throughout Europe acted similarly to Korczak and Wilczynska when their charges were taken to their deaths.

About Photos

Left: Janusz Korczak with several orphans in his institution, Warsaw, Poland. Yad Vashem Photo Archive 24AO2

Right: A sculpture in memory of Janusz Korczak, after the war, Warsaw, Poland. Yad Vashem Photo Archive 7941/6

Selections from "The Child's Right to Respect" (1929)

"The child is not foolish. There are no more fools among children than among adults. Draped in the judicial robes of age, how often we impose thoughtless, uncritical, impractical regulations. The wise child, sometimes stops short in amazement when confronted with the aggressive, senile, offensive stupidity.

The child has a future but also a past consisting of events, memories, long hours of highly significant solitary reflections. He remembers and forgets in a manner no different from our own, appreciates and condemns, reasons logically and makes mistakes born of ignorance. Thoughtfully, he trusts and doubts.

The child is a foreigner who does not understand the language or street plan, who is ignorant of the laws and customs. Occasionally, he likes to go sightseeing on his own; and, when up against some difficulty, he asks for information and advice. Wanted—a guide to answer questions politely.

Respect the ignorance of the child!"

* * *

"Not to trample upon, humiliate, handle as a mere slave to tomorrow; not to repress, hurry, drive on.

Respect for every single instant, for it passes never to return, and always take it seriously; hurt, it will bleed, slain, it will haunt with harsh memories.

Let him drink eagerly in the joy of the morning and look ahead with confidence. That is just how the child wants it to be. A fable, a chat with the dog, catching a ball, an intense study of a picture, the copying of a single letter—nothing is for a child a waste of time. Everything kindly. Right is on the side of the child."

Selections reprinted from Janusz Korczak, "The Child's Right to Respect," in *Selected Works of Janusz Korczak* (translated from Polish by J. Bachrach). Published for the National Science Foundation by the Scientific Publications Foreign Cooperation Center of the Central Institute for Scientific, Technical and Economic Information, Warsaw; [available from the U.S. Dept. of Commerce Clearinghouse for Federal Scientific and Technical Information, Springfield, VA], 1967, 484–490.

L1

GENEVA DECLARATION OF THE RIGHTS OF THE CHILD

By the present Declaration of the Rights of the Child, commonly known as 'Declaration of Geneva,' men and women of all nations, recognizing that mankind owes to the child the best that it has to give, declare and accept it as their duty that, beyond and above all considerations of race, nationality or creed:

(1) The child must be given the means requisite for its normal development, both materially and spiritually;

(2) The child that is hungry must be fed; the child that is sick must be nursed; the child that is backward must be helped; the delinquent child must be reclaimed; and the orphan and the waif must be sheltered and succored;

(3) The child must be the first to receive relief in times of distress;

(4) The child must be put in a position to earn a livelihood, and must be protected against every form of exploitation;

(5) The child must be brought up in the consciousness that its talents must be devoted to the service of fellow men.

GENOCIDE CASE STUDY

I. **Summary of the Event**
   (What happened: by whom, to whom, when, for how long, and where?)

II. **The Background**
   (What political, economic, social, and/or geographic factors led up to the genocide?)

III. **Perpetrators**
   (What group (or groups) of people was responsible for this genocide? What were their motives?)

IV. **Victims**
   (What group (or groups) of people was targeted by the violence? What survival tactics did they attempt? What was the ultimate death toll?)

V. **Children**
(What was the fate of children? Were children forced to perform violent acts? Were children the focus of violence? How many children died? How many were injured? How many children were left orphans? Which principles of the "Declaration of the Rights of the Child, 1959" were violated?)

VI. **World Response**
(How did other countries and the United Nations respond to the mass killing? Based on your research, do you think this genocide could have been prevented?)

VII. **Aftermath**
(How has this genocide continued to affect both the perpetrators and victims and their families? What is the general situation in this country or region today?)

DECLARATION OF THE RIGHTS OF THE CHILD, 1959

Proclaimed by General Assembly Resolution 1386(XIV) of 20 November 1959

Whereas the peoples of the United Nations have, in the Charter, reaffirmed their faith in fundamental human rights and in the dignity and worth of the human person, and have determined to promote social progress and better standards of life in larger freedom,

Whereas the United Nations has, in the Universal Declaration of Human Rights, proclaimed that everyone is entitled to all the rights and freedoms set forth therein, without distinction of any kind, such as race, colour, sex, language, religion, political or other opinion, national or social origin, property, birth or other status,

Whereas the child, by reason of his physical and mental immaturity, needs special safeguards and care, including appropriate legal protection, before as well as after birth,

Whereas the need for such special safeguards has been stated in the Geneva Declaration of the Rights of the Child of 1924, and recognized in the Universal Declaration of Human Rights and in the statutes of specialized agencies and international organizations concerned with the welfare of children,

Whereas mankind owes to the child the best it has to give,

Now therefore,

The General Assembly

Proclaims this Declaration of the Rights of the Child to the end that he may have a happy childhood and enjoy for his own good and for the good of society the rights and freedoms herein set forth, and calls upon parents, upon men and women as individuals, and upon voluntary organizations, local authorities and national Governments to recognize these rights and strive for their observance by legislative and other measures progressively taken in accordance with the following principles:

Principle 1

The child shall enjoy all the rights set forth in this Declaration. Every child, without any exception whatsoever, shall be entitled to these rights, without distinction or discrimination on account of race, colour, sex, language, religion, political or other opinion, national or social origin, property, birth or other status, whether of himself or of his family.

Principle 2

The child shall enjoy special protection, and shall be given opportunities and facilities, by law and by other means, to enable him to develop physically, mentally, morally, spiritually and socially in a healthy and normal manner and in conditions of freedom and dignity. In the enactment of laws for this purpose, the best interests of the child shall be the paramount consideration.

Principle 3

The child shall be entitled from his birth to a name and a nationality.

Principle 4

The child shall enjoy the benefits of social security. He shall be entitled to grow and develop in health; to this end, special care and protection shall be provided both to him and to his mother, including adequate pre-natal and post-natal care. The child shall have the right to adequate nutrition, housing, recreation and medical services.

Principle 5

The child who is physically, mentally or socially handicapped shall be given the special treatment, education and care required by his particular condition.

Principle 6

The child, for the full and harmonious development of his personality, needs love and understanding. He shall, wherever possible, grow up in the care and under the responsibility of his parents, and, in any case, in an atmosphere of affection and of moral and material security; a child of tender years shall not, save in exceptional circumstances, be separated from his mother. Society and the public authorities shall have the duty to extend particular care to children without a family and to those without adequate means of support. Payment of State and other assistance towards the maintenance of children of large families is desirable.

Principle 7

The child is entitled to receive education, which shall be free and compulsory, at least in the elementary stages. He shall be given an education which will promote his general culture and enable him, on a basis of equal opportunity, to develop his abilities, his individual judgement, and his sense of moral and social responsibility, and to become a useful member of society.

The best interests of the child shall be the guiding principle of those responsible for his education and guidance; that responsibility lies in the first place with his parents.

The child shall have full opportunity for play and recreation, which should be directed to the same purposes as education; society and the public authorities shall endeavour to promote the enjoyment of this right.

Principle 8

The child shall in all circumstances be among the first to receive protection and relief.

Principle 9

The child shall be protected against all forms of neglect, cruelty and exploitation. He shall not be the subject of traffic, in any form.

The child shall not be admitted to employment before an appropriate minimum age; he shall in no case be caused or permitted to engage in any occupation or employment which would prejudice his health or education, or interfere with his physical, mental or moral development.

Principle 10

The child shall be protected from practices which may foster racial, religious and any other form of discrimination. He shall be brought up in a spirit of understanding, tolerance, friendship among peoples, peace and universal brotherhood, and in full consciousness that his energy and talents should be devoted to the service of his fellow men.

Office of the United Nations High Commissioner for Human Rights
Geneva, Switzerland

L10